Destination Canada
Canada

Immigration Debates and Issues

Peter S. Li

OXFORD

UNIVERSITY PRESS

OXFORD
UNIVERSITY PRESS

70 Wynford Drive, Don Mills, Ontario M3C 1J9
www.oup.com/ca

Oxford University Press is a department of the University of Oxford.
It furthers the University's objective of excellence in research, scholarship,
and education by publishing worldwide in

Oxford New York
Auckland Bangkok Buenos Aires Cape Town Chennai
Dar es Salaam Delhi Hong Kong Istanbul Karachi Kolkata
Kuala Lumpur Madrid Melbourne Mexico City Mumbai Nairobi
São Paulo Shanghai Taipei Tokyo Toronto

Oxford is a trade mark of Oxford University Press
in the UK and in certain other countries

Published in Canada
by Oxford University Press

National Library of Canada Cataloguing in Publication

Li, Peter S.
Destination Canada : immigration debates and issues / Peter S. Li.
Includes bibliographical references and index.
ISBN 0-19-541374-1

1. Canada—Emigration and immigration. 2. Canada—Emigration and immigration—
Government policy. I. Title.

JV7225.L5 2002   325.71   C2002-903049-8

1 2 3 4 - 06 05 04 03

Cover design: Brett Miller
This book is printed on permanent (acid-free) paper ∞.
Printed in Canada

Contents

List of Tables and Figures

Tables

Figures

Preface

This is a book about immigration debates and issues in Canada. Questions of immigration have always captured the interests of Canadians in part because Canada is an immigrant country, and in part because Canada continues to accept a relatively large number of immigrants every year. The foreign-born population in Canada accounts for about 17 per cent of its total population, which is high compared to 10 per cent in the United States and 9 per cent in Germany, but low relative to the 23 per cent foreign-born in Australia, although the Australian figure also includes non-immigrant long-term residents. Canada has been a country of choice for international immigrants, after the United States, because it has a high standard of living, a healthy economy, publicly funded health care and education systems, as well as a citizenship policy that accepts new immigrants as citizens after three years of residence in Canada. However, Canada's taxation, scale of economy, and economic vitality are often seen as less favourable than in the United States. By world standards, Canada is a desirable destination; it has attracted roughly a quarter of a million newcomers every year to settle as immigrants and refugees.

International migration requires individuals and families to make decisions about uprooting, moving, and resettling in a new country. It also involves receiving countries guarding their gates—setting policies to separate desirable immigrants from undesirable ones in order to close the door to the latter. After the Second World War, advanced industrial countries such as Canada reformulated their immigration policies to attract immigrants with professional expertise and technical skills, and more recently, to encourage those with substantial investment to immigrate. Thus, highly developed countries have used immigration to supplement their skilled labour pools. The result has led to an international brain drain.

The expansion of the capitalist market and economic globalization has contributed to a process known as globalization, which has the effects of removing barriers of trade and investment as well as facilitating the flow of technology, information, capital, goods, and labour. In this brave new world, there is a high degree of mobility of people across national boundaries, especially those who have human capital or financial capital. But globalization has also displaced people in their home countries and marginalized those who are left out of the expansion of the free market. Other political and economic forces, too, have contributed to displacement and marginalization. The resulting tensions represent some of the contradictions of globalization: the need to dismantle national barriers of mobility of capital, trade and labour on the one hand, but, on the other hand, the need to strengthen national boundaries to keep asylum seekers, illegal immigrants, and pauperized migrants from entering the country.

This book examines the debates and issues of immigration from the vantage point of Canada. The immigration discourse in Canada has a rationale of its own: it operates on many assumptions that appear to be self-evident; it adopts concepts and their underlying subtexts without rigorous interrogation; it upholds objective facts and scientific findings but also allows normative values and cultural preferences to influence their interpretations. This book assesses that rationale. The debates and issues are examined systematically, beginning with the historical role of immigration to Canada and ending with a discussion of the relationship between immigration and Canadian society. The merits of immigration are assessed historically, demographically, economically, and socially. The weight of evidence indicates that Canada has benefited from immigration in many ways despite also having incurred some costs. In the long run, it is inconceivable that Canada would want to scale back its immigration program without also jeopardizing its national and international interests.

I have intended this book to be as accessible as possible to a wide audience; at the same time, I have tried to be comprehensive in reviewing most of the major arguments and available evidence that bear on the immigration debates and issues. Some of the arguments I present in the book have been published in academic papers before. Chapter 6 on human capital of immigrants is based primarily on two of my published papers, 'Earning Disparities between Immigrants and Native-born Canadians' (*Canadian Review of Sociology and Anthropology*, 2000, 37(3): 289–311) and 'The Market Worth of Immigrants' Educational Credentials' (*Canadian Public Policy*, 2001, 27(1): 23–38). Sections of Chapters 7 and 9 are based on another published paper of mine, 'The Racial Subtext in Canada's Immigration Discourse' (*The Journal of International Migration and Integration*, 2001, 2(1): 77–97). Permission to use these previously published materials in this book is gratefully acknowledged.

My interest on the topic of immigration began many years ago, but there have always been related areas that have captured my research interest and steered me away from the central debates of immigration. I wrote about many topics related to immigration, such as about the Chinese immigrants in Canada, race and race relations, multiculturalism, and ethnic inequality. But in the past 10 years I have reflected on more central immigration questions and initiated research projects to study these.

Several events have contributed to my intellectual development. Beginning in the late 1980s and early 1990s, several federal departments invited me to attend policy discussion sessions, conferences, and workshops, and these experiences have educated me a great deal about the intrigues of policy making, and have broadened my understanding about the difference in culture and practice of the academic world and the policy world. These encounters compelled me to develop strong arguments and to search for hard evidence to counteract what I saw was an emerging anti-immigration stance in some public quarters.

By the time the federal department of immigration was engaging in a nation-wide consultation on immigration in 1994, I found myself totally emersed in the immigration debate. I was appointed to two national expert panels to develop strategies regarding immigration and settlement issues, and was asked to co-chair a third panel on the integration of immigration. My frequent trips to Ottawa have further expanded my horizon about the complexity of the immigration debate, and have brought me face to face with many differences of opinions, some delivered with academic elegance and others with sensational emotion.

When the federal government, mainly under the initiative of Citizenship and Immigration, launched the Metropolis Project in 1996, I became deeply involved in this interesting venture. The project was ambitious since it provided funds of about $8 million to establish four centres of excellence on immigration and to support them for six years. There were many critics and skeptics. I remember Meyer Burstein, a director general in Citizenship and Immigration before he became the executive head of the Metropolis Project, saying to me that I should view the project as creating opportunities for policy makers, academics, and other stakeholders. In retrospect, I have to concur.

The Metropolis Project has given me many opportunities to meet policy makers, interact with academics, and listen to NGOs. Above all, the Metropolis Project, through the Social Sciences and Humanities Research Council, has supported the Prairie Centre of Excellence for Research on Immigration and Integration, which is headquartered at the University of Alberta and linked with six universities in Alberta, Manitoba, and Saskatchewan, including the University of Saskatchewan. My affiliation with the Prairie Centre has been rewarding and enjoyable. The Centre has provided me with the funding for both an individual and a team research project; as well, it gives me many opportunities to meet and work with colleagues elsewhere, in my capacity as the leader of the economic domain. Baha Abu-Laban, director of the Prairie Centre, has supported my work and has provided both financial and moral support to facilitate my job in the economic domain. I also worked with Baha, as well as Meyer Burstein and Howard Duncan, in the establishment of the *Journal of International Migration and Integration*. Despite many challenges, some totally unexpected, it was a very rewarding experience for me, as I witnessed how Baha managed to build consensus, lobby financial support, and make decisions about the future of the journal. I think the journal owes much to Baha, and I am proud to have been associated with such an outstanding colleague in this creation. I visited the head office of the Prairie Centre at the Humanities Building of the University of Alberta periodically on business, and every time, Kelly McKean and others in the office have provided me with all the assistance to make my visit pleasant and enjoyable.

Many people in the government have contributed in different ways to my intellectual development and have directly or indirectly helped me to formulate this book. I appreciate the colleagueship and friendship of Meyer Burstein, Howard Duncan, and others of the Metropolis Head Office, who have always valued my views even when they were radically different from theirs at times, and who have respected my academic freedom in pursuing my research interests and conclusions in the way I see fit. I have also enjoyed my association with others at Citizenship and Immigration, including Joan Atkinson, Rosalyn Frith, Elizabeth Ruddick, Martha Justus, Claude Langlois, Craig Dougherty, and many others who have maintained a high degree of professionalism, competence, and above all, humour, in their working relations with me. Claude Langlois first introduced me to the IMDB (Longitudinal Immigration Data Base)—an ambitious project to develop a longitudinal data set for immigrants. Claude and Elizabeth Ruddick provided opportunities to work on the complex data, beginning at an early stage of IMDB. My knowledge of the IMDB is indebted to Claude Langlois and Craig Dougherty, who painstakingly explained to me how the complex data were created and tested, and then within a week disappointed me by telling me that what I had just learned was now made obsolete by their latest ingenious creation. The project is intellectually intriguing and technically demanding, but I am grateful for the opportunities it gives.

Other academics have also provided me with intellectual inspirations, fruitful ideas, and helpful comments. Several colleagues in my home department, including Gurcharn Basran, Li Zong, Terry Wotherspoon, and Harley Dickinson, read various drafts of different chapters in the book and provided friendly and useful suggestions. Others, such as Shiva Halli, Lori Wilkinson, Derek Hum, and Wayne Simpson of the University of Manitoba, Richard Wanner of the University of Calgary, Ravi Pendakur of the Canadian Heritage, Krishna Pendakur and Don DeVoretz of Simon Fraser University, as well as David Ley and Daniel Hiebert of the University of British Columbia, shared their writing with me, from which I greatly benefited. Frances Henry of York University has been a source of inspiration, and her passion for discourse analysis and her commitment to anti-racism prompted me to venture into the world of language deconstruction—a fascination that quickly captured my attention. In addition, I have benefited from formal and informal conversations with colleagues in different universities, such as Paul Hjartarson, Madeline and Warren Kalbach, Vic Satzewich, Morton Weinfeld, Jeffrey Reitz, Danielle Juteau, Alice Nakamura, and others too many to name, who shared their ideas and insights with me on different occasions, and provided me with much inspiration. Naturally, I alone am responsible for any error and oversight in the book.

The Prairie Centre of Excellence for Research on Immigration and Integration has supported my research on immigration issues, and I have also received research grants from the Social Sciences and Humanities Research Council. I was also awarded a teaching release stipend from the Social Sciences and Humanities Research Council, which together with a matching component from the College of Arts and Science, University of Saskatchewan, provided me with a partial teaching release to finish the book. The Department of Sociology, under the headship of Terry Wotherspoon, has also been encouraging and supportive of my research and writing. The support of these academic institutions and granting agencies is greatly acknowledged. Keely Kinar and Qing Zhang were my assistants who helped in many ways in the course of researching and writing this book, such as locating materials in the library, compiling statistics, typing tables and charts, and checking references.

Finally, I wish to thank Oxford University Press for publishing this book. I have worked with the publisher in many capacities in the past, and I am happy to say that I have always enjoyed the professionalism, expertise, and collegiality of the editors and support staff. Euan White was the acquisition editor who first signed me up as the author of this book, and I appreciate his foresight, long before others, in seeing the great value of a new book on immigration. I worked mainly with Megan Mueller, the college division acquisition editor, in the course of finishing the book. I enjoyed my association and working relationship with Megan, who is methodical in regularly reminding late authors like me about impending deadlines, but at the same time is sensitive to how academics work. I appreciate her constructive suggestions about the organization of the book, as well as the helpful comments of three anonymous reviewers of the manuscript. Phyllis Wilson is an experienced editor at Oxford, who has skillfully and expeditiously supervised the production of this book, as she has several of my previous works. Pamela Erlichman copyedited the manuscript with care. I worked with her when she edited another book of mine when she was with another publisher. It was a pleasure working with her again. I sincerely thank the colleagues I have worked with at Oxford for making the publication of a book such a rewarding experience.

For Terence—
son of immigrant parents

Chapter 1

Questions of Immigration

Immigration is an international issue in that it involves the migration of people from one country to another on a permanent basis. Historically, frontier societies such as Australia and the New World of America relied heavily on immigration for growth and development during the initial period of settlement, but immigration continues to be an important means by which advanced capitalist societies address their labour needs, especially during periods of rapid industrial expansion.[1]

Immigration, in fact, predates the modern settlement of frontier societies—if forced migration in the form of slavery and indentured servitude were to be included.[2] Conceptually, one could argue that immigration in the contemporary context should only include the movement of people out of free choice, since migration that is not free, such as the slave and coolie trades, is a feature of colonialism and the outdated plantation economy. In reality, although forced migration is associated with pre-capitalist or early capitalist modes of production that benefit from slavery, indentured servitude, and sharecropping, advanced capitalism also witnesses the coexistence of unfree labour along with the expansion of free labour (Miles, 1987; Satzewich, 1991). In other words, capitalist development produces conditions that enlarge the wage labour market and at the same time disintegrates conventional production and displaces individuals and families from their traditional livelihood. Thus, some people are compelled to move in search of a basic livelihood because they are displaced by forces beyond their control, even though their action appears to involve a free decision to move rather than to stay.

Capitalist expansion and economic globalization produce uneven development by incorporating previously undeveloped regions into the global capitalist economy, and they often exacerbate the inequality between rich and poor nations in the process. At the same time, globalization encourages international movements of people by integrating national and regional economies on the one hand, and by penetrating into traditional economies and displacing individuals and families associated with them on the other. It is a process that produces contradictory outcomes for international migration. In its review of global human development, the United Nations has noted that the opportunities of globalization are uneven and unbalanced and that the process is integrating global markets and concentrating power, while at the same time "marginalizing the poor, both countries and people" (United Nations Development Programme, 1999).

Globalization and Migration

The penetration of the capitalist mode of production on a world scale and the proliferation of communication technology have hastened the process of globalization that intensifies the flow of people, capital, information, goods, raw materials, and services across national boundaries. There were such international exchanges even before the age of globalization, but the speed, the scope, and the complexity of present-day cross-border interconnections mark the uniqueness of the global era. Globalization makes it possible to further economize the cost of production and distribution for firms by localizing economic activities in different countries and regions and taking full advantage of the local labour and market conditions. As well, digitalized technologies and transnational corporate structures and networks make it possible for firms to integrate localized economic activities in metropolitan headquarters. In short, free trade and globalization allow corporate firms to operate freely in a transnational market, one that is characterized by the increasing deregulation of local restrictions and the integration of national economies into a universal framework of free trade.[3] All indications suggest that the growth of the world market is ascertained; the rate of change is only subject to the extent and speed with which local barriers are to be removed and replaced by a global framework of trade and investment that is orderly, regulated, and predictable (see United Nations Development Programme, 1999; World Trade Organization, 2001).

The process of economic globalization has produced many contradictory tendencies. For example, the same process that promotes the dispersion of economic activities across national boundaries to capitalize on the relative advantage of market and labour for firms also hastens the integration of territorially dispersed economic activities in the hands of corporate concentrations in global cities (Sassen, 2001). At the same time, the demand and growth of specialized service firms in global cities have enriched the professionals and technocrats responsible for their success, but the informalization of economic activities, in production and distribution, have resulted in poor remunerations for those associated with them (Sassen, 2001).[4]

Economic globalization creates contradictory tendencies not only in different parts of the world and in global cities, but also in international migration. Capitalist expansion and economic globalization encourage the free movement of people across national boundaries, along with capital, technology, goods, and services. It is a freedom of movement that is closely associated with free trade, within which investments, exports, imports, information, and capital are encouraged to operate relatively unrestricted within a common trading zone, or a block of trade partners.

In other words, one of the outcomes of globalization is to soften national boundaries by internationalizing domestic markets and integrating them in production, distribution, and consumption. Within the global economy, there is an increasing degree of freedom of mobility for those who are associated with its creation and prosperity, including investors, capitalists, corporate professionals, and technical experts. For them, the global economy has created new opportunities for their financial capital, professional expertise, corporate experience, and business acumen, and has enabled them to operate relatively freely as *de facto* global citizens.

There is no doubt that economic globalization has created new opportunities for high-skilled labour and has encouraged the geographical mobility of many people. The World Bank estimates that at the beginning of the twenty-first century, 2 to 3 million people emigrated as legal immigrants every year, mainly to the United States, Germany, Canada, and Australia. About 2.5 per cent of the world population, or roughly 130 million people, live outside their countries of birth—mostly in North America, Western Europe, Oceania, and the Middle East (World Bank, 2000: 37–8). In these high-immigrant-receiving regions, 1 of every 13 persons is estimated to be foreign-born (World Bank, 2000: 37–8). Immigrants or foreign-born workers make up a substantial part of the labour force in some highly developed countries. For example, immigrants account for 9.8 per cent of the population and 11.7 per cent of the labour force in the United States, and 17.4 per cent of the population and 19.2 per cent of the labour force in Canada (see Table 1.1). In Europe, the foreign population makes up 9.1 per cent of the labour force in Germany, 6.1 per cent in France, 17.3 per cent in Switzerland, and 57.7 per cent in Luxembourg. Australia also relies heavily on immigrants, which constitute 23.4 per cent of its population and 24.8 per cent of its labour force.[5]

Immigrants today are attracted to the highly developed regions of the world because of the material affluence and economic prosperity of these regions, and because of the resulting occupational opportunities and financial rewards for individuals. Economically developed regions such as Europe, North America, and Oceania—mainly Australia—have net gains in international migration, whereas Asia, Latin America, and to a lesser degree Africa, are migrant- or immigrant-sending regions that are experiencing net loss in international migration (see Figure 1.1). Between 1990 and 1995, North America had a net gain of 971,000 immigrants and Europe had a net gain of 739,000 migrants; in contrast, Asia had a net loss of 1.4 million emigrants.

Advanced capitalist countries such as the United States, Canada, and Australia are benefiting from international migration, especially from draining the highly trained human capital from developing regions of the world. The brain drain often benefits the advanced capitalist countries at the expense of the sending countries. For example, Africa today has only one scientist and engineer per 10,000 people, but as many as 30,000 Africans with doctorate degrees are estimated to live abroad (United Nations Development Programme, 1999: 32).

The economic prosperity of Europe and North America explains why many developed countries are able to attract a large annual inflow of immigrant or

Table 1.1   Foreign or Foreign-Born Population and Labour Force in Selected OECD Countries, 1998

OECD Countries	Foreign or Foreign-Born Population as % of Total Population	Foreign or Foreign-Born Labour Force as % of Total Labour Force
Australia	23.4	24.8
Austria	9.1	9.9
Belgium	8.7	8.8
Canada	17.4	19.2
Denmark	4.8	3.2
Finland	1.6	—
France	6.3	6.1
Germany	8.9	9.1
Ireland	3.0	3.2
Italy	2.1	1.7
Japan	1.2	0.2
Luxembourg	35.6	57.7
Netherlands	4.2	2.9
Norway	3.7	3.0
Portugal	1.8	1.8
Spain	1.8	1.2
Sweden	5.6	5.1
Switzerland	19.0	17.3
United Kingdom	3.8	3.9
United States	9.8	11.7

Source: Adapted from SOPEMI: *Trends in International Migration*, Annual Report 2000 Edition. Table 1.5, p. 41 (Paris: OECD Publications Service). Reprinted by permission of OECD.

foreign population. For the year 1998 alone, the inflow of foreign population was 138,100 to France, 605,500 to Germany, 111,000 to Italy, and 236,900 to the United Kingdom (see Table 1.2). Similarly, the economic strength and financial capacity of the United States account for its large volumes of immigration, in the magnitude of about 1 million immigrants yearly on average throughout the 1990s (World Bank, 2000: 178). Canada, too, admitted about 200,000 to 250,000 immigrants a year in the same period (see Table A.1).

Different kinds of immigrants are drawn to highly developed countries for similar reasons. For those with advanced skills and human capital that are in rising demand because of the expansion of the digitalized technology and professional specialties, the technologically advanced capitalist economies offer the best remuneration levels and job opportunities. But the robustness of the highly developed economies also attracts others to venture to move, including those who are marginalized and displaced in their own countries as a result of economic globalization, capitalist expan-

Figure 1.1 Annual Net International Migration Totals and Migration Rates in the World's Major Areas, 1990–5

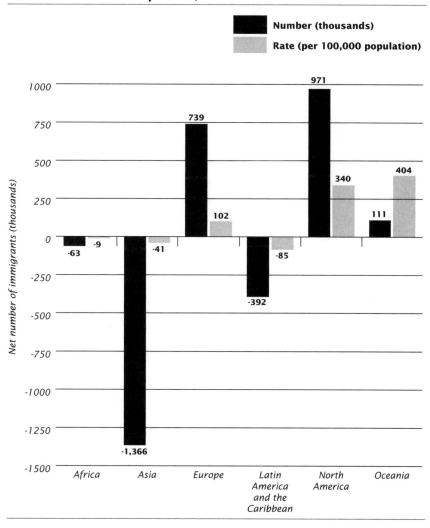

Source: *International Migration Policies, 1995*, United Nations 1996, Sales No. E.96.xl11.7 (ST/ESA/SER.A/154, © United Nations 1996).Reprinted by permission of the United Nations. Available at <http://www.un.org/esa/population/pubsarchive/migpol95/impcht3.htm>.

sion, and other social and political forces. For them, the advanced capitalist countries provide a chance to improve their livelihood, even though their lack of educational expertise and technical skills is likely to land them only in marginal sectors and in low-paying jobs. In short, in comparison to the harsh conditions, limited options, and growing uncertainty in their home countries, any slim chance of migrating to affluent countries is attractive, even if it means working in menial jobs.

Table 1.2   Inflows of Foreign Population and Asylum Seekers into Selected OECD Countries, 1998

OECD Countries	Inflows of Foreign Population (thousands)	Inflows of Asylum Seekers (thousands)
Australia	77.3	7.8
Austria	—	13.8
Belgium	50.7	22.1
Canada	174.1	25.2
Denmark*	20.4	5.7
Finland	8.3	1.3
France	138.1	22.4
Germany	605.5	98.6
Greece	38.2	2.6
Hungary	12.8	7.4
Ireland	20.8	4.6
Italy	111.0	11.1
Japan	265.5	—
Luxembourg	10.7	1.6
Netherlands	81.7	45.2
New Zealand	36.2	2.9
Norway	26.7	7.7
Sweden	35.7	12.5
Switzerland	74.9	41.2
United Kingdom*	236.9	58.0
United States	660.5	55.0

* Note: Foreign population inflow figures for UK and Denmark are for 1997.

Source: Adapted from *SOPEMI: Trends in International Migration*, Annual Report 2000 Edition. Tables A.1.1, A.1.4, pp. 304, 305 (Paris: OECD Publications Service). Reprinted by permission of OECD.

It is difficult to estimate the current number of people being dislocated economically and politically. But as of 1995, 23 million refugees are estimated to have crossed national borders, in addition to 20 million persons displaced within their own countries (World Bank, 2000: 37). Many advanced industrial countries that draw immigrants and foreign workers also attract asylum seekers. In 1998, 98,600 asylum seekers went to Germany; 22,400 to France; 45,200 to the Netherlands; and 58,000 to the United Kingdom (see Table 1.2).

A distinction is sometimes made between political or convention refugees and economic refugees; the latter group is composed of those who are economically displaced and not necessarily politically persecuted. Whether driven by political factors or economic forces, the displacement of large numbers of people globally also encourages desperate attempts to seek entry to highly developed countries that offer better opportunities of survival. Many advanced capitalist countries today are faced with the rising problem of undocumented immigrants, that is, those who are without legal status because they either extend their legal stay without authorization or who enter the country illegally. The United States is estimated to have 4 million undocumented immigrants, and European countries estimate that half of their immigrants are undocumented, in contrast to only a quarter in the mid-1980s. The undocumented immigrants are in a vulnerable position subject to exploitation and abuse, and they often provide a source of cheap labour for developed countries (United Nations Development Programme, 1999: 33).

The contradictory effects of economic globalization on international migration are well summarized by the United Nations as follows:

> Global employment opportunities may be opening for some, but they are closing for most others. The global market for high-skilled labour is now more integrated, with high mobility and standardized wages. But the market for unskilled labor is highly restricted by national barriers, even though it accounts for a larger share of the international migration (United Nations Development Programme, 1999: 32).

These migration flows produce different tendencies for immigrant receiving countries. On the one hand, there is an intense competition among these countries for immigrants with professional expertise and highly specialized human capital that are in growing demand in the information age and digitalized economy. On the other hand, advanced industrial countries have common concerns and adopt similar strategies in trying to block the entry of unwanted immigrants and illegal migrants who are seen as having little value to offer and constituting a social and financial burden to the receiving society. These tendencies influence the way the receiving society approaches the immigration question and how it assesses the merits of immigration.

Scope of the Book

It is clear that international migration issues include not only the decisions to move that individuals and families make, but also the legal restrictions that receiving countries place on prospective newcomers regarding who might be admitted as legal immigrants and who should be barred from entry. Further issues analyze how receiving countries construct a discourse on immigration regarding the merits of immigration, the impact of immigrants on the host society, the performance of immigrants, and the relationship between old-timers and newcomers.

Thus, the immigration debate in advanced capitalist countries is articulated in a particular discourse, one that is largely expressed in terms of benefits to the receiving society, and not in terms of costs to the sending countries. In such a debate, the self-interest of the receiving country is taken for granted, and the merits of immigration are mainly evaluated in light of the demographic and economic needs of the receiving society, and not in the context of global inequality.

This book is about the domestic debate of immigration in Canada. It does not address broader questions pertaining to economic globalization and uneven capitalist developments and their resulting effects on brain drain and labour migration on a global basis. Nor does it examine more fundamental social and political questions of international migration, which require analyzing the global capitalist economy and understanding how the same process of capital accumulation impoverishes and displaces people at the margin of development while enriching other people at the centre of development. Such questions are fundamental if immigration is to be understood as a global issue, and they help to provide a more complete picture of international migration. They also help to explain the contradictions of economic globalization that involve on the one hand removing national barriers to encourage the free flow of labour and capital and on the other hand reinforcing border controls of highly developed countries to keep away unwanted immigrants and refugee claimants from less-developed regions. Such interesting questions take the debate in a different direction.

The intent of the book, however, is to engage the immigration debate in the context of Canada as a receiving society. It will systematically examine the objective facts and scientific findings, as well as dispel the myths and biases that often distort the facts and their interpretation. It is also an attempt to study the immigration discourse in Canada—how it is constructed, what assumptions are adopted, what arguments are commonly accepted.

It is difficult to present the immigration debate in a nutshell, as it raises many complex questions. For example, should Canada follow an expansionist policy of immigration in view of its demographic trends and prospects? Has Canada benefited or been harmed by immigration, and how can such costs and benefits be assessed objectively? Is increased diversity, for which recent immigrants are believed to be responsible, a blessing or a curse for Canada? How can ideological biases be separated from rational arguments to assess racial diversity, urban growth, and Canada's future development as part of the immigration question? Can such complex debates somehow be resolved with the existing knowledge and scientific evidence? Even if they can't, more informed debates could at least help to clarify erroneous predispositions and misguided conclusions about immigrants and immigration. Before discussing the immigration debate in Canada, it is helpful to understand some fundamental features of Canadian society—especially how Canada has been constituted as an immigrant society.

Canada as an Immigrant Nation

There are many ways to understand the history of a nation. One is to think of it in terms of the origin of its people and the development of its population over time. In this context, a distinction can be made between what Suryadinata (1997: 3) calls 'indigenous nations' and 'immigrant nations'; the former are constituted mainly on the basis of an original population that may actually have several origins, whereas the latter are shaped largely by the arrival of waves of settlers or migrants from the outside. The distinction is only a matter of degree. It is difficult to imagine a nation in which migration and settlement of people from elsewhere have no part in its history. Nor is it realistic to expect that a country would not have some groups of people whose ancestors can be traced far back in history on the land they first inhabited and passed on to subsequent generations. Thus, indigenous nations and immigrant nations do not exist in pure forms. In short, the populations of indigenous nations are mainly made up of descendants of original settlers with a long history on the land; in contrast, immigrant nations are constituted by waves of settlers and immigrants from the outside such that the majority of the population is not indigenous to the land.

Using such a broad distinction, North America, or the New World, is an immigrant society. The term *the New World* signifies a recent history dating back to the beginning of the sixteenth century, as opposed to the longer history of the Old World of Europe from where many North Americans originate. As well, the New World is new in that its population mainly comes from settlements from the outside, principally from Europe, and recently from Africa, Asia, and elsewhere. This is not to deny the fact that indigenous peoples have been in North America long before the arrival of European settlers.[6] But the colonization of North America by Europeans in the seventeenth and eighteenth centuries has marginalized the indigenous peoples and reduced them to a minority that remained tangential to the development of their ancestral land (see Frideres, 1993; Patterson, 1972; Wotherspoon and Satzewich, 2000). Thus, the New World was framed principally by European settlers and their descendants, and only later by other waves of immigrants. In view of the role played by settlers and immigrants from outside North America in shaping its history and constituting its people, and given the continuing importance of immigration in renewing its population, it is indeed accurate to describe the New World as an immigrant society.

Like the United States, Canada is a country of immigrants in that most of its people originated from another country and moved to Canada either in their generation or in previous generations. The only ones who can legitimately claim an aboriginal entitlement of the land are the native peoples. Thus, Canada's population can be seen as having three components: the aboriginal peoples, descendants from previous generations of immigrants, and recent immigrants.

If recent immigrants are understood as those who have moved to Canada in their lifetime, then such first-generation immigrants accounted for about 5 million people or 17.4 per cent of Canada's population in 1996 (Statistics Canada, 1997). By comparison, aboriginal peoples, that is, those who claimed an aboriginal identity in the census, made up only 2.7 per cent of Canada's population (Statistics Canada, 1998a). Together, recent immigrants and aboriginal peoples accounted for about 20 per cent of Canada's population. In other words, four out of every five Canadians in 1996 were descendants of previous generations of immigrants. They made up the majority of Canada's population as native-born Canadians not of aboriginal ancestry.

Old-timers and Newcomers

Since most Canadians are either descendants of immigrants or first-generation immigrants, one would expect the merits of immigration to be taken for granted by the people in Canada. This is not always the case. Over time, earlier immigrants and their descendants become old-timers of the land, and their charter status places them in a privileged position vis-à-vis the newcomers who must accept the conditions of entry and rules of accommodation laid down by those who came before them. The distinction between old-timers and newcomers might seem trivial, since it is the duration of residence in the land that separates the two groups. In reality, it is a difference between those who have the power and control to decide who the newcomers should be, and others who have to demonstrate their worth in order to gain entry and earn their place in the receiving society.

For a country like Canada that enjoys a high living standard, a robust economy, and social and political stability, it is sometimes difficult for its existing population to see why the country should want to bring in more new arrivals from the outside. The resident population does recognize the country's history and its people's past as being intertwined with immigration; but it does not always see the relevance of immigration to the country's future prosperity and vitality, given the current material and social accomplishments.

The debate of immigration in Canada is a debate among old-timers about how they see themselves and newcomers: Will immigration benefit the existing population or will it undermine social and economic security, and cultural complacency? Thus, part of the immigration debate has to do with constructing social boundaries with which old-timers define who they are and who others are not. In this debate, the racial difference between old-timers and newcomers further contributes to the distinction between the two groups. Such superficial difference can easily become a source of tension, since it adds to the uncertainty of old-timers about newcomers, especially in a homogeneous country like Canada with extensive European ancestral roots.

The topic of immigration is always sensational and controversial in Canada because it touches on many sensitive issues; some relate to economic benefits and local changes and others relate to cultural sensitivity and national symbols. It is sometimes difficult for Canadians to be impartial about the immigration question, despite the best efforts of academics and policy makers to search for objective answers about how immigrants perform and what immigration means. Typical Canadians are likely to filter scientific findings and objective facts about immigrants through their subjective experiences, and reinterpret the immigration question in light of whether they see immigrants as a threat to their immediate economic or cultural well-being rather than in the context of Canada's future half a century away.

The Immigration Question

Since the arrival of the British and the French in the seventeenth century, Canada as a nation has been influenced by the continuous arrival of new immigrants, and the cultures and languages that they brought with them. Over time, immigrants to Canada and their Canadian-born descendants have built a nation of distinct characteristics, reflecting in the main, the bicultural and bilingual features of the

British and the French as founding peoples of Canada as a confederation. The dominance of the British and to a lesser extent, the French, as charter groups of Canada meant that historically they were much more influential than other immigrant groups in shaping Canadian society, and in setting the terms and conditions under which newcomers were to be admitted into the country.

To highlight the differential power relationship between the British and the French versus other immigrant groups who came after them, Porter (1965) coined the notions of charter status and immigrant status to describe the privileged position of the charter members vis-à-vis the entrance position of the latecomers. These concepts underscore the *de facto* difference between old-timers and newcomers, as the former claimed the dominance and legitimacy of their position and asserted their right in framing the terms of incorporation for newcomers.

To this very day, much of the debate in immigration has to do with how native-born Canadians view the country that they and their predecessors have built, and how they see their lives and the future of Canada in relation to newcomers. Thus, prospective immigrants are seen as outsiders whose admission to Canada is a privilege granted by those well entrenched in Canada based on birthright, even though their predecessors may have been immigrants themselves at one time. Such a perspective is well grounded, since a nation-state has the right to determine who should be admitted and excluded. Furthermore, Canada's high living standard makes it easy for Canadians to think of future immigrants as marginal rather than central to Canada's continuing prosperity. Further, the risks of immigration are seen as unwelcome hordes of asylum seekers, occasional criminal elements, and mounting costs of immigrant settlement and security control. Thus, immigration is often seen as helpful but not indispensable to Canada's future. Longtime residents also react at the first sign that newcomers are reducing their entitlements or competing with them for economic and social benefits.

The social worth of immigrants is largely evaluated as their ability to augment the country's productivity so that those already in the country can benefit from immigration. Accordingly, immigrants at the very least cannot be burdens to those already in the country. It is a utilitarian mentality, but one that has been popularly adopted as a basis to erect and to defend a national boundary to keep away unwanted immigrants.

Utilitarianism, however, is not the only grounds used in debating the immigration question, since Canada's immigration program is also premised upon humanitarian considerations to enable family reunion as well as to provide refugee status to those politically persecuted in another country. Often, the debate has less to do with humanitarianism than with Canada's leniency in allowing what are perceived as unscrupulous entrants taking advantage of the fairness of the system and the generosity of its people. Even for those properly accepted as *bona fide* family members and refugees, the debate sometimes has to do with whether these 'unsolicited' immigrants add value to Canada or drain resources from it.

The immigration debate also touches on some fundamental demographic questions, such as whether Canada as a nation can maintain its capacity to grow in population by itself, or whether it has to rely on net migration to keep pace with an aging population. At times, the demographic debate also shifts to other queries, such as whether Canada even needs to have a growing population, or whether a larger economy brought about by an expanding population is necessarily the most desirable path for Canada to follow. It is clear that these debates are difficult to resolve, in part because they are premised upon social values whose 'price' to people is often subjectively based and not objectively determinable.

Since the changes in immigration regulations in the late 1960s, there have been some noticeable changes in the ethnic and racial composition of new immigrants. These changes are cast in the immigration debate as the question of 'diversity'. In essence, it is a debate of race in the sense that Canada is still wrestling with the question of whether it should preserve itself as a racially homogeneous society of Europeans with diverse ethnic backgrounds, or whether it is prepared to accept different racial groups as equals in Canadian society. It is a debate that takes shape not only in immigration, but also in the context of multiculturalism in Canada. But it is in the context of immigration that the arguments for and against diversity are honed, because immigration is seen as the factor that is responsible for bringing about the racial diversity that is becoming entrenched in today's Canada.

The immigration question has many facets. Some have to do with economic costs and benefits of immigration; others are related to short-term problems and long-term gains; still others touch on subtle but sensitive issues of cultural security and racial difference.

Conclusion

Immigration is a global issue involving the movement of people across national boundaries. Capitalist expansion and economic globalization have increased such movements, both among the advanced industrial countries as well as from less-developed areas to the highly developed regions of the world. There are many reasons why globalization encourages international migration.

Economic globalization has enabled corporate firms to localize economic activities in different parts of the world to economize the cost of production and distribution, and at the same time, to integrate global operations in headquarters located in global cities. The expansion of digitalized technology and the growth of the corporate sector are some of the driving forces of globalization. Along with the enlargement of free trade and the global market is the rising demand for specialized services, investment capital, and highly trained human capital, and the resulting opportunities for professionals, technocrats, financiers, and capitalists. Globalization creates new opportunities and increases mobility for those in possession of technical skills, professional expertise, and investment capital. At the same time, however, economic globalization penetrates regions that have been marginal to capitalist development, disintegrates the traditional economy of these regions, and displaces individuals and families associated with them. Thus, globalization both creates new opportunities for highly skilled labour and for investment capital and limits the survival capacity of those with few skills or resources.

Immigration touches on many fundamental questions related to global inequality. However, the immigration debate in advanced capitalist countries is typically framed in a narrow context that approaches immigration from the vantage point of the receiving country's self-interest. To understand such an immigration discourse requires studying the assumptions, biases, and the facts and findings underlying the immigration question.

The objective of the book is to engage the immigration debate in the context of Canada as an immigrant-receiving society. Immigration has always played an important role in the development of Canada as a nation, and Canadian society has been framed largely by European traditions, notably the British and the French. Thus, an important aspect of the immigration discourse has to do with how old-timers see themselves and their country in relation to newcomers, who are increasingly coming from non-European source countries such as from Asia and Africa. The immigration debate is also a debate about cultural complacency and social change, as old-timers adjust to the changing racial and social compositions in metropolitan centres of Canada.

The immigration debate has many dimensions, but in essence, it has to do with whether the existing population defines newcomers as creating a net benefit or a net cost for Canada. Unfortunately, such a debate cannot be resolved entirely on the grounds of academic research or scientific findings, since typical Canadians are likely to filter the arguments of immigration through their own experiences. Ultimately, the debate has to do with how native-born Canadians view themselves and their future, in relation to those they see as newcomers and outsiders. It also has to do with how much social value Canadians are prepared to attach to a Canada of greater diversity as opposed to one that is European-based in ethnic homogeneity and cultural uniformity. In the immigration discourse, short-term considerations and short-sighted perspectives often eclipse the long-term significance of immigration. In the final analysis, the immigration question also determines Canada's future, especially in light of the demographic, economic, and social changes in Canadian society, as well as Canada's evolving position in an increasingly globalized world.

Chapter 2

Immigration and Canada

Immigration has been a key component in the nation building and social development of Canada. Initially, it was colonization of North America by France and Britain that prompted the Europeans to cross the Atlantic Ocean. The French who arrived in the seventeenth century came as indentured labourers, craftsmen, settlers, and colonists, some with the intention to stay and others only to sojourn (Moogk, 1994). The development of fur trade stimulated the growth of the French and later the British colony, and encouraged continuous immigration from Europe. The founding of Canada as a confederation in 1867 represents a compromised union of two immigrant societies made up of British and French settlers and their descendants, and of two languages and cultural traditions. Successive waves of immigrants in different historical periods have also come to Canada, and have helped to build the nation, its economy, and its social system (Easterbrook and Aitken, 1988; Pentland, 1981; Porter, 1965).

Undoubtedly, immigration involves individuals, families, and groups making choices about uprooting and resettling. It also involves immigrants responding to two sets of factors—the 'push' factors that drove emigrants away from their home country and the 'pull' factors that lured immigrants to the country of destination. The combination of these two sets of factors explains much of the history of international migration. Like the indentured workers and colonists who embarked for New France in the ports of La Rochelle and Nantes in France throughout the seventeenth and early eighteenth century, subsequent emigrants from Britain and later from other parts of the world also left because of harsh conditions at home and opportunities in Canada (Moogk, 1994). International migration, however, is also selective; it requires those who move to overcome physical and social barriers, as well as to attend to government policies regarding crossing national boundaries.[1]

In the era of digitalized technology and economic globalization, advancements in communication and transportation have greatly reduced the physical hardship of international migration, but formal restrictions and legal barriers set by the receiving states, and sometimes also by the sending countries, continue to serve as legal controls of international migration flows. Immigration in the contemporary context is heavily regulated; the receiving state often resorts to its legislative and other powers to stipulate what constitutes desirable and legal immigrants, as opposed to the undesirable and illegal ones.

A country's immigration policy, like other public policies, often reflects national priorities and class interests of the country. The main function of the Canadian state, as Whitaker (1977: 43) puts it, has been to facilitate capital accumulation in private hands, to construct a necessary infrastructure, to provide a framework of public order, and to communicate the symbols of legitimacy. However, the state also retains a relative degree of autonomy, as it has to mediate the conflicting interests among fractions of the capitalist class, as well as between capital and labour (see Doern and Phidd, 1983; Panitch, 1977).[2]

Throughout the history of Canada, the state plays a heavy role in setting its immigration policy, using immigration as a means to address the problems of labour shortages and economic development, and to regulate the social, cultural, and symbolic boundary of the nation. In his study of the incorporation of foreign labour in Canada after the Second World War, Satzewich (1991: 43) suggests that the Canadian state is a gatekeeper, whose intervention in the process of exclusion, inclusion, and allocation of foreign labour 'is structured by a range . . . of economic, political and ideological relations associated with the reproduction of the relations of production'. Satzewich's observations are well supported by historical facts that show that the Canadian state has constantly tailored the immigration policy to the economic needs of the nation—from using foreign labour to build infrastructure, to recruiting settlers to open up the West, to admitting skilled workers in periods of rapid industrial development. But economic interests are also carefully balanced by the state with ideological and political considerations in regard to maintaining the cultural and symbolic boundary of the nation. Thus, even during periods of 'open-door' immigration policy when the demands for immigrants were high, Canada excluded racial and religious elements (Tulchinsky, 1994: 4), not necessarily because they were redundant to the economic development of the country, but because they were deemed not to possess the right pedigree for Canada's social formation.

Immigration and Nation Building

Immigration has been central to the nation building of Canada. Since the seventeenth century, traders and settlers from France and Britain had established settlements in Canada. The growth of fur trade brought more artisans, traders, missionaries, and settlers from France and Britain. The subsequent rivalry of Britain and France and the competition between their colonies in North America became enduring features in the development of Canadian society (Easterbrook and Aitken, 1988). The tensions and relations of the British and the French produced and maintained the linguistic and cultural duality of what was to become Canada. In this sense, the defining characteristics of Canada as a nation of two charter groups, each with distinct linguistic and cultural features, emerged over time as the two immigrant societies challenged and accommodated each other.

The *Constitution Act* of 1791 that divided Canada into Lower Canada and Upper Canada further institutionalized the governance of the two immigrant societies under the British rule, which was firmly established after the British conquest of 1760 (Naylor, 1987). However, troubles continued throughout the nineteenth century in Upper and Lower Canada, and the confederation of 1867 represented a constitutional compromise between the two settler societies. The founding of Canada as a nation clearly underscores its cultural and linguistic duality that was part of the history of immigration and settlement of the British and the French. As Porter (1965: 60) characterized it, the British and the French are charter groups of Canada in the sense that they were the first outside groups to settle in a previously sparsely populated territory, and, since their positions were well entrenched before other groups came, they were able to set the conditions of entry and rules of accommodation for subsequent immigrant groups.

Throughout Canada's history, many immigrant groups had arrived, propelled by conditions of desperation of the home countries and attracted by opportunities in the New World. Undoubtedly, the expanding economic opportunities in Canada, first in mercantile trade, then agricultural settlement and later industrial growth, and the vast territory of open land and resources, created many conditions to 'pull' immigrants to come. At the same time, emerging desperate economic and political conditions in sending countries, ranging from famines to political instability, provided the driving forces to 'push' emigrants to the New World to seek a better life.

For example, the Irish exodus to Canada in the middle of the nineteenth century was driven by the potato crop failure in Ireland in 1845 and 1846. This 'famine migration' brought approximately 140,000 Irish to Canada in 1848, 200,000 in 1852, and 280,000 in 1861 (Pentland, 1981: 104). Earlier, during the period of 1827 to 1832, Irish Catholic immigrants had formed the majority of the thousands of workers hired in the building of the Rideau Canal, and the 'famine migration' further provided Canada with the much needed labour in railroad construction and in other industrial development (Avery, 1990; Pentland, 1981: 96–121). Some of the Irish who immigrated to Canada, like others who came during the nineteenth and early twentieth century, eventually left for the United States in response to better economic conditions there, but many stayed and became a part of the Canadian mosaic.

Non-British and non-French immigrants have also contributed to the social development of Canada. Ukrainians began coming to Canada in significant numbers in 1896, mainly to homestead and to farm in the prairie provinces (Porter, 1965: 68; Potrebenko, 1977). Their endurance contributed not only to the settlement of Western Canada and the expansion of prairie agriculture, but also to the enrichment of political and cultural life Canada. It has been noted that between 1904 and 1975, 886 Canadians of Ukrainian origin participated as candidates in federal and provincial elections and 249 were elected (Canada, House of Commons, 1983). About 10,000 Ukrainians served in the Canadian armed forces during the First World War, and about 40,000 of them were in the Canadian military forces in the Second World War. As well, Ukrainians have enriched pluralism in the Prairies and other parts of Canada with their artistic and cultural traditions (Canada, Debates of the Senate, 1964, p. 53).

Visible minorities have also been a part of Canada throughout its history, despite the relatively small numbers. For example, blacks have been in Nova Scotia since the eighteenth century, and Chinese migration to British Columbia began in the middle of the nineteenth century (Henry, 1973; Li, 1998). These groups have contributed to the economic and social development in many parts of Canada. The completion of the Canadian Pacific Railway in 1885 was facilitated largely as a result of Chinese labour brought over from China. Over 10,000 Chinese workers came to work on the western section of the Canadian Pacific Railway between 1881 and 1884, and between 1886 and 1904, another 45,000 Chinese immigrants paid a head tax, levied only on the Chinese, in order to work in Canada and escape poverty at home (Li, 1998). Despite the persistence of anti-Orientalism and racial discrimination, many Chinese remained in Canada and helped to build the nascent industries of mining, lumbering, and manufacturing in British Columbia. Many of the Chinese pioneers endured hardship and long years of separation from their families in China because of restrictive immigration law in Canada, and only reunited with the families in Canada after the Second World War. With the change of immigration regulations in Canada in the postwar period, a new generation of Chinese immigrants was able to come, and many of them made significant contributions in art, culture, science, and public service in Canada (Huang and Jeffery, 1992).

Historically, many immigrant groups to Canada have made numerous contributions to the development of Canadian society. Together with the British and the French who came before them, successive waves of immigrants to Canada from many countries of origin have helped to transform what began as a settler society of mainly Europeans into a mosaic of many cultures. The history of Canada is a testimony to how immigration has contributed to the linguistic duality and cultural diversity of the nation.

Immigration Policies in Historical Periods

Immigration to Canada since the late nineteenth century can be classified into four phases, each governed by a state policy regarding the type of people who would be accepted as desirable immigrants. During the first phase, from 1867 to 1895, Canada maintained a laissez-faire philosophy towards immigration in allowing market forces of supply and demand to determine migration flows into Canada (Manpower and Immigration Canada, 1974b: 3–4). Immigration was a component of Prime Minister Macdonald's National Policy, which involved increasing tariffs to encourage domestic production and completing the transportation infrastructure to open up the West for agricultural settlement (Kelly and Trebilcock, 1998: 110).

Immigration strategy was essentially an open-door policy towards those of European origin, especially those from Britain and the United States. But when the volume of immigration remained relatively low, the government encouraged group settlement by setting aside land reserves for immigrant groups; among those who responded were Mennonite, Scandinavian, and Hungarian immigrants (Kelly and Trebilcock, 1998: 72–7).

The *British North America Act* of 1867 specified that matters related to 'naturalization and aliens' were within the exclusive legislative authority of the Parliament of Canada, but it also indicated that in addition to the Parliament of Canada having the right to pass immigration laws, a province could make laws regarding immigration to the province provided that such laws were not repugnant to federal laws.[3] In 1869, Canada passed its first legislation on immigration, by which immigration agents were established in Canada, Britain, and elsewhere; but the act was silent on admissible classes (Manpower and Immigration, 1974b). In practice, most immigrants were from Britain and the United States. Between 1867 and 1895 about 1.5 million immigrants, mostly from Europe, came to Canada (Statistics Canada, 1983), most coming to work on the land but also in factories, mines, and other non-agricultural sectors (Manpower and Immigration, 1974b: 5). The fact that the responsibility of immigration was initially placed under the Department of Agriculture suggests the government considered immigration to be important to agricultural development and land settlement. However, even during this period of open-door immigration policy, severe restrictions were placed on non-white immigrants such as those from Asia. As early as 1885, the Parliament of Canada passed an act to restrict and to regulate Chinese immigration and to impose a head tax of $50 on practically every Chinese who came to Canada (see Li, 1998).

The second phase of immigration extended from 1896, just before the 'wheat boom' at the turn of the century, to the beginning of the First World War in 1914. During this period, Canada experienced the highest level of immigration in history, a level unmatched by any year throughout the twentieth century. Several factors contributed to an expansion of economic activity and an unprecedented growth of immigration: improved agricultural production in the prairies, higher staple prices, declining transportation rates, higher European demand of Canadian produce, and intensive industrialization (Kelly and Trebilcock, 1998: 111–63). Under the policy developed by Clifford Sifton, minister of the interior responsible for land administration and immigration, Canada was in favour of massive immigration for agricultural settlement, especially in the prairie provinces. When the supply of emigrants from England and Western Europe trailed behind the demand of workers and settlers, Canada began bringing in Eastern and Southern Europe immigrants, such as Poles, Ukrainians, Hutterites, and Doukhobors. Canada's immigration policy for this period was well summarized by a government report in 1910:

> The policy of the Department (of Interior) at the present time is to encourage the
> immigration of farmers, farm labourers, and female domestic servants from the United
> States, the British Isles, and certain Northern European countries, namely, France, Bel-

gium, Holland, Switzerland, Germany, Denmark, Norway, Sweden and Iceland. On the other hand, it is the policy of the Department to do all in its power to keep out of the country undesirables . . . those belonging to nationalities unlikely to assimilate and who consequently prevent the building up of a united nation of people of similar customs and ideals (Manpower and Immigration Canada, 1974b: 9–10).

In this context, Asians and other non-whites were seen as those 'unlikely to assimiliate', because of their superficial racial and cultural differences. By the first decade of the twentieth century, Canada had already established explicit policies aimed at excluding those it deemed undesirable as immigrants. For example, the head tax levied on the Chinese coming to Canada was raised to $500 in 1903 (Li, 1998), and the stipulation of a continuous journey from a home country to Canada was imposed in 1908 largely as a measure to prevent the voyage of East Indians from India to Canada (Basran, Gill, and MacLean, 1995: 15; Johnston, 1989). Thus, even in periods of acute labour shortage, Canada maintained an immigration policy that used race as a basis to restrict non-whites who were deemed socially questionable and racially undesirable (see Roy, 1989; Ward, 1978).

The volume of immigration reached its peaked during this second period. In addition to agricultural expansion, the labour market in Canada also grew substantially as a result of the consolidation of corporate capitalism between 1900 and 1913 in the United States and Canada (Clement, 1977). These developments increased the national production and in turn, the demand for labour. During the economic boom at the turn of the century, Canada experienced a substantial net gain of immigration over emigration, after four decades of a net loss (Timlin, 1960). Between 1900 and 1910, 1.7 million immigrants came to Canada, producing a net gain of 715,000 immigrants for Canada for this period (Naylor, 1975: 8; Statistics Canada, 1983: A350; Timlin, 1960). The net gain of immigration over emigration, albeit in smaller magnitudes, was to persist for two more decades (Statistics Canada, 1983: D498-511).[4] In all, over 3 million immigrants came to Canada during the period 1896 to 1914. However, in the four years prior to the beginning of the First World War alone, from 1910 to 1913, about 1.4 million immigrants landed in Canada, setting the highest record of average annual immigration for the entire twentieth century (see Figure 2.1 and Table A.1 in the appendix). The volume of immigration for these few years relative to Canada's total population is even more astounding. Throughout much of the 1890s, the yearly arrival of immigrants accounted for less than 1 per cent of the country's population. However for 1910 and 1911, immigrant arrivals made up 4.1 and 4.6 per cent of Canada's population, and for 1912 and 1913, the figures reached 5.1 and 5.3 per cent (see Figure 2.1). The large volume of immigrants to Canada in the first decade of the twentieth century substantially raised the immigrant population in Canada, which reached 22 per cent in 1911, as well as in 1921 and 1931. In absolute numbers, the foreign-born rose from about 1.6 million people in 1911 to 2 million in 1921, and to 2.3 million in 1931 (see Table 2.1).

In the third period of immigration, from 1915 to 1945, Canada continued to follow

Figure 2.1 Number of Immigrants Admitted Annually to Canada, and Immigrants Admitted as a Percentage of Population, 1867–2000

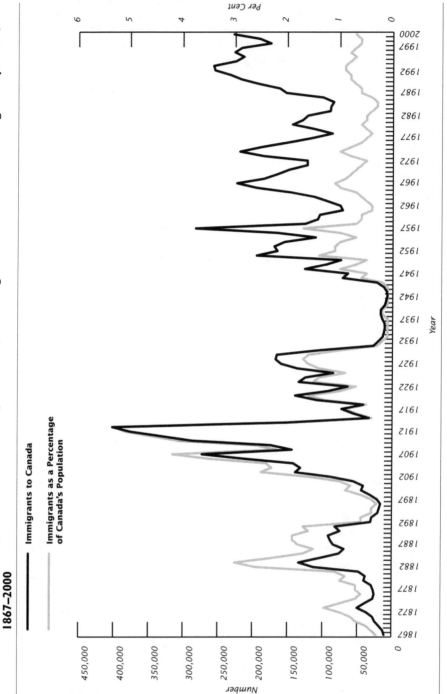

Immigrants to Canada

Immigrants as a Percentage
of Canada's Population

Source: Table A.1 in the appendix to this book.

Table 2.1   Immigrant Population as a Percentage of Canada's Population, 1911–96

Year	Canada's Population	Number of Immigrants	Number of Native-Born	Immigrants as % of Canada's Population
1911	7,206,643	1,586,961	5,619,682	22.0
1921	8,788,483	1,955,736	6,832,747	22.3
1931	10,376,786	2,307,525	8,069,261	22.2
1941	11,506,655	2,018,847	9,487,808	17.5
1951	14,009,429	2,059,911	11,949,518	14.7
1961	18,238,247	2,844,263	15,393,984	15.6
1971	21,568,310	3,295,530	18,272,780	15.3
1981	24,083,500	3,843,335	20,240,165	16.0
1986	25,022,005	3,908,150	21,113,855	15.6
1991	26,994,045	4,342,890	22,651,155	16.1
1996	28,528,125	4,971,070	23,557,055	17.4

Source: Statistics Canada, 1996 Census, Table n01_0411.ivt, *Profile of Total Population by Immigrant Status (4A), for Canada, Provinces and Territories, 1911–1996 Censuses*, 93F0023XDB96001, released 4 Nov. 1997, available at <http://library.usask.ca/data/social/census96/nation/immigration.html>.

a policy of accepting immigrants for land settlement. As in the past, British and American immigrants were considered the most desirable, followed by North European and then Central Europeans. Southern and Eastern Europeans were tolerated; at the bottom were Jews and non-white immigrants who were not welcome (Kelly and Trebilcock, 1998: 442; Li and Bolaria, 1979). It was a period that witnessed drastic events such as the two World Wars and the Great Depression, which hampered immigration to Canada. In the years between 1915 and 1918, slightly over 200,000 immigrants came to Canada, a far cry from the record level of over 400,000 arrivals in 1913 alone (see Table A.1). The immigration level rebounded after the First World War, but the return of a quarter of a million soldiers and the decline of war-related industries strained Canada's capacity to place large numbers of workers in the growing economy (Kelly and Trebilcock, 1998: 183). The volume of immigration rose during the 1920s, but it never reached the record levels of the 1910s. Throughout the 1930s and the first part of the 1940s, immigration to Canada declined to the lowest annual level of the twentieth century. In total, slightly fewer than 2 million immigrants came to Canada between 1915 and 1945, but for the 15-year period between 1931 and 1945, only about 220,000 immigrants were admitted (Table A.1). The slowing down of the immigration flow during this period gradually diluted the foreign-born population in Canada, which declined to 17.5 per cent in 1941, and then 14.7 per cent in 1951 (see Table 2.1).

The end of the Second World War marked the beginning of a new era of industrial growth, and the development of a postwar immigration policy that culminated in the adoption of a universal selection system in 1967. Throughout the 1950s and

1960s, Canada enjoyed a relatively low unemployment rate, a real increase in household income, and an expansion of the national economy (Kelly and Trebilcock, 1998: 311–45). Between 1951 and 1971, there was a net gain of 3.3 million jobs in Canada, 23 per cent of which were in the sector of education, health and welfare, and another 28 per cent in the service sector and government sector (Li, 1996: 46). Canada's labour force grew from 5.2 million people in 1951 to 8.8 million people in 1971, and then to 12 million people in 1981 (Li, 1996: 34). The increasing labour demand was met by several sources: natural population increases, more women joining the labour force, as well as relatively large intakes of immigrants in the postwar years (Li, 1996). Between 1946 and 1955, over 1.2 million immigrants came to Canada, about 87 per cent came from Europe (Manpower and Immigration Canada, 1970). Another 1.7 million immigrants arrived in Canada in the next 12 years, from 1956 to 1967, and European immigrants accounted for 80 per cent.[5] The changes in immigration regulations in 1967 brought a new wave of immigrants from non-European sources. Between 1968 and 1978, 1.7 million were admitted, with 21 per cent coming from Asia. The last quarter of the twentieth century brought a higher level of immigration, bringing a total of 3.7 million immigrants to Canada in the 21-year period between 1979 and 2000, with over half originated from Asia. In all, Canada admitted 8.3 million immigrants in the second half of the twentieth century after the end of the Second World War; among these, 48 per cent originated from Europe, and 30 per cent from Asia.

Changes in Post–World War II Canadian Immigration Policy

Historically, Canada had relied upon Western Europe, in particular Great Britain, as the major supplier of immigrants to Canada. In the two decades after the end of the Second World War, Canada maintained an immigration policy of favouring immigrants from the United Kingdom, the United States, and other European countries, and restricting the entry of those from non-traditional sources such as Asia and Africa to limited admission categories. However, in the 1960s, there were major changes in the Canadian immigration policies; they moved away from national and racial origins as grounds of admission, and emphasized educational and occupational skills as selection criteria for admitting immigrants, although sponsored immigrants under family unification remained an important component in the immigration program.[6]

Until the immigration regulations of 1962 were adopted, the postwar immigration policy of Canada was guided by the statement of Mackenzie King, the prime minister of Canada in 1947. On 1 May 1947, Mackenzie King stated in the House of Commons:

> The policy of the government is to foster the growth of the population of Canada by the encouragement of immigration. The government will seek by legislation, regulation, and vigorous administration, to ensure the careful selection and permanent settlement of such numbers of immigrants as can advantageously be absorbed in our national economy . . .

There will, I am sure, be general agreement with the view that the people of Canada do not wish, as a result of mass immigration, to make a fundamental alteration in the character of our population. Large-scale immigration from the orient would change the fundamental composition of the Canadian population. Any considerable oriental immigration would, moreover, be certain to give rise to social and economic problems of a character that might lead to serious difficulties in the field of international relations. The government, therefore, has no thought of making any change in immigration regulations that would have consequences of the kind (Canada, House of Commons Debates, 1 May 1947, pp. 2644–6).

In his statement, King indicated that the government viewed immigration as a source of population and economic growth, but did not wish to alter the fundamental composition of the Canadian population as a result of immigration. He further stated that the government was not prepared to change 'the existing regulations respecting Asiatic immigration' except to remove the discriminatory *Chinese Immigration Act*, and an order-in-council regarding naturalization (Canada, House of Commons Debates, 1 May 1947, p. 2646). It was a policy in favour of expanding the intake of immigrants from traditional sources of Europe and the United States and maintaining a tight control of immigration from Asian countries.

In 1952, the Government of Canada passed the *Immigration Act*, which laid down the framework for managing Canada's immigration policy and gave sweeping power to specially designated immigration officers to determine what kinds of people were admissible (Hawkins, 1988: 101–7). But a decision in the Supreme Court of Canada compelled the government to refine the categories of admissible people that were listed in an order-in-council, which excluded Asian countries as among those where immigration to Canada were permitted (P.C. 1956–785). By the 1960s, it had become clear that although Europe was still the main source of immigration to Canada, there were indications that the quality of immigrants, in terms of their occupational and educational qualifications, had been diluted by the increased number of unskilled immigrants from Southern Europe, and a corresponding decrease in the proportion of skilled immigrants in professional and managerial jobs. The 1962 immigration regulations revoked the special provisions of admission that applied to British, French, and American citizens and replaced it with a policy in favour of immigrants with educational, professional, and technical qualifications. Of the four categories of immigrant admission, the first two were given to independent immigrants with educational and professional skills. The remaining two were for sponsored immigrants; but sponsorship of immigrants outside of Europe and America was restricted only to close relatives (P.C. 1962–86).

Further changes in the immigration regulations in 1967 finally resulted in a universal point system of assessment that was to be applied to all prospective immigrants, irrespective of country of origin or racial background (P.C. 1967–1616). Under the point system, an immigrant could apply either as an independent or as a nominated relative sponsored by a Canadian citizen or permanent resident. In either case, the immigrant would be assessed as well on the basis of his or her education, occupational demand, and age. The point system was further modified in 1978 (P.C. 1978–486). The new regulations reaffirmed the importance of educational and occupational qualifications in the selection of independent immigrants; of the maximum 100 points used in the assessment, 60 were given to educational level, vocational training, work experience, and occupational demand.

There is evidence to indicate that the changes in immigration regulations in 1962 were prompted, in part at least, by the influx of unskilled immigrants from Southern Europe, who were able to immigrate as relatives of Canadian citizens and permanent residents. At the same time, there were also concerns over the potential of an influx of unskilled non-white immigrants once national origin was not being considered in assessing prospective immigrants. Such worries were well summarized by Dr Davidson, deputy minister of immigration, in an internal memorandum in 1962:

> Our prime objective in the proposed revision is to eliminate all discrimination based on colour, race or creed. This means that, if we continue to allow Greeks, Poles, Italians, Portuguese and other Europeans to bring in the wide range of relatives presently admissible, we will have to do the same for Japanese, Chinese, Indians, Pakistanis, Africans, persons from the Arab world, the West Indies and so forth. The only possible result of this would be a substantially larger number of unskilled close relatives from these parts of the world to add to the influx of unskilled close relatives from Europe (quoted in Hawkins, 1988: 130).

The subsequent amendments in 1962 reflected these concerns. On the one hand, the 1962 immigration regulations allowed individuals with educational qualifications and technical skills to immigrate to Canada, and on the other hand, they restricted the range of immigrant sponsorship for those from outside of Europe and America.

There is further evidence to suggest that the changes in the Canadian immigration policy in the 1960s were prompted by the shrinking supply of immigrants from Europe and the rising demand and competition of skilled labour from the United States. In particular, there was a decline in the supply of European immigrants with managerial and professional expertise. Several factors explain this dramatic shift in the postwar immigration pattern from Europe to Canada. The rapid postwar economic recovery and subsequent industrial expansion in Western Europe resulted in a surging demand for skilled labour. In the process of economic growth and demographic changes, Western European countries met the labour shortage partly by relying on guest workers from Southern European and Third World countries, and partly by absorbing emigrants from Soviet bloc countries. Rather than a major supplier of emigrants to Canada, Western Europe became a competitor for the same short supply of skilled labour in Europe.

The economic prosperity in the United States in the 1950s and 1960s also substantially increased the demand for skilled labour. In the two decades prior to

1967, Canada had been losing many professional and technical workers to the United States. Between 1953 and 1963, there was a net outflow of 41,263 professionals and 38,363 skilled workers from Canada to the United States (Parai, 1965: 47–57). However, Canada was able to benefit from a net gain of 125,242 professionals and skilled workers for the same period only because of a large volume of incoming immigrants from around the world. Between 1950 and 1963 Canada was experiencing an average annual outflow of 5,476 professionals to the United States and the United Kingdom. Despite an average volume of 7,790 professionals immigrating to Canada annually from around the world, the average net gain per year was only 2,314 professionals (Parai, 1965: 33). These structural conditions compelled Canada to revise its immigration policy in 1962 to facilitate the international migration of skilled workers to Canada.

In 1965, the United States passed a new immigration act to replace the *McCarran-Walter Act* of 1952. The 1965 Act abolished immigrant selection based on national origin quota and used a preferential system to facilitate the entry of immigrants with professional and technical qualifications, and those with skills in demand. The changes in the US immigration policy made it even more urgent for Canada to broaden its recruitment of skilled immigrants. The amendments in the 1967 immigration regulations reflected Canada's attempt to compete for skilled labour around the world, although sponsored immigrants under family reunification continued to be a core component of immigration.[7]

The impact of the changes in the 1967 immigration regulations can be seen from immigration statistics (Li, 1992: 153–7). Between 1954 and 1967, 423,638 people emigrated from Canada to the United States, and 173,873 people immigrated from the United States to Canada; thus, Canada experienced a net loss of 249,755 people. For the 19-year period after 1967, until 1986, Canada had a moderate gain of 55,393 people from immigration to and from the United States. This pattern is particularly evident in the migration of skilled labour. Prior to the 1967 changes in immigration regulations, the exodus of skilled labour from Canada to the United States reached a climax. In total, for the 13 years between 1954 and 1967, Canada lost 60,230 people in professional, technical, managerial, and entrepreneurial occupations to the United States. In return, Canada received 33,119 immigrants in these occupations from the United States. Thus, the net loss of skilled labour for Canada for this period was 27,111 people. No doubt this exodus was related to the economic boom and the corresponding employment opportunities in the United States during the fifties and sixties, as well as the relative ease with which immigrants from Canada were accepted by the United States. One of the consequences of the changes in the 1967 immigration regulations was a reversal of this trend, as Canada placed more emphasis on professional and educational qualifications as bases of immigration. For the 19-year period between 1968 and 1986, Canada experienced a net gain of 16,349 immigrants in professional, technical, managerial, and entrepreneurial occupations from the United States (Li, 1992).

The point system adopted in 1967 has remained the framework for selecting immigrants until as late as 2001 when the immigration act was revamped and new immigration regulations were developed, although there were periodic modifications to the selection grid. However, the point system only applies to the selection of economic immigrants, while family-class applicants are processed on the basis of close family relationship with citizens and permanent residents, and refugee claimants are assessed on humanitarian grounds (see Chapter 3).

In 2001, the Parliament of Canada passed a new immigration bill (Bill C-11), entitled the *Immigration and Refugee Protection Act* (S.C. 2001, c. 27), which replaced the 1976 *Immigration Act* (S.C. 1976–7, c. 52) and the more than 30 amendments that were made to the Act. As in previous immigration legislation, the new Act sets out the general framework and empowers the governor-in-council to make regulations pertaining to immigration and refugee matters. However, the Act also requires the minister responsible for immigration to table before each House of Parliament proposed regulations for referral to appropriate House committees (S.C. 2001, c. 27, s. 4.2). The Act clearly distinguishes between immigration and refugee protection, and devotes a separate part of the Act to each. As well, the Act lists 10 objectives with respect to immigration and 8 objectives regarding refugees. The first two objectives for the immigration program are 'to permit Canada to pursue the maximum social, cultural and economic benefits of immigration' and 'to enrich and strengthen the social and cultural fabric of Canadian society' (S.C. 2001, c. 27, s. 3.1). Thus, there is an emphasis to frame immigration in terms of Canada's benefits and its social and cultural boundaries. The importance of skilled immigrants and economic benefits to Canada is clearly stated in a document published by Citizenship and Immigration Canada to justify the new act as follows:

> Canada needs young, dynamic, well-educated skilled people. It needs innovation, ideas and talents. Canadian employers want to take advantage of opportunities offered by the fast-moving pool of skilled workers. The global labour force can benefit Canadians through job creation and the transfer of skills. Immigration legislation must be adapted to enhance Canada's advantage in the global competition for skilled workers (Citizenship and Immigration Canada, 2001a: 1).

On 14 June 2002, the government published the new immigration regulations to update the point system (*Canada Gazette*, Part II, vol. 136, no. 9, pp. 1–449). The new point system for selecting skilled workers or economic immigrants places an even greater emphasis on human capital as providing flexible skills rather than on specific job demands in the labour market (see Chapter 3).

Canada's Business Immigration Program

Since 1978, Canada has also amended its immigration policy to allow the admission of entrepreneurs and those in self-employment as immigrants without being assessed on the basis of occupational demand or arranged employment. To qualify as an entrepreneur immigrant, a person has to establish or purchase a controlling interest in the ownership of a business in Canada, which can provide employment to at least five Canadian citizens or permanent residents; the entrepreneur is also required to participate in the daily management of the business. For a self-employed person to be admitted as an immigrant, the person must plan to establish a business in Canada that will provide employment for the immigrant and no more than five Canadian citizens or permanent residents. The applications of entrepreneurs and self-employed persons would be placed in the fourth and fifth priority in the processing of immigrant visas (P.C. 1978–486). Between 1978 and 1985, 4,109 entrepreneurs and 8,630 self-employed persons, not counting their family members, were admitted into Canada (Employment and Immigration Canada, 1990: 8).

In 1985 the policy of admitting business immigrants was expanded to include entrepreneurs, self-employed persons, and investors; applications for immigrant visas under these categories were moved up to the second priority for processing (P.C. 1985–3246). To qualify as an investor, a person must have a successful track record in business or commercial undertakings, and have accumulated a net worth of at least $500,000, and have made a business investment of at least $250,000 in Canada in direct business ventures or through private investment syndicates or government administered venture capital funds (P.C. 1985–3246). The government stated that the intent of the Immigrant Investor Program was 'to provide a means for admitting to Canada people who had business skills and experience that would benefit Canada, and who were prepared to make an investment in business in Canada that provinces considered important to their economic development and that would create or maintain employment opportunities' (P.C. 1989–2440: 4944). The changes in immigration policy to broaden the recruitment of business immigrants made it easier for immigrant capital to move to Canada, either as direct investments, or as partnerships through venture capital funds or investment syndicates. As the Immigration Regulations indicate, the purpose of having syndicates or investment funds was to 'provide equity or loan capital to establish, purchase, expand or maintain business or commercial ventures', and the reason for not permitting immigrant investments to be revoked within three years is to 'contribute to the creation or continuation of employment opportunities for Canadian citizens or permanent residents other than the investor and his dependents' (P.C. 1985–3246, s. 4).

In 1989 and 1990 the investors' component of the Business Immigration Program was further amended to ensure that larger capitals would be invested by business immigrants in Canada for a longer holding period. In 1989, a tier structure was developed as an administrative device for controlling the minimum qualifying investment (P.C. 1989–2440).[8] The 1990 amendment changed the minimal required from $150,000 to $250,000 for Tier I investments, which, before the change, were available to provinces having less than 3 per cent of business immigrants in the previous year, and which, after the change, were permitted for provinces sharing less than 10 per cent of business immigrants.[9] The minimal requirement for Tier II, which applied to all other areas outside of Tier I, was raised from $250,000 to $350,000. The minimal level of $500,000 remained the same for Tier III, which applied in any part of Canada that provided investment guarantees. The 1989 amendment also modified the definition of 'eligible business or commercial venture' to mean a business or venture operated in Canada with a total asset not exceeding $35 million (P.C. 1989–2440). The purpose of this change was to ensure that immigrant investors' investment capital would be channelled into small- and medium-size business ventures in Canada that would have more difficulty in raising venture funds. As the government explained, this policy would 'ensure that the benefits of the program remain directed toward small to medium size businesses. . . . It is thought that companies beyond this size can readily obtain financing without the benefit of the Immigrant Investor Program (P.C. 1989–2440: 4946). The 1990 amendment also increased the locked-in period of investments from three to five years to provide more flexibility to investment syndicates or capital funds (P.C. 1990–2317).

Further amendments to Immigration Regulations were made in 1993 (P.C. 1993–1626). The changes involved putting immigrant investors into a special class, clarifying the Business Immigration Program, and stipulating tightening controls over how venture funds were to be organized (P.C. 1993–1626). The regulations reaffirmed that investor immigrants must have a successful business background and a minimum net worth of $500,000, or $700,000 if subject to an investment guarantee, accumulated through their own endeavour, and must invest a prescribed minimum amount ranging from $250,000 to $500,000 in a business or fund approved by the government (P.C. 1989–2440). The minimum investment must be invested in the 'active business operations' of eligible businesses; the term *active business operations* means 'business operations that create or continue employment for Canadian citizens or permanent residents and that actively foster the development of a strong and viable economy and regional prosperity in Canada', and the term *eligible business* refers to 'a business that is operated in Canada, the total assets of which . . . do not exceed $35,000,000, as calculated without subtracting from those total assets the liabilities of the business or the associated corporations' (P.C. 1993–1626, s. 6.2.1).[10]

In 1999, the federal government made further changes to the Immigrant Investor Program, aimed at centralizing the administration of investors' funds and reducing the potential for abuse. Under the redesigned program, the federal government would collect all the investors' investments initially and then redistribute them to provinces based in part on the level of provincial gross domestic product. An investor's minimum net worth was raised to $800,000 and the required investment became $400,000, which would remain locked for five years before the principal would be returned to the investor (P.C. 1999–525).

The Business Immigration Program, in particular the component under the Immigrant Investor Program, has been able to attract offshore capital to invest into Canada. The government has referred to the Immigrant Investor Program as 'making significant and growing contributions to regional and provincial economic development' (P.C. 1990–2317: 4896). In its report, the 1995 Immigrant Investor Program Advisory Panel also indicated that between 1986 and 1994, immigrant investors made about $2.5 billion in subscriptions to the program, about 32 per cent went to Quebec, and 20 per cent to Saskatchewan. However, more recent statistics indicate that since its inception in 1986 until 2000, immigrants have subscribed over $5.8 billion in investment funds, about 54 per cent of which were allocated to Quebec and 12 per cent to Saskatchewan (Citizenship and Immigration Canada, 2001b).

The development of the Business Immigration Program has to be interpreted in light of the economic development of Canada in the 1980s. Economic stagnation, high unemployment, and mounting government debts made it difficult for the government to use fiscal policies to create industrial demand and stimulate the economy. Revised immigration policy in the 1980s allowed the government to address the fundamental economic contradictions of the time, just as change was needed in the 1960s to recruit skilled immigrants for industrial expansion. The 1980s shift focuses on international investment capital migration, in contrast to the pre–World War II emphasis on labour migration and in the postwar demand for human capital migration. The government seems to have in mind securing offshore capital to support small- and medium-size businesses and commercial ventures that have difficulties in raising venture capital. The program does not require immigrant investors to participate actively in the operations of businesses they invest in, but their minimum investment is required to lock into the businesses for an extended period of time. This arrangement provides investment fund managers and Canadian business owners the maximum flexibility in using and controlling immigrants' capital to engage in business ventures, while shifting the risk of capital loss to the immigrant investors. Immigrant investors who do not wish to take investment risks and choose to invest in venture funds that provide guarantees are required to have more capital assets. Until the changes in Immigration Regulations in 1993, Canadian fund managers and entrepreneurs marketing investment schemes to immigrant investors encountered few restrictions from the government in devising investments with substantial risks to capitalize on the desire of offshore investors to become immigrants to Canada.[11] The regulations governing the Immigrant Investor Program attempt to ensure that small and medium business ventures in prosperous provinces and less-developed regions of Canada can benefit from this windfall of international capital, rather than to protect the interests of immigrant investors.

In 1985, the total number of business immigrants admitted, including dependants, was 6,481, or 7.7 per cent of all immigrants to Canada. It increased to 11,069 in 1987; 17,564 in 1989; and 18,445 in 1990, before tapering off to 16,948 in 1991. For the period between 1985 and 1991, Canada admitted a total of 16,984 entrepreneurs, 4,427 self-employed and 3,093 investors, who, together with their dependants, made up about 93,137 immigrants, or 8.2 per cent of all immigrants to Canada during this period (Employment and Immigration Canada, 1989a, 1991a). More recent statistics show that from 1986 to 2000, Canada accepted 73,586 principal applicants as business immigrants to Canada; about 33 per cent were from Hong Kong and another 15 per cent from Taiwan (see Table 2.2).

A large proportion of business immigrants to Canada have been from Asia. In

Table 2.2   Source Countries of Business Immigrants (Investors, Entrepreneurs, and Self-Employed) Landing by Country of Last Permanent Residence (Principal Applicants Only), 1986–2000

Rank	Source Country	Number	%
1	Hong Kong	24,404	33.2
2	Taiwan	11,330	15.4
3	South Korea	6,203	8.4
4	China	2,826	3.8
5	Germany	1,995	2.7
6	Iran	1,545	2.1
7	USA	1,503	2.0
8	England	1,433	2.0
9	United Arab Emirates	1,327	1.8
10	Switzerland	1,235	1.7
	Top Ten	53,801	73.1
	Other	19,785	26.9
	Total	73,586	100.0

Source: Citizenship and Immigration Canada, *Business Immigration Program Statistics 2000,* released 20 Aug. 2001, available at <http://cicnet.ci.gc.ca/english/immigr/bus-stats2000.html>.

1983, 19 per cent of the business immigrants, including dependants, came from Hong Kong, and another 4 per cent from Taiwan (Employment and Immigration Canada, 1983). Within two years, the number of business immigrants from Hong Kong more than doubled to 2,821, which made up about 44 per cent of all business immigrants admitted in 1985 (Employment and Immigration Canada, 1985). The volume of business immigration to Canada continued to increase after 1986; in 1989 alone, Canada admitted 17,564 business immigrants and their dependants—about 30 per cent came from Hong Kong and another 13 per cent from Taiwan (Employment and Immigration Canada, 1989a). For the entire period between 1986 and 2000, business immigrants from Hong Kong and Taiwan accounted for about 49 per cent of all business immigrants admitted to Canada (see Table 2.2).

Although business immigrants made up only a small percentage of the total volume of immigration, they made significant economic impacts in Canada. In 1987, the 2,484 approved applicants as entrepreneurial immigrants had a net worth of $2.5 billion; their investments were to create about 12,000 jobs and to retain another 2,155 jobs.[12] In total, between 1987 and 1990, the 11,000 approved applicants of entrepreneurial immigrants brought to Canada an estimated net worth of about $14.3 billion; their investment was estimated to create 48,000 jobs. For the two years 1999 and 2000, immigrant entrepreneurs coming to Canada invested about $429 million in Canada, which according to official statistics created 4,589 full-time jobs and 1,945 part-time jobs (Citizenship and Immigration Canada, 2001b).

The capital invested in Canada by investor immigrants was also impressive. Between 1987 and 1990, the 1,933 cases of approved applicants of investor immigrants were estimated to have a net worth of about $3.2 billion; $753 million was estimated to have been directly invested in various Canadian investment funds (Li, 1993). As noted earlier, more recent data indicate that about $5.7 billion was subscribed by investor immigrants between 1986 and 2000 (Citizenship and Immigration Canada, 2001b).

An evaluation of the Immigrant Investor Program for the period 1986 to 1991 (excluding Quebec) that was funded by the Department of Employment and Immigration and conducted by Informetrica Limited indicates that by the middle of 1992, $722 million out of $1.1 billion that was subscribed by immigrants through the program had been invested (Employment and Immigration Canada, 1993a). The evaluation study concludes that although the real capital impact that was triggered by immigrant investors' capital investment only accounted for an estimated 0.6 per cent of the total private, non-residential business investment for the period, the program had produced positive employment effects. In total, about 10,000 permanent jobs had been created by the investment activity of this program during the period under review, of which about 45 per cent of the permanent jobs created were located in British Columbia (Employment and Immigration Canada, 1993a). Another study by Ernst and Young Associates shows that of 82 practitioners related to the Immigrant Investor Program, 51 per cent indicated that the businesses in which they had invested the immigrants' capital funds did not attract other investors (Employment and Immigration Canada, 1992a: 36). However, studies based on actual interviews with business immigrants suggest that structural constraints and blocked mobility confront them, especially in the non-ethnic business sector (Ley, 1999; Wong and Ng, 1998).

Canada continues to admit immigrants under the Business Immigration Program, although the number has declined in the late 1990s: 9 per cent of all immigrants were admitted as business immigrants in 1997, 8 per cent in 1998, 7 per cent in 1999, and 6 per cent in 2000 (Citizenship and Immigration Canada, 2000, 2001b). In actual numbers, this represents a decline from 19,927 in 1997 to 13,655 in 2000 (Citizenship and Immigration Canada, 2000, 2001c).

Postwar European Immigration to Canada

Although European immigrants to Canada made up the majority of immigration to Canada in the postwar period, their importance, particularly in terms of the proportion of the total number of immigrants admitted, declined after 1967. In the 1940s and 1950s, immigration to Canada was made up almost exclusively of immigrants from Europe. For example, in the postwar years from 1946 to 1955, Canada admitted about 1.2 million immigrants to Canada, about 87 per cent of whom came from Europe; British immigrants alone accounted for 29 per cent of the total number of immigrants (Table 2.3). Between 1956 and 1967, Canada admitted 1.7 million immigrants, 79 per cent from Europe, and 29 per cent from the United Kingdom alone (see Table 2.3). However, this relatively high percentage of postwar European immigration was largely a result of Canada's preferential policy towards European immigration to Canada prior to 1967. After the changes in immigration regulations, European immigrants to Canada declined to about 740,000 between 1968 and 1978, or 44 per cent of the total 1.7 million immigrants admitted to Canada during this period (see Table 2.3). The percentage decline for British immigrants to Canada was from 29 per cent for 1956 to 1967 to 17 per cent for 1968 to 1978. The importance of European immigrants to Canada continued to wane in the last two decades of the twentieth century. Between 1979 and 2000, European immigrants accounted for 23 per cent of the total 3.7 million immigrants admitted, and those from the United Kingdom only 5 per cent. In contrast, Asian immigrants reached 54 per cent of the total number of immigrants for this period (see Table 2.3).

There is evidence to indicate that the changes in the Canadian immigration regulations in 1967 had facilitated the recruitment of immigrants in managerial and professional occupations. In the few years prior to 1967, between 1961 and 1967, new immigrants in professional, technical, managerial, and entrepreneurial occupations made up 22 to 27 per cent of all immigrants entering Canada and destined to the labour force every year. Between 1968 and 1972, this type of skilled immigrants increased to 30 to 34 per cent of the annual number of immigrants coming to Canada and entering the labour force. Furthermore, although the number of immigrants in managerial and professional occupations fluctuated from year to year in the postwar decades, the percentage from Europe declined from about 80 per cent in the 1950s to less than 50 per cent after 1967. In contrast, from 1968 to

Table 2.3   Immigrants Admitted to Canada by Selected Regions of Origin, 1946–2000

Year	Total Immigrants Admitted	Immigrants from Europe Including Britain		Immigrants from Britain		Immigrants from Asia	
	N	N	%	N	%	N	%
1946–55	1,222,319	1,064,118	87.1	358,681	29.3	26,990	2.2
1956–67	1,699,320	1,344,124	79.1	486,266	28.6	84,411	5.0
1968–78	1,675,007	739,855	44.2	292,107	17.4	352,713	21.1
1979–2000	3,794,009	853,957	22.5	192,340	5.1	2,039,365	53.8
Total	8,390,655	4,002,054	47.7	1,329,394	15.8	2,503,479	29.8

Source: Data from 1946 to 1955 are based on Department of Manpower and Immigration, *Immigration Statistics*, 1970, Catalogue M22-1/1970, Table 13, p. 21 (Ottawa: Information Canada, 1971); data from 1956 to 2000 are based on *CANSIM*, Label: D27-28, D36-D41, D125596-D125598 (updated 25 Sept. 2001), Title: Immigration by Country of Last Residence (original source: SDDS 3601 Employment and Immigration Canada).

the 1990s, the proportion of immigrants in professional and technical occupations from non-European countries exceeded more than 50 per cent of the annual number of immigrants in these occupations; for some years, for example, between 1987 and 1992, professionals and technical workers from non-European countries accounted for more than 70 per cent of all immigrants in professional and technical occupations entering Canada every year.[13]

Despite the improvement of educational qualification of new immigrants as a result of changes in immigration regulations in 1967, there is also evidence to suggest that the quality of human capital gradually declined over time since the late 1970s because of the relatively large intake of non-selected immigrants, as opposed to independent immigrants selected under the point system (see Bloom, Grenier, and Gunderson, 1995; Bloom and Gunderson, 1991; Coulson and DeVoretz, 1993). As a result, it was estimated that it would take much longer for immigrants who came to Canada in the 1980s to reach income parity with native-born Canadians than earlier immigrant cohorts (Bloom, Grenier, and Gunderson, 1995).

The evidence is clear that the volume and proportion of European immigrants to Canada had declined since the peak in the 1950s. The changes in the immigration regulations in the 1960s enabled Canada to abandon national origin as a selection criterion, and to select and admit immigrants from all over the world, especially those in managerial and professional occupations. After 1967, the supply of this source of labour had broadened to include non-European countries. Throughout the 1980s and 1990s, immigrants from Asia, Africa, and other non-traditional sources had made up more than half the total number of immigrants to Canada.

Emergence of 'Visible Minorities' in Canada

In Canada, the emergence of visible minorities to constitute a sizable segment of the population is a rather recent phenomenon that resulted mainly from the changes in immigration regulations in 1967; historically, however, Canada had relied on waves of Oriental labour in the development of major industries and megaprojects in Western Canada (Li, 1998). The term *visible minority* received official recognition in 1984 when Rosalie Abella identified visible minority as one of the designated groups in the *Royal Commission Report on Equality in Employment* (Canada, Royal Commission on Equality in Employment, 1984). The subsequent *Employment Equity Act* of 1986 included visible minority as one of the target groups for which contract compliance in government regulated businesses would be used to improve the employment opportunities of racial minorities (S.C. 1986, c. 31). The 1986 *Employment Equity Act* defines the four designated groups as 'women, aboriginal peoples, persons with disabilities and persons who are, because of their race or colour, in a visible minority in Canada' (S.C. 1986, c. 31, s. 3). In the 1986 Census of Canada, Statistics Canada defined visible minorities to include ten origins: Blacks, Indo-Pakistani, Chinese, Korean, Japanese, South East Asian, Filipino, Other Pacific Islanders, West Asian and Arab, and Latin American, excluding Argentinean and Chilean (Statistics Canada, 1990: 71–2).

In the 1991 Census of Canada, slightly over 2 million people were classified by Statistics Canada as belonging to the visible minority, which was made up of largely immigrants from Third World countries. Members of the visible minority constituted 7.6 per cent of the total population, or 10.7 per cent of the population that declared a single origin only; they do not include the 470,615 individuals who chose aboriginal origin as a single ethnic origin in the 1991 Census (Statistics Canada, 1993).

No doubt, the single most important factor contributing to the growth of the visible minority in Canada has been immigration since the 1970s. The changes in immigration regulations in 1962 and then in 1967 removed national origin as a consideration in selecting immigrants. Since 1967, immigrants have been able to enter Canada on the basis of educational and occupational qualifications, and of family ties with Canadians and permanent residents of Canada. Prospective immigrants from Asia, Africa, and other non-white regions that historically were restricted to enter Canada have been evaluated for admission under the same immigration regulations as applicants from Europe. The removal of racial or national barriers in immigrant selection has facilitated immigration from Third World countries.

As noted earlier, immigration statistics for the period after 1967 show that there has been an increase in the proportion of immigrants from Asia and Africa, and a corresponding decrease in the proportion of immigrants from Europe (see Figure 2.2 and Table 2.3). In the five years after 1967, between 1968 and 1971, Canada admitted 737,124 immigrants, of which slightly over half came from Europe, 15.5 per cent from the United States, and 15 per cent from Asian countries. Thereafter, the proportion of immigrants from Europe continued to decline: from 38 per cent for 1973 to 1977 to 22.6 per cent for 1988 to 1992. In contrast, Asian immigrants increased from 25.4 per cent for the period between 1973 and 1977 to 40 per cent between 1978 and 1982, and then further to 51.8 per cent between 1988 and 1992. Similarly, African immigrants, who made up only 5 per cent of immigrants between 1973 and 1977, rose to 6.7 per cent between 1988 and 1992.

In total, for the period of 25 years from 1968 to 1992, Canada admitted 3.7 million immigrants, of which 35.7 per cent came from Asia, 4.8 per cent from Africa, and 7.4 from the Caribbean. If immigrants from these regions were estimated to be members of racial minorities in Canadian society, then about 48 per cent of the 3.7 million immigrants coming to Canada between 1968 and 1992 would have been members of the visible minority. In addition, if some of the immigrants from central and South America were also counted as members of racial minorities, then the proportion of the visible minority among immigrants to Canada between 1968 and 1992 would exceed 50 per cent. For the same period, European immigrants made up 33.9 per cent of all immigrants entering Canada, and immigrants from the United States accounted for 9 per cent.

The immigration statistics suggest that about 1.8 to 1.9 million members of the visible minority were added to the Canadian population between 1968 and 1992. In view of the fact that in the 1991 Census about 2 million individuals belonged to

Figure 2.2 Immigrants Admitted Annually to Canada by Selected Regions of Last Permanent Residence, 1955–2000

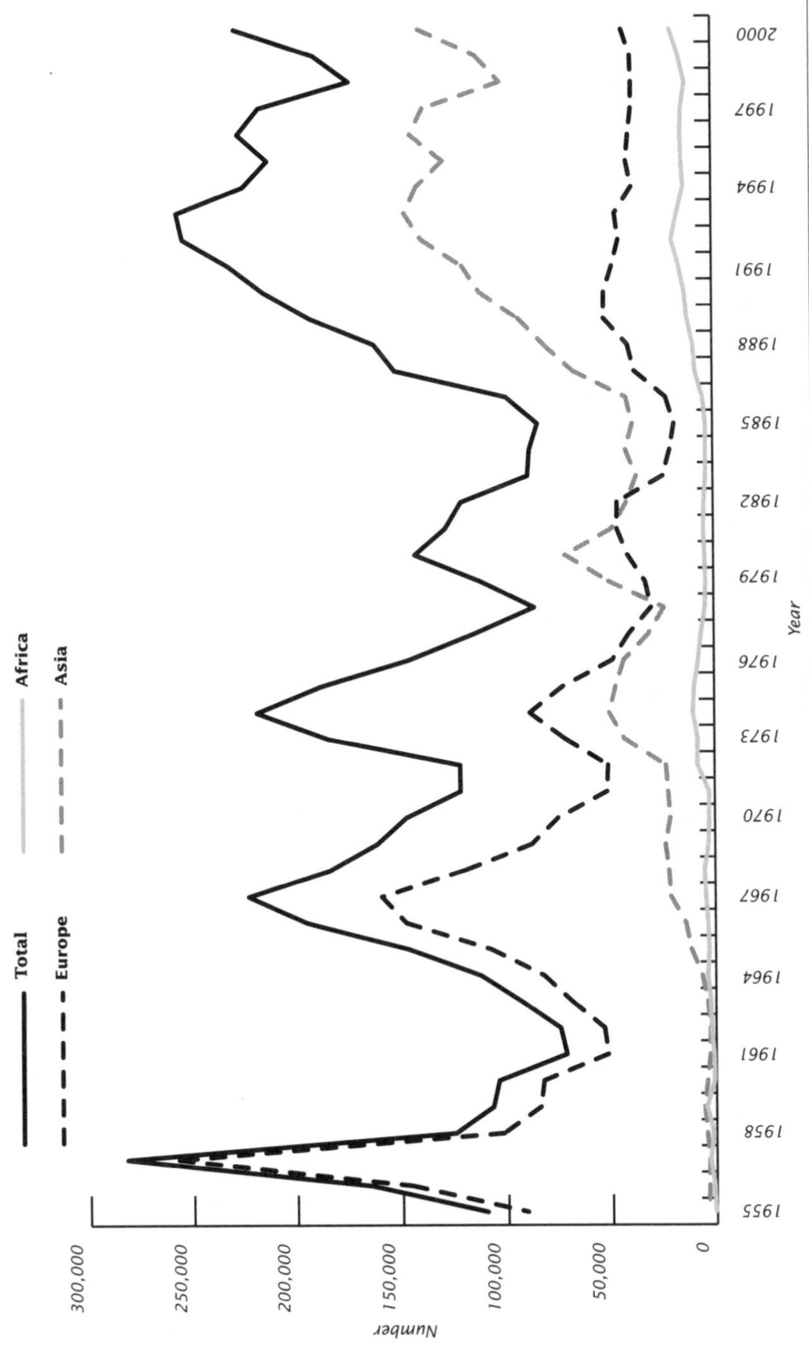

Source: Table A.2 in the appendix to this book.

the visible minority in Canada, then it is clear that most of the growth in the population of the visible minority took place in the period from the late 1960s to the 1990s. The immigration pattern also means that most members of the visible minority are first-generation immigrants born outside Canada, in contrast to most European-Canadians who, because of a historical immigration policy in favour of their admission, tend to be native-born in Canada.

By the time the 1996 Census was taken, the number of visible minority members in Canada had reached 3.2 million people, or about 11.2 per cent of Canada's total population (Statistics Canada, 1998b). It is clear that the visible minority population grew at a faster rate than Canada's population, since the visible minority population increased from 6.3 per cent of Canada's population in 1986 to 9.4 per cent in 1991 and then to 11.2 per cent in 1996. There is no doubt that immigration since the late 1960s has contributed principally to this growth. The increase in the visible minority population is more conspicuous in metropolitan areas, since immigrants have a tendency to move to large urban centres. Thus in 1996, British Columbia and Ontario accounted for three-quarters of the visible minority population in Canada, even though these two provinces accounted for only half of Canada's population. In particular, 42 per cent of Canada's 3.2 million visible minority members resided in Toronto, and they accounted for 32 per cent of Toronto's population. Visible minority members also made up 31 per cent of Vancouver's population in 1996, and 17 per cent of Calgary's (Statistics Canada, 1998b). It is this concentration of the visible minority population in some urban areas of Canada that gives the exaggerated impression that the immigration policy has substantially altered the cultural and racial composition of Canada.

Conclusion

The immigration discourse sometimes overlooks that Canada is an immigrant society in two senses. First, Canada's founding, history, and development are intimately linked to immigration. Second, Canada's existing population is made up of the descendants of earlier immigrants and of current immigrants. Therefore, immigration has been an integral component in the nation building and social development of Canada.

¶Although immigration involves individuals and families making choices about uprooting and moving, international migration is also highly selective. In particular, receiving countries develop immigration policies to regulate and to control the flow of people across national boundaries. Throughout the history of Canada, it has framed immigration policies to address economic needs and to regulate the social, cultural, and symbolic boundary of the nation. Immigration policies provide the gate-keeping function in designating the types of people who are deemed to be desirable immigrants as well as those who are considered unacceptable.

The history of Canada clearly shows that the confederation was founded on the two settler societies of the British and French. Both societies have helped to define the social institutions and the political framework, and have given the nation the characteristic of bilingualism and biculturalism. At the same time, the predominance of European settlement throughout the history of Canada has also given the nation a strong European tradition, in ethnic identity, culture, and ideology.

Prior to the end of the Second World War, Canada has maintained a consistent policy of welcoming immigrants from Europe and the United States and restricting the entry of those outside these regions, notably from Asia and Africa. Four periods of immigration can be demarcated in the history of immigration to Canada. The first one, from 1867 to 1895, represents a period of open immigration from England and the United States. The second phase extends from 1896 to the 1914, covering the 'wheat boom' at the beginning of the twentieth century and attracting a record number of immigrants from Europe to Canada. The third period runs roughly from 1915 to 1945, during which time Canada continued to accept European settlers for agricultural development. The end of the Second World War marked the beginning of major changes in immigration, cumulating eventually in the overhaul of the immigration regulations in 1967 that resulted in a universal system of selecting immigrants irrespective of national or racial origin.

There were many changes in the immigration pattern to Canada in the period after the Second World War. The most noticeable change has to do with the relative decline of immigration from Europe and the corresponding rise of immigration from Asia, Africa, and other non-Europe source countries. No doubt, the changes in immigration policy in the 1960s facilitated non-white immigrants coming to Canada. The changing racial origin of new immigrants to Canada opens up another dimension in the immigration debate, which is related to cultural and racial diversity of immigrants and to how native-born Canadians react to such diversity.

The changes in immigration policy in the 1960s had to do with the changing industrial demand of labour in Canada and the country's shortage of professional and technical workers. Canada abandoned its historical emphasis on national or racial origin as an admission criterion and adopted a universal point system in 1967 for selecting independent immigrants. The immigration policy of Canada in the last quarter of the twentieth century continued to stress the importance of occupational skills and educational credentials as important selection criteria for economic immigrants. In the 1980s, Canada expanded a Business Immigrant Program as another means to attract international investment capital and immigrants with business expertise and experience. Further changes to the immigration policy were made in 2001 with the adoption of the Immigration and Refugee Protection Act. The new policy further stresses the need for Canada to have highly skilled immigrants, that is, those with adaptable human capital to meet the changing needs and labour demands of Canada's increasingly globalized economy.

Chapter 3

The Social Construction of Immigrants

The immigration debate frequently focuses on immigrants and their features—their earning capacity, educational qualifications, and cultural values—and seldom on those who pass judgment on them. Thus, immigrant characteristics are believed to provide the key to understanding immigrants and their impact on Canadian society. Such a belief is not unfounded. Social and economic features of immigrants do influence their performance in the labour market and adjustment in Canadian society. For example, the demographic profile of an immigrant stock and its human capital content in terms of educational level, occupational skill, and linguistic capacity, can be rather informative as to how well immigrants will fare in the economy and society. But how immigrants are incorporated into Canadian society also depends on the ideological preference and conceptual bias of long-time Canadians. In this regard, assessments of immigrants and their influence on Canadian society are contingent not only on immigrants' social features, but also on who the assessors are and what conceptual yardstick they use to benchmark immigrants. In short, how immigrants are socially constructed has a serious bearing on the outcome of the assessment. In this chapter, the notion of immigrant is discussed from three vantage points: the bureaucratic, the folkloric, and the analytic. The chapter shows that the notion of immigrants is socially constructed; such construction often uses a conceptual boundary that stresses the concerns and emphases of the assessors more than the characteristics of immigrants.

The Ambiguity of the Term *Immigrants*

Academic research and policy discussion often make two assumptions regarding immigrants. First, the term *immigrants* is widely assumed to be unambiguous, referring to those who have immigrated to Canada, and who, as newcomers from different backgrounds with unequal individual abilities, have varying degrees of success in adapting to Canadian society. Second, it is believed that the social and economic worth of immigrants can be gauged by immigrants' performance in reference to native-born Canadians. Thus, what native-born Canadians do and think become the benchmarks to measure the success or failure of immigrants. In reality, both assumptions are problematic, but they affect the image of immigrants and their place in Canadian society. In this sense, the social construction of immigrants plays a role in influencing how they are evaluated and ultimately how they are incorporated into Canadian society.

The notion of immigrants is often used inconsistently, depending on whether one applies a bureaucratic or legal definition, a folk understanding, or an analytical standard. These three approaches produce different boundaries in mapping out who immigrants are and what to expect of them. Consequently, assessments of immigrants are influenced by how the notion of immigrants is socially constructed.

The social construction of immigrants delineates who should be considered as immigrants, and places social and economic values on them. The social construction of immigrants also makes fine distinctions among immigrants, in terms of how they are viewed as contributing to the well-being of Canadians and to the cultural harmony of Canadian society. In this respect, the benchmark by which the social worth of immigrants is assessed becomes important, since normative assumptions of the evaluation criteria can affect and indeed distort the evaluation itself.

The Bureaucratic Definition of *Immigrants*

Immigrants are admitted into Canada under different legal categories as defined by immigration regulations and statutes.[1] The definition may occasionally change, but three categories are clear: the family class, the independent or economic class, and refugees.[2] The *Immigration and Refugee Protection Act* explicitly states that the family class, the economic class, and the refugee class are to be used in the selection of permanent residents (S.C. 2001, c. 27, s. 12). Selection criteria differ for these categories. For example, admissions under the family class are usually restricted to close family members of a resident or citizen of Canada, such as a spouse, common-law partner, child, parent, or other prescribed family member. Independent or economic class admission, also referred to as the skilled-worker class, is selected on the basis of education and educational skills or financial and investment capacity of the principal applicant; in the new immigration regulations, some consideration is given to the educational qualifications of the spouse or common-law partner (*Canada Gazette*, Part II, vol. 136, no. 9, p. 58).

There are finer classifications within the economic class, which typically includes skilled workers, business immigrants (self-employed, investors, and entrepreneurs) and those independent immigrants admitted as provincial or territorial nominees. The selection of economic immigrants is made under a point system by which a visa officer assigns 'points' or 'units' to applicants using prescribed selection criteria. The system assigns substantial weight to educational and occupational factors. Under the assessment grid used to assess economic immigrants until 2001, 16 units could be assigned to education, 8 units to experience, 10 units to occupation, and 18 units to education and training (see Table 3.1). The immigration regulations announced in December 2001 establish a new grid, whereby a maximum of 25 points could be given to formal education, 20 points to knowledge of official languages, 25 points to a skilled worker's experience and 35 points to experiences for investors and entrepreneurs (see Table 3.1). In all, between 70 to 80 points, depending on whether it is working experience or business experience being assessed, are now used to assess factors related to human capital. In addition, for skilled worker applications, the new grid allows points to be given to educational and working experiences in Canada, as well as to the education qualification of the applicant's spouse. For an applicant applying for admission under the economic class, the applicant has to meet the minimum points set by the minister in charge of immigration. At the time of writing, the passing mark for skilled workers is set at 75 points. It is clear from the selection criteria that the selection of economic immigrants places substantial emphasis on educational and occupational qualifications, official language ability, as well as the age factor. The system is designed to select working-age immigrants with substantial human capital.

Since the mid-1990s, there has been a strengthening of policy to increase the proportion of economic immigrants admitted annually. Throughout the late 1990s, economic-class immigrants made up more than half of all immigrants admitted, whereas in the mid-1980s they accounted for 30 per cent to 36 per cent of the total annual immigration.[3] In the year 2000, of the total 227,209 immigrants and refugees admitted, 132,118 individuals or 58 per cent were placed under various categories of the economic class; 60,515 individuals or 27 per cent were under the family class; and 30,030 individuals or 13 per cent were accepted as refugees (Citizenship and Immigration Canada, 2001c). The relative decline in the admission of family-class immigrants is particularly noticeable. In 1983 and 1984, family-class immigrants made up close to half of the total immigrants admitted; by the late 1990s, family-class immigrants accounted for 30 per cent or less of the total annual immigration (see Table 3.2).

Since the admission categories are premised on bureaucratic decisions based on regulatory admission criteria, individuals are granted admission if they are deemed to have fulfilled the criteria. However, unequal economic and social values are placed on immigrants depending on whether they are seen as 'selected' or 'self-selected'. In general, those admitted under the family class or the refugee class are deemed as not having met the labour market selection criteria that are applied to economic immigrants, but are granted admissions on the grounds of close family ties or humanitarian considerations. For this reason, family-class immigrants and refugees are often seen as 'unsolicited' or 'self-selected' immigrants, as opposed to those who have the human capital or investment capital to meet the labour market criteria to be admitted under the independent class.

The difference between *selecting* independent class immigrants and *admitting* family-class immigrants and refugees underscores the thinking that economic

Table 3.1   New and Previous Selection Grid for Selecting Skilled Workers and Business Immigrants

Selection Criteria	New Grid For Skilled Worker Immigrant	For Investor and Entrepreneur	Previous Grid
Education (maximum points)	25	25	16
Official Language (maximum points)	24	24	15
Experience (for skilled worker)	21		8
Business Experience (for investor and entrepreneur)		35	
Age (21–49 years of age at time of application, less 2 points for each year of age over 49 years or under 21 years)	10	10	10
Arranged Employment in Canada	10		10
Adaptability (maximum points)	10	6	10
For Skilled Worker:			
Spouse's or common-law partner's education	3 to 5		
Minimum 1 year full-time authorized work in Canada	5		
Minimum 2 years post-secondary study in Canada	5		
Have received points under Arranged Employment in Canada	5		
Family relationship in Canada	5		
For Investor and Entrepreneur:			
Business exploration trip to Canada within 5 years of application		6	
Participation in designated Joint Federal-Provincial Business Immigration Initiatives		6	
Other Criteria Used in Previous Grid			
Education and training			18
Occupation			10
Demographic factor			10
Bonus for assisted relatives			5
Bonus for self-employed immigrants			30
Maximum Points	100	100	
Pass Mark For Skilled Worker Immigrant	75		70

Source: Immigration and Refugee Protection Regulations, Canada *Gazette*, Part II, vol. 136, no. 9, 14 June 2002; Citizenship and Immigration Canada, *Canada's Immigration Law,* Ottawa: Minister of Public Works and Government Services Canada, released Feb. 2000, updated Nov. 2000, available at <http://cicnet.ci.gc.ca/english/pub/immlaw.html>.

Table 3.2   Family Class by Category, 1996–2000

Year	Spouse		Fiancé		Son or Daughter		Parent or Grandparent		Other	
	N	%	N	%	N	%	N	%	N	%
1996	31,628	46.80	3,889	5.75	5,384	7.97	24,417	36.13	2,261	3.35
1997	30,119	50.24	3,079	5.14	4,552	7.59	20,213	33.71	1,990	3.32
1998	28,313	55.64	1,918	3.77	4,010	7.88	14,199	27.91	2,442	4.80
1999	32,824	59.40	1,734	3.14	3,984	7.21	14,481	26.20	2,239	4.05
2000	35,234	58.22	1,519	2.51	3,946	6.52	17,741	29.32	2,077	3.43
Total	158,118	53.75	12,139	4.13	21,876	7.44	91,051	30.95	11,009	3.74

Source: Citizenship and Immigration Canada, *Facts and Figures 1996*, Catalogue MP43-333/1996E, p. 32 (Ottawa: Minister of Supply and Services Canada, 1997); *Facts and Figures 1999*, Catalogue MP43-333/1999E, p. 36 (Ottawa: Minister of Supply and Services Canada, 2000); *Facts and Figures 2000*, Catalogue MP43-333/2000E, p. 41 (Ottawa: Minister of Supply and Services Canada, 2001).

immigrants are more valuable and desirable. This point is often stressed in the official discourse. For example, the 1996 annual report to Parliament by the minister of citizenship and immigration made this point: 'Research shows that economic immigration is the component that benefits Canada and Canadians most quickly and to the greatest extent' (Citizenship and Immigration Canada, 1996: 7). A similar rationale was adopted by the government when it articulated in 1993 its concerns over losing control of the immigration flows that were increasingly dominated by what the government called 'self-selected persons', and as a result produced 'a squeeze on economic migration' (Employment and Immigration Canada, 1993b: 2, 7). In short, there is no doubt that the government places a higher premium on independent or economic immigrants because they are deemed to bring a greater economic value to Canada than those admitted under the family class or the refugee class.

In her analysis of the immigration policy, Abu-Laban (1998) argues that in the mid-1990s, there was a strong emphasis of economic self-sufficiency as a measure of immigrants' worth, and a corresponding shift in assigning priority to economic immigrants over family immigrants and refugees. The policy choice reflects what Abu-Laban (1998: 205) calls 'the problematization of immigrant families', which provides 'legitimacy for the idea that immigrants are a social/welfare/economic cost to Canadians and Canadian society'. The policy emphasis on selecting immigrants who do not drain public resources also has the tendency of pitting independent immigrants against family-class immigrants.

Despite the official distinction between selecting economic immigrants and admitting family-class immigrants, the actual processing of immigrants as the economic or family class can be rather arbitrary. For example, under the current policy, members of a family who immigrate to Canada with the principal applicant processed as an independent-class immigrant are automatically classified as economic immigrants as well, but the same family members who apply to come to Canada after the principal applicant immigrates to Canada are processed as family-class immigrants. For the five-year period between 1996 and 2000, over half of those admitted under the family class were a spouse or fiancé, and another 7 per cent were a son or daughter (see Table 3.2). Thus, about 60 to 70 per cent of those admitted as family-class immigrants between 1996 and 2000 were either a spouse or fiancé or a child, and they probably could have accompanied a principal applicant to immigrate to Canada and would have been classified under a different admission category. Furthermore, some prospective immigrants to Canada may choose to apply for admission under the family class or refugee class for practical reasons, and not necessarily because of lacking educational qualifications or occupational skills. In short, the bureaucratic categories may be useful for understanding how immigrants are processed, but they do not necessarily transpire into logically constituted social groupings that meaningfully reflect the experiences of immigrants.

The bureaucratic classification also raises the question of what type of people should be officially classified as immigrants. For the purpose of obtaining Canadian citizenship through naturalization, those who are permanent residents and have fulfilled three years of domicile in Canada may apply for Canadian citizenship. Once granted Canadian citizenship, naturalized citizens enjoy identical rights and privileges as native-born Canadian citizens. Thus, the granting of the Canadian citizenship is sometimes used to demarcate the transition from the immigrant status to the citizen status. The *Immigration and Refugee Protection Act* appears to indicate that the immigrant status applies to permanent residents. For example, it states that one of the objectives regarding immigration has to do with promoting 'the successful integration of permanent residents into Canada', and that another objective pertains to working 'in cooperation with the provinces to secure better recognition of the foreign credentials of permanent residents' (S.C. 2001, c. 27, s. 3.1). In practice, many immigrant settlement services financed by the federal government explicitly stipulate that recipients have to be permanent residents who have not obtained Canadian citizenship in order to qualify. For example, the settlement program Language Instruction for Newcomers to Canada (LINC), designed to provide basic language instruction to adult immigrants, is open only to immigrants or those whom Canada intends to grant permanent resident status, but not to those who have acquired Canadian citizenship.[4] Thus, from the bureaucratic and legal vantage point, immigrants seem to include those who have been admitted to Canada under various immigration admission classes but who have not yet acquired Canadian citizenship, notwithstanding the fact that a distinction is often made between the selected immigrants and the unsolicited ones in the official immigration discourse.

The Folk Version of *Immigrants*

The folk version of the concept 'immigrants' is also ambiguous in that in its current usage, the term is frequently associated with people who appear foreign-looking to most Canadians. Since Canada was settled mainly by Europeans, notably from France and England, descendants of European immigrants who are now long-time Canadians do not think of themselves as immigrants. In contrast, immigrants from Asia, Africa, and other non-European countries only began to immigrate to Canada in large numbers after the 1960s as a result of changes in immigration regulations. These racially different newcomers pose a challenge for Canada because unlike their predecessors from Europe who are considered similar to native-born Canadians in values and traditions, non-white immigrants are viewed as outsiders who are, by implication of their skin colour, deemed to be too culturally and normatively removed from mainstream Canadians. With the growth of non-white immigrants in Canada in recent decades, the term *immigrants* has increasingly assumed a folk meaning that associates it with newcomers from a different racial and cultural background. This point is also made by Kobayashi and Peake (1997: 7) as follows: 'The popular conception of immigrants refers to people of colour who come from "Third World" countries, who do not speak fluent English and who occupy lower positions in the occupational hierarchy. White, middle-class professionals from British or the United States are not commonly perceived as "immigrants".'

In this popular interpretation of who immigrants are, skin colour is the basis for social marking. Accordingly, members of the visible minority, irrespective of whether they were born in Canada or not, are more likely than those of European origin to be considered immigrants because of their superficial physical features. In this context, the term *immigrants* also implies undesirable newcomers who are too culturally and racially removed from mainstream Canadians of European origin.

The changing pattern of immigration in recent decades probably contributes to the social image of immigrants as being made up of mainly non-whites. There is the prevailing view that changes in immigration policy since the 1960s have triggered a torrent of immigration from 'non-traditional' source countries of Asia and Africa to Canada, and that the sudden surge of non-white population has forced Canada to cope with the problem of increasing racial and cultural diversity. Specifically, the increase in non-white immigrants is seen as the source of rising tension in major cities where immigrants tend to concentrate, based on both real and alleged differences between long-time residents of Canada and immigrants from different cultural backgrounds. There is no doubt that rapid population increases in urban centres like Toronto and Vancouver have put pressure on housing, transportation, schools, neighbourhoods, and public services. But international migration is only one of the sources that contribute to the urban expansion of people and households. Since the growing pressure on the cities is associated with the surge of a non-white segment of the population, the foreign-looking newcomers are sometimes singled out as the cause of urban problems. In this folk interpretation, facts and myths are often muddled. It does not really matter whether non-white immigrants are singularly responsible for exacerbating many typical problems of urban development, but they do provide a convenient albeit simplistic answer regarding why so many unpredictable changes take place within a short period of time. Thus, the immigration question becomes a *de facto* question about non-white newcomers, and about the racial and cultural tension such immigrants are presumed to have brought to Canada.

Throughout the 1990s, the public discourse on immigration has adopted the folk interpretation regarding the immigration problem (see Chapter 7). The interpretation sees Canada and its major cities being swamped by too many non-white immigrants arriving at a pace that exceeds Canada's capacity to absorb them. In this view, Canada's capacity is believed to be stretched to the limit not only because of finite resources, but also because non-white immigrants are seen as particularly costly to integrate as a result of their linguistic and cultural differences. In other words, the immigration question is not just about having a higher or lower level of immigrants coming to Canada, but also about whether Canada should continue to admit large numbers of non-white immigrants whose cultural diversity is seen as incompatible with the cultural and social fabric of traditional Canada.

The folk version of *immigrants* and *the immigration problem* is also reflected in opinion surveys, which often solicit public opinions regarding whether respondents consider that there are too many visible minority immigrants coming to Canada (*Globe and Mail*, 2000a; *Vancouver Sun*, 2000). Based on such polling results, it is sometimes suggested that a segment of the Canadian population opposes raising the immigration level not because of opposition to immigration *per se*, but because of reservations towards too many non-white immigrants (Public Policy Forum, 1994). Media reports are often sympathetic towards the folk interpretation of the immigration problem, and attribute citizens' reservations towards non-white immigrants not so much to racism as to cultural insecurity of long-time Canadians who see their tradition and heritage being encroached by newcomers different from them (*Globe and Mail*, 1994a, 1994b).

In the immigration discourse and in the folk version of the immigration problem, there is a considerable overlap between the concepts 'immigrants' and 'non-whites' or 'visible minorities'. The term *immigrants* frequently becomes a code, in the sense that it contains a subtext, to refer to non-white immigrants, their cultural diversity, and indeed, the urban problems they are believed to have created. Pollsters and reporters, too, tend to accept the folk interpretation of the immigration problem and treat public opinions against higher levels of immigration as the public's opposition to accepting more non-white immigrants. Over time, the folk meaning of *immigrants* assumes a negative connotation that applies mainly to non-white newcomers who are seen as altering the racial composition of immigration, and in turn, changing the racial composition of traditional Canada.

Immigrant as an Analytical Concept

The term *immigrants* can also be treated as an analytical concept. Conceptually, researchers usually use the term to refer to people who have moved from one country to another permanently. Yet in actual studies, it is a person's nativity, or place of birth, that is typically used to determine whether the person is an immigrant or a native-born person. The assumption is that if a person was not born in the same country where the person resides, the person would have to move to the current country of residence, presumably as an immigrant. In reality, children of Canadian citizens could have been born overseas. Using nativity as a measurement would misclassify such people as immigrants when they are Canadian citizens who may have made a decision to move back to Canada.

The analytical notion of immigrants as ones who have moved internationally is not always applied rigorously; for example, children of immigrants are sometimes referred to as second-generation immigrants, even though the so-called host country is their country of birth, and not one to which they have migrated in their generation (see Epstein and Kheimets, 2000; Pereira and Tavares, 2000). Similarly, the notion of returned immigrants suggests that the analytical definition of *immigrants* may not account for those who have immigrated to another country but have returned to their country of origin.

It is in the context of illegal immigration that the analytic and bureaucratic concepts differ the most. By law, those who enter Canada illegally are not considered officially to be immigrants, even though analytically they may share some characteristics with those who immigrated legally, and even though some individuals who enter Canada illegally do end up becoming legal immigrants. The vulnerable status of illegal immigrants also means that they are difficult to document. The analytical concept of immigrants does not exclude illegal immigration as a component, but in practice, academic studies usually do not account for this stream of immigration because data are not readily available.

The notion of illegal immigrants also raises the question about those who may have entered Canada as visitors, foreign students, temporary workers, or refugee claimants, but who eventually may seek an immigrant status and become a legal immigrant. The size of this transient population can be substantial, especially compared to the volume of legal immigration to Canada. For example, between 1980 and 1988, the annual stock of temporary resident and refugee claimant population ranged from 100,000 to 200,000 people, including foreign workers, foreign students, and those classified as humanitarian cases (see Table 3.3). The annual stock measures the total number of people for a given date every year, who have a temporary status in Canada. From 1989 to 1999, the annual stock of such population was well over 200,000, and in some years, over 300,000.

These statistics do not include those who entered Canada using a visitor visa. For example, in 1998 Canada issued 560,003 visitor visas, in addition to granting 42,222 student visas, and allowed 65,148 foreign workers in various occupations to work in the country; for the same year, Canada admitted 174,072 legal immigrants (Citizenship and Immigration Canada, 1999a). It is not clear how many of the foreign workers, visa students, or visitors eventually may become legal immigrants; nor is it apparent how many of the legal immigrants came into Canada initially under a temporary visa. One of the changes made in the *Immigration and Refugee Protection Act* is to permit a foreign national applying to enter Canada as a temporary resident to also have the intention to become a permanent resident, in recognition of the practical difficulty of insisting that an applicant have a single fixed intention regarding their stay in Canada (S.C. 2001, c. 27, s. 22.2). The movement of people across national boundaries as a global trend suggests the need to conceptualize immigration to incorporate many more types of people than the legal immigrant admission categories entail.

Expectations about Immigrants

The three interpretations of immigrants—bureaucratic, folk, and analytical—produce different expectations and approaches about immigrants. For example, the bureaucratic classification inevitably results in immigrants being evaluated in a dichotomy: (1) chosen immigrants who bring in human capital to benefit Canada; and (2) unsolicited immigrants who lack the language capacity and marketable skills to do well in Canadian society. It follows that unsolicited immigrants are by implication a burden to the state since their successful integration to Canada is seen as depending on the state's capacity to provide adequate settlement services to them. The implicit expectation is that unsolicited immigrants do not bring as much value as chosen immigrants to Canada, and that they are costly to integrate into Canadian society. This rationale can easily be used to justify targeting their admission to how much resources the state is prepared to allocate to settle them to avoid undue hardships for the unsolicited immigrants themselves and for Canadian society.

Table 3.3   Temporary Resident and Refugee Claimant Population by Primary Status, Stocks on 1 June 1978–99[1]

Year	Foreign Workers[2]	Foreign Students[3]	Humanitarian[4]	Other	All
1978	9,501	6,124	509	15,812	31,946
1979	33,858	30,587	2,906	29,071	96,422
1980	38,322	33,260	3,957	29,630	105,169
1981	45,679	41,015	8,983	31,790	127,467
1982	48,967	49,077	9,610	29,725	137,379
1983	47,129	49,932	10,004	27,048	134,113
1984	46,943	47,144	13,905	25,577	133,569
1985	49,412	43,260	21,184	25,791	139,647
1986	57,559	39,789	29,754	27,269	154,371
1987	64,425	38,657	44,031	29,632	176,745
1988	73,992	41,781	47,877	29,302	192,952
1989	84,741	46,609	113,025	26,008	270,383
1990	100,100	55,167	145,842	33,150	334,259
1991	105,074	63,147	160,301	36,560	365,082
1992	97,936	67,247	84,776	31,244	281,203
1993	81,885	67,493	79,947	27,694	257,019
1994	71,795	65,630	78,540	27,330	243,295
1995	70,415	64,831	79,015	29,979	244,240
1996	70,833	70,962	81,350	33,861	257,006
1997	71,817	78,249	79,293	35,348	264,707
1998	73,810	79,693	72,331	36,292	262,126
1999	76,853	86,718	69,201	38,863	271,635
Total	1,421,046	1,166,372	1,236,341	656,976	4,480,735

Note: (1) This table shows the annal stock statistics measured on the first of June from 1978 to 1999. The figures are broken down by primary status. A person is included in these stock counts regardless of the type of permit or authorization he or she is in possession of. A person who has been given permanent resident status on or before the date of observation is excluded from the stock calculation on that date. (2) *Foreign Workers* are shown according to whether they hold an employment authorization or another type of document on the observation date. For example, in 1999, 76,853 Foreign Workers were deemed to be present in Canada on June 1. Of those people, 71,834 were authorized to work and 5,019 were authorized to reside in Canada by virtue of being in possession of some other type of authorization. (3) *Foreign Students* are shown according to whether they hold a student authorization or another type of document on the observation date. For example, in 1999, 86,718 Foreign Students were deemed to be present in Canada on June 1. Of those people, 83,510 were authorized to study and 3,208 were authorized to reside in Canada by virtue of being in possession of some other type of permit or authorization. (4) A refugee claimant who has not been issued a permit or authorization by CIC is included in these stock counts as a *Humanitarian case* for two years following the date of his or her most recent appearance in the CIC system.

Source: Citizenship and Immigration Canada, *Facts and Figures 1999*, Statistical Overview of the Temporary Resident and Refugee Claimant Population, available at <http://cicnet.ci.gc.ca/english/pub/facts99-temp/facts-temp-3.html>.

The bureaucratic approach to immigrants means that immigrants, whether chosen or not, are expected to perform as well as native-born Canadians in order to prove their social and economic worth. For selected immigrants, they are expected to match the performance of the average Canadian since they are selected on the basis of their potential labour market contribution. For unsolicited immigrants, their social worth is measured by their not having to rely on the state for settling in Canada and by their ability to catch up with the average Canadian. Given that bureaucratically the immigrant status only applies to those before Canadian citizenship is granted, immigrants, chosen or not, are racing against time to demonstrate their economic contribution in the first few years after arrival before they are 'de-classified' as non-immigrants for bureaucratic purposes.

The folk version of immigrants also produces social expectations, which often reflect less on immigrants themselves but more on how race is constructed in Canadian society. In this sense, the notion of immigrants has been racialized in that the term has become a codified concept for some Canadians to focus their opposition to having more non-whites immigrating to Canada. Oppositions to increases in the immigration level take on the social significance of defending the social cohesion in Canadian society, as some Canadians see traditional Canada and its occidental values and symbols being destroyed by hordes of non-white immigrants from countries that represent incompatible values and different traditions (Li, 2001). Since the 'immigration problem' is popularly seen as a 'race problem' in the sense that 'non-white' immigrants and their concentration in urban centres are frequently perceived as producing social stress and tensions that undermine the social cohesion of Canada, the immigration problem is therefore depicted as caused by 'too many' non-white immigrants flooding to Canada at a pace faster than Canada can absorb them. The idea of a finite absorptive capacity is exacerbated by the belief that non-white immigrants are more difficult to integrate because of their fundamental differences in language, culture, tradition, and values. In short, the superficial racial differences of non-white immigrants are normatively transformed into fundamental cultural obstacles that hinder the integration of newcomers.

The folk version of 'immigrants' and 'their cultural problem' also suggests that despite the official policy of multiculturalism, new immigrants from a different culture are expected to comply with the cultural and normative standards of Canadian society. After all, it is the distinctiveness of the recent non-white immigrants that is seen as causing adjustment problems in Canadian society, unlike European immigrants who are deemed to integrate more easily into Canadian society because of their cultural proximity to native-born Canadians. The undue emphasis on cultural differences creating settlement tensions means that the cultures of new immigrants are not given the same value as Canadian culture and values. These differences, whether superficial or substantive, are made into social problems that are considered to hinder the social cohesion of Canada. It follows that in finding their new place in Canadian society, new immigrants must abandon their cultural distinctiveness in order for them and for Canadian society to avert the problem of integration. In short, the folk version of 'immigrants' and 'immigration problem' calls for cultural conformity and not acceptance of pluralistic cultures and values.

Compared to the bureaucratic classification and the folk version of immigrants, the analytical understanding of *immigrants* as people who have immigrated appears to be unproblematic. However, the analytical approach has made certain normative assumptions about how best to evaluate immigrants. The current state of research is preoccupied with empirical comparisons between immigrants and native-born Canadians. Comparisons are also typically made between those who arrive more recently with those who immigrated earlier to see if the length of residence in Canada makes immigrants more similar to native-born Canadians. To the extent that immigrants, over time, are becoming more like native-born Canadians, immigrants are considered to have assimilated or integrated into Canadian society. Conversely, the display of behavioural patterns and psychological profiles among immigrant groups, which are distinct from that of the majority, is interpreted as the persistence of cultural diversity or ethnicity and a resistance to assimilation. Academic research has implicitly followed the theoretical framework of assimilation in studying the speed and manner by which immigrants become similar to native-born Canadians, despite the popular belief that official multiculturalism has enabled immigrants to preserve their cultural distinctiveness in the process of becoming Canadians. Much research has adopted a benchmark that uses the behavioural standards of those born in Canada to gauge the performance of immigrants.

The Science of 'Benchmarking' Immigrants

Several terms have been used in the literature to refer to the process by which immigrants are incorporated into Canadian society. In policy debates, the term *integration* is often used, although there is no universally accepted standard to determine what successful integration entails. A working group appointed by the minister of immigration in 1994 to examine the question of integrating newcomers defined integration 'as a policy objective in Canada that ideally involves a two-way process of accommodation between newcomers and Canadians' and it suggested that 'the concept integration implies a political desire and commitment to encourage newcomers to adapt to Canadian society and to be received by Canadians and their institutions without requiring newcomers to abandon their cultures to conform to the values and practices of the dominant group, as long as the adherence to immigrants' cultures does not contravene Canadian laws' (Citizenship and Immigration Canada, 1994a: 7). Social scientists have used terms such as adaptation (Goldlust and Richmond, 1974; Richmond, 1974), adjustment (Richmond and Kalbach, 1980), acculturation (Kalbach and Richard, 1990), ethnic identification (Driedger, 1978) and ethnic survival (Reitz, 1980) to refer to the process of change that immigrant groups experience in Canada. By and large, the terms have provided the theoretical directions for gauging the performance of immigrants with respect to how well they integrate into Canadian society.

Although successful integration is difficult to assess without resorting to some value judgments, researchers have suggested that there are definite social advantages for immigrants who are similar or become similar to the two charter groups. As

Kalbach and Richard (1990: 179–80) said, '[I]mmigrants who have been in Canada the longest and who came from cultural backgrounds most similar to the two charter groups have always been favourably regarded as well as those more recent immigrants who have been quick to assimilate with respect to language, social and economic behaviour and have been able to diminish their "visibility".' In short, despite the absence of official policies for immigrants to have to assimilate in Canada, there are favourable social consequences for immigrants who become assimilated with the dominant groups in language, social, and economic behaviours.

Much of the research on the integration of immigrants attempts to find out how immigrants are similar to or different from native-born Canadians with respect to linguistic, social, religious, and economic characteristics. A detailed study using the 1971 Census data uncovered both similarities and differences between the native-born and foreign-born populations of Canada (Richmond and Kalbach, 1980). For example, when age and gender were taken into account, cohorts of postwar immigrants between 1946 and 1960 had similar or higher median earnings than their Canadian-born counterparts in 1961 and 1971; as well, the labour force participation rates among immigrants were higher than those born in Canada. The same study also showed that immigrants tended to be better educated than native-born Canadians, but in terms of family type, first generation immigrants and their children differed little from those of third and subsequent generations (Richmond and Kalbach, 1980: 204–15). Richmond (1984) also reported findings from the 1971 Census that indicated that native-born men and women had higher unemployment rates than foreign-born men and women respectively; however, the 1971 Census data also showed that more recent immigrants had higher unemployment levels than those who had been in Canada longer (Richmond, 1988: 78). Other differences and similarities have been noted; for example, Kalbach and Richard (1990) found that for first-generation immigrants in the 1981 Census, ethnic church affiliation tended to be associated with less acculturation and lower socioeconomic status, but that ethnoreligious differences became minimal after the first generation.

Adjustments of immigrants have also been studied in terms of the speed with which they found jobs, comparing in particular, immigrants who entered Canada under different categories of admission. A longitudinal study that tracked a 1969 cohort of immigrants to Canada for three years found that on average immigrants took four weeks to find work after arrival, and that about 47 per cent of those who found work did not change jobs in the first three years (Manpower and Immigration Canada, 1974d). The study also showed that the proportion of immigrant wives in the paid labour market was higher than that of non-immigrant wives in Canada. Those men who entered Canada as nominated immigrants experienced a higher rate of unemployment initially than those who came as independent immigrants, but the disparity became smaller over time so that by the third year after arrival, the unemployment rates for the two groups were very similar. After the first three-year period, both the nominated and independent male immigrants had lower unemployment rates than that found in the Canadian labour force (Manpower and Immigration Canada, 1974d: 22). The study concluded that by the end of the third year after arrival, the differences between immigrants and native-born Canadians 'on a variety of economic measures had become rather small' (Manpower and Immigration Canada, 1974d: 11). Another commissioned study (Ornstein and Sharma, 1981), cited by Thomas (1990: 10), confirmed that immigrants who arrived in 1976 had similar economic experiences to those who came in 1969. However, another study showed that immigrants who arrived in 1981 did not have lower unemployment rates as compared to native-born Canadians after three years (Samuel and Woloski, 1985).

Studies of immigrants' adjustment have been extended to many facets of life, such as patterns of linguistic retention, family structure, rates of endogamy, religious affiliation, and residential segregation (deVries, 1990; deVries and Vallee, 1980; Driedger, 1978; Kalbach and Richard, 1990; O'Brien, Reitz, and Kuplowska, 1976; Reitz, 1980; Richard, 1991a; Richmond and Kalbach, 1980). The general findings indicate that there are variations according to ethnic origin and nativity. However, over time, immigrants and native-born Canadians become similar in many social and economic aspects of life; children born in Canada of immigrant parents often displayed linguistic and social patterns different from the immigrant generation. These studies suggest that the forces of assimilation are strong in Canadian society, and that over time immigrants do become similar to native-born Canadians in many aspects of life.

Much of the research effort on the integration of immigrants focuses on the process of assimilation, with the implicit assumption that conformity represents 'successful' integration. The theoretical corollary is clear: immigrants who adhere to their linguistic, social, and cultural patterns have yet to conform to the behaviourial standards of native-born Canadians in order to integrate into Canadian society. Thus, despite the policy objective of defining integration as a two-way street that requires the accommodation and adaptation on the part of immigrants as well as Canadian society, it is immigrants and not Canadian society or institutions that are seen as needing to change. In fact, social changes in metropolitan centres that are attributed to immigration are generally not interpreted as desirable, as they are often viewed as urban problems brought about by increases in the immigrant population beyond the 'absorptive capacity' of Canada. Such capacity is hard to define, and is often assumed rather than objectively established. Thus, the scientific approach to studying the integration of immigrants amounts to measuring how immigrants change in accordance to the benchmarks established by native-born Canadians. In this way, the study of 'successful' adjustment is based on the expectation of immigrants becoming similar to native-born Canadians, and rarely based on the understanding that Canadian society and its social institutions also need to accommodate to immigrants and their needs.

Ideological Biases in Benchmarking Immigrants

Empirical research suggests that eventually, immigrants resemble, and in some instances outperform, those born in Canada in a wide variety of comparisons (Li, 1996). Recent immigrants appear to maintain more distinct patterns of behaviour, especially in terms of choice of neighbourhoods, language characteristics, occupational status, and earnings. Over time, however, these differences attenuate and immigrants and their children develop similar behavioural profiles to native-born Canadians. Research also shows that compared to immigrants of European origin, minority immigrants from Asia, Africa, and the Caribbean are more likely to be racialized or stigmatized, because of racial discrimination and a greater reluctance on the part of native-born Canadians to accept them as legitimate Canadians or Canadians of equals (Basavarajappa and Verma, 1985; Beaujot, Basavarajappa, and Verma, 1988; Henry and Ginzberg, 1985; Li, 2000, 2001b; Reitz and Breton, 1994: 90–124).

The research community has also been interested in assessing immigration in terms of the cost and benefit of immigrants to Canada, with the assumption that an optimal level of immigration can be estimated to maximize the benefit and minimize the cost to Canadian society (see Chapter 5). This type of research has succeeded in developing highly constrained statistical models used to calculate the impact of various levels of immigration on the size of the population, and in turn, on the increase in economic aggregates. The best conclusion this type of study has suggested is that given a hypothetical level of immigration every year and assuming a constant fertility rate, the Canadian population will peak at some point, beyond which the increase in population will only bring a diminishing rate of return on productivity. The general conclusion is that high levels of immigration would increase economic aggregates such as production, but the real per capita impact is relatively small (deSilva, 1992; Economic Council of Canada, 1991; Marr and Percy, 1985; Rao and Kapsalis, 1982; Seward, 1987). This type of research aims at placing an economic value on immigration by studying immigrants and their economic impact in terms of selective quantifiable indexes. Thus, contributions by immigrants that cannot be readily quantified are not considered; and on the basis of limited measurements that purport to estimate the economic benefits brought by immigrants and to the extent that relatively high levels of immigration only bring small changes in these quantifiable measurements, immigrants are considered to be able to generate only small economic benefits for Canadian society.

Academic research has not been concerned with the implicit normative standards that have been adopted to evaluate the integration of immigrants, their performance, and their contribution to Canadian society; neither have academics placed a high priority in developing an objectively based and explicitly justified normative standard for assessing immigrants and immigration.

Conceptually, the immigrant population may be seen as a product of Canada's immigration policy. However, the immigrants' place in Canadian society is more than just a product of admission policy, as immigrants interact after arrival with people already residing in Canada, and participate in varying degrees and capacities in the social institutions and social relations of Canadian society. In the long run, immigrants in Canada and their identifiable social features are as much a product of what they were when they first settled in Canada as what Canada made them to be.

The notion of an interaction process between Canadian society and its newcomers also suggests that the former is able to exert changes on the latter, but in time, newcomers would also be able to make changes in Canadian society. However, the reciprocal relationship is not symmetrical in that immigrants are much more vulnerable and powerless in relation to those already established in Canadian society to chart the future course of the country. The influence of Canadian society on its newcomers is more overpowering, given the dominance of those already well secured, and their claim of legitimacy in values, norms, practices, and in short, their way of life, that are reflected in Canadian institutions and virtually every aspect of society.

As Breton (1984: 128) argued, historically immigrants and their children 'were being progressively incorporated into a collective identity and an institutional system whose symbolic character was fundamentally British, but regarded as Canadian'. According to Breton, the changes in bilingualism and multiculturalism policies in the 1960s and 1970s represented state intervention in the reconstruction of a symbolic order and redistribution of social status among ethnic groups that undermined the cultural dominance of British-origin Canadians and the complacency of their symbolic order. Thus, the conflict between those who claim they are a founding people of Canada and others who have immigrated more recently to Canada arises in part out of the former group's endorsement and the latter group's rejection of this status criterion (Breton, 1984: 137).

Others have echoed elements of Breton's thesis; for example, Mercer (1995: 171–2) described how immigrants to Canada in the 1980s and early 1990s have brought many changes to Canadian cities, which become a challenge to Canadians who have historically assumed a 'white tenor' and a 'Eurocentric perspective' in interpreting themselves and the immigration experience. Mercer (1995) also noted that the absorption of immigrants occurs in the areas of housing, labour market, schools, and health and social services, but also in the area of identity that is becoming more racialized. Breton's thesis and Mercer's observations clearly suggest that there is pressure to conform in Canada for newcomers, and there is enduring resistance by old-timers to quash challenges to conformity.

This imbalance of power and influence between those well entrenched in Canadian society and others who enter Canada as latecomers affects every aspect of incorporating immigrants. This fact has to be taken into account, but not taken for granted, by academics if they are to understand the process by which immigrants become a part of Canada. It cannot be presumed, because of the dominance of those already established in Canada and their claim of legitimacy, that their predominance in social institutions and in other aspects of life, and therefore their ability to dictate the terms and conditions of incorporating newcomers, constitutes, *ipso facto*, a logical and natural benchmark against which immigrants must be measured and evaluated. The fact that there are powerful forces assimilating and transforming immigrants in accordance with the conditions and expectations set by the dominant group reflects only the power of those who have maintained their economic and political privileges and have successfully claimed their legitimacy in Canadian society.

It is precisely in 'benchmarking'—the science of gauging the performance of immigrants, their accomplishments, and failings—that many academics take much for granted. Such a scientific endeavour, if it is to be objectively based, requires at the very least, making a distinction between the force of assimilating newcomers as a social fact and the social expectation of their doing so as an ideology. Academics have failed to make this distinction in part because they have accepted the nominal value of another ideal that cherishes the multicultural character of Canadian society. Thus, the existence of the multiculturalism policy is accepted by academics to mean that immigrants in Canada are not socially expected to succumb to the forces of assimilation, unlike immigrants to the American melting pot. The reality, as Reitz and Breton's (1994) comparative study of American and Canadian societies has shown, is that Canadian society is no less assimilating than American society.

Academics' acceptance and defence of the multiculturalism ideal make them oblivious to the normative forces of Canadian society that expect immigrants not to deviate from the benchmark set by those who have legitimized their way of life as Canadians. As many empirical studies have shown, immigrants do not deviate much from the expected Canadian benchmark. Their voluntary conformity is celebrated as immigrants' success in Canadian society, and the occasional failure of some to do so is seen as a problem of integration. Thus, in their unquestionable acceptance of a normative yardstick to measure the performance of immigrants in terms of the behavioural profiles of those already well established in Canadian society, academics have internalized the social norms of those who have the power to set the terms and conditions of incorporating newcomers as though these norms have academic merits of their own.

The problem of benchmarking suggests that academics have to find a more defensible normative standard in studying immigrants. At the very least, immigrant society has to be studied in its own merit in that its creation, its social relations, and its institutions have to be examined as an integral part of Canadian society, and not as a primordial transplant from an ancient land, or as a form of social deviance, only to be eventually converted into the form and manner of mainstream society to which long-time Canadians are more accustomed.

The search for a normative standard also calls into question the reliance of a universal framework in assessing the merits of immigrants in terms of how much they conform or deviate from the expected performance of typical Canadians. If immigrants were to be accepted by old-timers as equal partners in the building of a nation's future, it would have to be a partnership that is premised on a respect and an appreciation of difference, and not an imposition of uniformity as defined by those who have successfully claimed and defended their charter status. The social construction of immigrants and the biases in benchmarking them produce the unrealistic expectation that immigrants are useful to Canada if only they are similar to Canadians. Such a narrow perspective has stifled the thinking that differences can complement what Canada does not have, and not necessarily undermine what it already possesses as a nation.

Conclusion

In the immigration discourse, it is commonly assumed that immigrants' contribution to Canadian society and their successful integration into Canadian society depend on immigrants' individual features, in particular their educational and occupational skills, linguistic capacity, and cultural proximity to the majority of Canadians. Rarely are the conceptual preferences and biases used in assessing immigrants considered as relevant in influencing the assessment itself. This chapter argues that the notion of immigrants is rather ambiguous because it is socially constructed. There are at least three versions of social construction that should be considered: the bureaucratic definition, the folk interpretation, and the analytical application.

The bureaucratic definition defines immigrants according to law as those who have been legally admitted as immigrants under the economic class, the family class, and the refugee class, and who for the purpose of settlement programs, have not acquired the Canadian citizenship. Such a definition is obviously not incorrect, but it narrowly defines the term *immigrants* as applying only to those who have immigrated for a few years until they become Canadian citizens. In the official discourse, there is also a distinction between economic immigrants who are 'selected' on the basis of human capital and 'unsolicited' family-class immigrants and refugees who are admitted because of family ties or humanitarian consideration. Selected immigrants are believed to have more to contribute to Canada and unsolicited immigrants are seen as a greater burden to Canada because of the high cost that is believed to be associated with their settlement. Since the mid-1990s, there has been a strong policy emphasis to increase the intake of economic immigrants and to reduce the proportion of family immigrants.

In the folk interpretation, the term *immigrants* implies those of non-white origin, mainly from Asia and Africa. The term is used inconsistently, but it is often applied as a codified concept to refer to the 'immigration problem' created by large numbers of non-white immigrants coming to Canada within the past two to three decades, changing the social and cultural landscape of Canada. In the social construction of the immigrants and of the immigration problem, the emphasis is on the cultural and racial difference created by non-white immigrants and long-time Canadians of European origin, and on the challenge this diversity has created for the social cohesion of Canada.

The analytical construction of the concept 'immigrants' is mainly used to study people who have moved from one country to another. However, the concept is not rigorously applied when studying second-generation immigrants. Nor is it comprehensively adopted to include the study of temporary residents, refugee claimants, and illegal immigrants.

The various ways of constructing the notion immigrants mean that there are rather different expectations placed on immigrants depending on the specific social value being emphasized. The bureaucratic definition stresses the importance of immigrant selection, and places a higher value on selected immigrants than on unselected ones. The official discourse of immigrants also suggests the worth of immigrants is measured by the human capital they bring to Canada so that those admitted without being subjected to selection determination are seen as not contributing, or indeed as a burden, to Canada. The folk interpretation of 'immigrants' stresses the importance of racial homogeneity and highlights the social cost of diversity. In this approach, cultural and racial differences between newcomers and long-time Canadians are seen as liabilities for Canadian society, and non-white Canadians are believed to be transforming Canada at too fast a pace.

In the analytical approach to studying immigrants, academics adopt an assimilationist approach by using the behaviourial standard of native-born Canadians as a benchmark with which to measure the success and failure of newcomers. Thus, the proximity of immigrants to native-born Canadians, with respect to educational level, earnings, linguistic patterns, and other behaviours, is often used as an indicator of immigrants' successful integration in Canadian society. Despite the policy of multiculturalism, immigrants' behaviourial deviations from that of native-born Canadians are interpreted as a lack of assimilation, and not as immigrants' capacity and success in building a lifestyle in Canada that may deviate from that of long-time Canadians.

The different ways with which the notion of immigrants can be constructed suggest that the assessment of the social worth and economic contribution of immigrants depends not only on the social features of immigrants, but also on who the assessors are and what values are adopted in the assessment. Different social boundaries and normative standards have been used in the social construction of immigrants, and the outcome of the assessment reflects as much the characteristics of immigrants as the ideological preferences and biases of the assessors.

Chapter 4

Immigration and Canada's Population

Immigration is one of the demographic factors that influence a country's population size and its composition. In the case of Canada, immigration has played a key role in augmenting the population of Canada, especially in periods of settlement and expansion such as at the beginning of the twentieth century when the West was developed. For example, during the economic boom of the first decade of the twentieth century, the record level of immigrants coming to Canada substantially raised the foreign-born stock of Canada's population from 13 per cent in 1901 to 22 per cent in 1911 where it remained until 1931 (Manpower and Immigration Canada, 1974c: 13; see also Table 2.1).

The importance of immigration in the early process of nation building does not mean that a country has to continue to rely on immigration for population growth and economic productivity. Indeed, the demographic effect of immigration varies, depending on a population's capacity to replace itself naturally, as measured by the difference between births and deaths, as well as on the volume of net international migration, as measured by the difference between in-migration and out-migration. When a country experiences a high fertility rate and a relatively low death rate, such as in the period of baby boom shortly after the Second World War in Canada, natural increase can play a decisive role in expanding a country's population. Conversely, when a population fails to replace itself naturally because of low fertility and aging of the population, then net immigration would remain the larger source or only source from which a population can continue to grow or even to maintain its current size.

The debate on the importance of immigration to Canada's population growth and economic vitality has been expressed in several ways. For example, the effect of various levels of immigration on Canada's population change has been studied using different methods, producing conflicting results. The debate also questions whether Canada needs a larger or smaller population, given that the country is highly industrialized and that the economy is increasingly based on information and digitalized technology. The future of Canada's population and the role of immigration are also debated, especially in view of declining fertility and the aging of Canadians. The nature of these debates often involves not just objective facts and rigorous analyses, but also value judgments concerning the optimal size of the economy, the desirable quality of life, and the social and environmental sustainability of Canada. Thus, the discourse assessing the effect of immigration on population is also influenced by social values that often lack a consensus. The chapter reviews the scientific studies and demographic trends in Canada to see what kind of conclusions can be drawn about the relationship between immigration and population; it also assesses the likely impact such trends will have on the future of Canada, given the changing age composition and fertility pattern.

The Nature of the Debate

The short-term effect of immigration on population change can be illusive, since the annual flow of immigrants can vary dramatically. As discussed in Chapter 2, Canada has witnessed some large fluctuations in the annual intake of immigrants in the twentieth century, ranging from a peak of three to four hundred thousand a year in the early 1910s to a trough of less than ten thousand a year during the Great Depression (see Figure 2.1). The period after the Second World War saw an increase in the annual flow of immigration to Canada, although relative to the larger total population base in the second half of the twentieth century, the absolute increase in annual immigration only produces an annual flow less than 1 per cent of Canada's population in most years after the Second World War (see Figure 2.1).

The cumulative effect of the yearly arrival of immigrants on the population profile becomes more apparent over an extended period of time. Looking at the foreign-born segment of Canada's population, it is clear that with the exception of the first three decades of the twentieth century, the foreign-born population has remained a rather stable component in Canada, in the range of 15 per cent to 17 per cent of the total population between 1941 and 1996 (see Table 2.1). During the same period, Canada's total population has more than doubled from 11.5 million people in 1941 to 28.5 million in 1996. In other words, immigration has played a consistent role in contributing to Canada's population growth, since Canada's population has been steadily climbing in the latter half of the twentieth century and since the foreign-born population has remained at a steady level relative to Canada's population.

As noted in Chapter 1, Canada is among the few highly industrialized countries with a relatively large percentage of foreign-born population, reaching 17.4 per cent in 1996; the comparative figure is 23 per cent for Australia, about 10 per cent for the United States and 4 per cent for the United Kingdom (see Table 1.1). In short, the fact that more than one-sixth of Canada's population is made up of the foreign-born is yet another indication of the relative weight of immigration in influencing the demographic composition of Canada.

The relevance of immigration to Canada's population growth in the past is well recognized in the immigration discourse. However, the debate revolves around the effectiveness of immigration to augment the population, since the current level of annual immigration is less than 1 per cent of Canada's population, and given that natural increases have historically played a greater role than immigration in influencing population growth. As well, the debate questions the value for Canada to have to maintain population growth in a technological and information age: Does Canada need to rely on an increasingly expanding population to maintain its economic productivity and well being, given that it has achieved one of the highest standards of living in the world and has developed an economy based more on knowledge and global exchange than farming and manufacturing?

This debate is well summarized in a 1974 report by the Department of Manpower and Immigration as follows:

> The traditional arguments are well known: the need to open a new land of vast resources to agriculture and commerce; the development of a population base adequate to sustain a vigorous and diversifying economy; the forging of a national entity that both demographically and culturally could flourish independently on a continent shared with a much larger neighbour. Forcible as they were in the past . . . , the validity of these arguments in contemporary circumstances is now being questioned. To many Canadians, living a modern industrialized and increasingly urbanized society, the benefits of high rates of population growth appear dubious . . ." (Manpower and Immigration Canada, 1974a: 4–5).

In short, the report questioned the need for Canada as a highly industrialized and technological-based society to have to depend on population expansion as an engine of growth, as it had done during the period of land settlement and agricultural development. However, the report was careful not to reject the relevance of immigration to population change; rather, it questioned the need for Canada to rely on population growth to sustain its productivity, thus implicitly questioning the need to sustain a high rate of immigration.

The recognition of immigration as having a role to play in helping Canada to attain its demographic goals was clearly stated in the 1976 *Immigration Act*, which remained in effect until 2001 (S.C. 1976–7, c. 52). However, in the 2001 *Immigration and Refugee Protection Act*, there is no mention of immigration serving the demographic goals of Canada (S.C. 2001, c. 27, s. 3). The Immigration Legislative Review, a federal task force that reviewed the immigration framework for the future of Canada and whose 1997 report greatly influenced the framing of the 2001 immigration act, pointed out that demographic changes in Canada would influence its immigration policy. The report suggests that immigration would be critical to Canada in the face of a declining birth rate and a rising elderly population, but at the same time, indicates that only a significantly large annual intake of immigrants would alter the demographic structure of Canada (Immigration Legislative Review, 1997: 9).

In sum, there is little dispute about the demographic pressures that Canada is facing as result of declining fertility and population aging. The debate analyses the effectiveness of immigration in affecting population growth and the relevance of an enlarged population base to sustain a continuous economic growth.

Conflicting Assessments of Immigration

Several studies have attempted to assess the effects of annual immigration on Canada's population by making assumptions about the volume of annual migration flow and then projecting its likely outcome on Canada's population size and demographic structure (Economic Council of Canada, 1991; Health and Welfare Canada, 1989). These studies have mixed conclusions. Immigration is seen as a factor that can influence Canada's population growth and demographic structure, but its impact is small compared to natural increase if the annual volume of immigration remains at its current level.[1]

The above conclusion is best illustrated by the findings of the Economic Council of Canada in 1991. The Council examined the historical effect of immigration on population change by considering the net effects of immigration on population growth. It offered the following observation:

> Immigration has not contributed continuously to Canada's population growth. Some initial net immigration was necessary well before Confederation to initiate the process of population growth through natural increase. However, from the 1860s to the end of the 19th century, net immigration was negative, on average. Then there was a short-lived but large burst of immigration between 1900 to 1914, as the West was settled. Between the two world wars, however, total net immigration was once more very small, making hardly any contribution to population growth. It is only after the Second World War that immigration became a significant and durable factor in population growth (Economic Council of Canada, 1991: 19).

It is obvious that the Council has stressed the short-term effect of annual immigration on population growth by focusing on whether immigration in a given period contributes in a significant way to population increase of that period, and as a result, concluded that the historical impact of immigration on population growth has been intermittent and inconsistent. This conclusion is understandable in view of the fact that the volume of annual immigration fluctuated widely and that the contribution of in-migration to population growth is counteracted by out-migration in establishing what is known as the net effect of immigration.

The Council also adopted a rather mechanical view regarding the effect of immigration on Canada's population and its economy. Essentially, it estimated the effect of a given level of annual immigration on the size of the population and in turn, on the scale of the economy. It suggested that if Canada were to maintain roughly the immigration level of the late 1980s, which was about 0.4 per cent of Canada's population, the country would reach a population of 32 million people in 2015. Assuming a high level of annual immigration equivalent to about 0.8 per cent of the population size, Canada's population would be 36 million by 2015. Under either scenario, the Council concluded that Canada would remain a country of small influence demographically speaking, compared to European countries, and that immigration would make almost no difference to Canada's relative power in comparison with the United States (Economic Council of Canada, 1991: 64). It is clear that the Council was assessing the effect of immigration to augment Canada's population to a point that would compare favourably to the population size and economic scale of the United States and some European countries. Using a highly constrained model that limits the annual level of immigration to below 1 per cent of Canada's population and comparing Canada to the United States, it is obvious that immigration to Canada could not be effective in changing Canada's world position as a sizable nation.

The federal government created a Demographic Review in 1986 to examine the demographic changes of Canada. In its 1989 report, the Demographic Review considered the scenario of change that involved zero net migration and a total fertility rate of 1.7. The total fertility rate in a given year measures the average number of births a woman would have in her life if she were to go through her entire reproductive years in accordance with the reproductive pattern set by all women of that year. Under this scenario, Canada's population would peak at 28 million in 2011, followed by a slow but persistent decline that would eventually bring Canada's population to 19 million by 2086. If this trend were to continue, the last Canadian would be expected to disappear in 2786 (Health and Welfare Canada, 1989: 2). In short, the report of the Demographic Review suggested that given Canada's declining fertility rate, Canada's population will eventually cease to exist under the scenario of no immigration.

Both studies used innovative ways to study the relationship between immigration and population that resulted in interesting findings. However, they have offered somewhat conflicting assessments about the role of immigration in shaping Canada's past and its future. On the one hand, immigration is seen as ineffective in improving Canada's world stature as a sizable and powerful nation compared to the United States and European countries; on the other hand, immigration is considered the only likely source of population growth for the future of Canada. The reason that the two studies have led to conflicting conclusions is because different benchmarks are used. If the objective is to use immigration to augment Canada's population to a level that can compete with superpowers in terms of population size and economies of scale, then there is little hope that immigration at any realistic level can produce such an outcome. At the same time, given the decline of the fertility rate below the replacement level, immigration is the only source from which Canada can maintain its population.

Immigration and Population Growth

One way to assess the impact of immigration on population is to decompose the change in population size in terms of natural increase and net migration, and to determine the role played by net migration in influencing the population growth. The decennial changes in Canada's population from 1861 to 2000 are shown in Table 4.1. In the 130 years between 1861 and 1991, Canada's population grew about 8.3 times from about 3.2 million in 1861 to 26.7 million in 1991 (Table 4.1, column 1).

Table 4.1 Principal Components of Canada's Population Change, 1861–2000

Period	Population at End of Decade [1]	Population Change from Beginning to End of Decade [2]	Births [3]	Deaths [4]	Natural Increase [5]=[3]-[4]	Immigration [6]	Estimated Emigration [7]=[6]-[8]	Estimated Net Migration [8]=[2]-[5]	% Population Increase Due to Natural Increase [9]=[5]/[2]	% Population Increase Due to Net Migration [10]=[8]/[2]	% Reduction in Population Growth with No Immigration [11]=[6]/[2]
					(in thousands)						
1851–61	3,230										
1861–71	3,689	459	1,369	718	651	183	375	-192	142	-42	40
1871–81	4,325	636	1,477	754	723	353	440	-87	114	-14	56
1881–91	4,833	508	1,538	824	714	903	1,109	-206	141	-41	178
1891–1901	5,371	538	1,546	828	718	326	506	-180	133	-33	61
1901–11	7,207	1,836	1,931	811	1,120	1,759	1,043	716	61	39	96
1911–21	8,788	1,581	2,338	988	1,350	1,612	1,381	231	85	15	102
1921–31	10,377	1,589	2,415	1,055	1,360	1,203	974	229	86	14	76
1931–41	11,507	1,130	2,294	1,072	1,222	150	242	-92	108	-8	13
1941–51	14,009	2,502	3,186	1,214	1,972	548	18	530	79	21	22
1951–61	18,238	4,229	4,468	1,320	3,148	1,543	462	1,081	74	26	36
1961–71	21,568	3,330	4,105	1,497	2,608	1,429	707	722	78	22	43
1971–81	24,083	2,515	3,576	1,664	1,912	1,429	826	603	76	24	57
1981–91	26,678	2,595	3,803	1,830	1,973	1,374	752	622	76	24	53

Source: Citizenship and Immigration Canada, *Citizenship and Immigration Statistics 1994*, Catalogue MP22-1/1997, Table G1, p. 3 (Ottawa: Minister of Public Works and Government Services Canada, 1997); Manpower and Immigration, *Immigration and Population Statistics*, Catalogue MP23-37-1974-3, Table 1.4, p. 8 (Ottawa: Information Canada, 1974).

Undoubtedly, natural increases have played a key role in population increases, but immigration has also contributed in varying capacities to the population growth.

During the latter half of the nineteenth century, Canada's population grew in the magnitude of 460,000 to 640,000 persons every 10 years (Table 4.1, column 2). However, natural increases, or the difference between births and deaths, produced a surplus of 650,000 to 720,000 persons every decade (Table 4.1, column 5). In other words, during the latter half of the ninetheenth century, Canada was able to increase its population by having more births than deaths, but the full impact of natural increases was discounted because there were more people leaving Canada than moving into Canada (Table 4.1, column 8). During the period from 1861 to 1901, net migration produced a population loss, but natural increases more than compensated for the loss. Thus, it would be accurate to say that net migration during this period did not increase Canada's population, but immigration did help to reduce the impact of emigration by offsetting some of the people leaving the country.

From 1901 to 1931, Canada's population gained about 1.6 to 1.8 million persons every decade. Although both natural increase and net migration contributed to such an expansion, it was natural increase that was mainly responsible for enlarging the population. For example, for the periods 1911 to 1921 and 1921 to 1931, natural increases were responsible for 85 per cent and 86 per cent of the population growth (Table 4.1, column 9). Even for the first period between 1901 and 1911 with a high rate of immigration, net immigration only accounted for 39 per cent of the population increase because emigration reduced the full impact of immigration on the population gain.

For the next period, from 1931 and 1941, the level of immigration was low because of the Great Depression and then the Second World War, and the small effect of immigration on population change was counteracted by an even larger flow of emigration that resulted in a net migration loss. However, Canada's population continued to grow because of natural increases.

The postwar period witnessed a sustained growth in population that was produced by both natural increases and net migration gains. The population grew substantially between 1951 and 1961 as a result of the postwar baby boom, coupled with a high level of immigration and a relatively low level of emigration. Overall, net migration accounted for 21 per cent of Canada's population growth for 1941 to 1951, 26 per cent for 1951 to 1961, and 24 per cent for 1971 to 1981 as well as for 1981 to 1991 (Table 4.1, column 10). More recent statistics indicate that immigration has been playing a larger role than in the past in contributing to Canada's population growth. For example, from 1983 to 1986, immigration to Canada was less than 100,000 a year; after 1986, the level of immigration began to rise, reaching over 250,000 in 1992 (see Table A.1 in the appendix). The combined effect of higher immigration levels and persistent low fertility rate results in net immigration accounting for an increasingly larger share of Canada's population growth. Between 1991 and 1996, net immigration accounts for 46.8 per cent of the increase in Canada's total population and 71 per cent of the increase in Canada's total labour force (Denton, Feaver, and Spencer, 1999).

Historically, there is no doubt that compared to natural increases, net migration produced mixed results in terms of being able to augment Canada's population consistently (Table 4.1, column 10). Even in the postwar period, net migration can only be described as accounting for about one-quarter of Canada's growth, while natural increases were responsible for the rest of the population expansion. However, the conventional approach to use net migration to estimate the effect of immigration tends to underestimate the full impact of immigration since the total weight of in-migration is inevitably reduced by the flow of out-migration. In other words, even in periods of high levels of in-migration, the net effect of immigration may be small or nil if an equally large number of people emigrated.

Another way to assess the importance of immigration is to see how much Canada's population increase would have reduced if there had been no immigration (Table 4.1, column 11). For the latter half of the nineteenth century, Canada's population gain would have been trimmed substantially without immigration, and the reduction in population growth ranges from 40 per cent of the gain for 1861 to 1871 to 178 per cent for 1881 to 1891. Thus, if no immigrants came to Canada for the period 1881 to 1891, there would have been a net loss in Canada's population because natural increases were not large enough to offset the great number of people emigrating from Canada.

The effect of immigration on the potential reduction in population gain is particularly evident during periods of high volumes of immigration. For example, during periods of economic boom in 1901 to 1911 and for 1911 to 1921, almost all of Canada's population gain would have dissipated had it not been for the high levels of immigration. It was only in the period between 1931 and 1941 that Canada's population would not have declined without immigration because the volume of immigration during this period was small.

For the postwar periods since 1951, the scenario of no immigration would have reduced Canada's decennial population increase from more than one-third to more than one-half, depending on the decade. Without immigration, 57 per cent of Canada's population gain in the period 1971 to 1981 and 53 per cent in 1981 to 1991 would have disappeared.

If the effects of immigration were assessed in terms of the potential reduction in population growth, then for much of Canada's history, decennial population increases would have shrunk substantially without immigration. The only period that immigration would not have produced a large reduction in population increase was between 1931 and 1941. Simply put, immigration produces a much larger effect on population change than is revealed in net migration figures; it slows down a population decline by making up at least some of the population loss that results from people moving out of the country.

Demographic Trends of Canada

The question whether an industrialized and technically advanced Canada requires a large immigration flow to sustain population and economic growth, as it once did during agricultural development, arises from the idea that sheer labour is ineffective in increasing productivity in a technological age and knowledge-based economy (Manpower and Immigration Canada, 1974a: 4–5). Such an argument, however, tends to consider additional people only in terms of efficiency and pro-ductivity. In reality, the demographic composition can adversely affect the size and shape of a population such that a persistent trend of population decline can even-tually affect its productivity even in a knowledge-based, technological economy.

Several demographic trends have emerged in Canadian society, and will likely affect Canada's future (Immigration Legislative Review, 1997: 9). For some time, the fertility rate of most industrial countries has been declining to levels below the benchmark of 2.1—a level of births that is needed for a population to replace itself over time.[2] Canada is no exception to what European countries have experienced in fertility. Indeed, it is the alarming decline in the fertility rate in Canada since the late 1950s that prompted the Demographic Review to comment as follows:

> Canadian fertility rates are below the replacement level, but because a large proportion of the population is currently in the childbearing ages, the population would, if current rates continue, grow until 2026. At that time, the population would begin a long, slow decline. It would return to the level of the 1986 Census—25 million—in 2086 and would continue to decline, eventually stabilizing at about 18 million or roughly the size of the country in the late 1950s (Health and Welfare Canada, 1989: 1).

The above projection of Canada's population decline is premised on the expec-tation that the fertility rate will at least maintain a given level. However, there are indications that Canada's fertility rate has been falling, and there is no assurance that the decline will stabilize at the current level.

Figure 4.1 charts the total fertility rate of Canada from 1921 to 1996. The figure shows a dramatic shift in fertility over the 75-year period. Except for the decade between the late 1940s and the late 1950s when the postwar prosperity brought about a short period of baby boom, the overall trend has been declining. In 1921, the total fertility rate was 3.5, but it fell slowly and steadily to 3.2 in 1931, and then to 2.8 in 1941, before rising to 3.4 in 1946, when the postwar baby boom period began. The era of baby boom peaked at around 1956 when the total fertility rate reached 3.9, and the period of boom ended roughly in 1966 when the rate fell to 2.8. The total fertility rate continued to decline to 2.2 in 1971, and to 1.8 in 1976. Between 1976 and 1991, the total fertility rate stayed between the level of 1.7 and 1.8, but by 1996, it declined again to 1.6, which is well below the level of 2.1 that is needed for a population to replace itself through births. More recent data indicate that the fertility rate dropped further in 1997 to 1.56, and the decline is expected to continue using different prediction scenarios (George et al., 2001: 8). The continuous decline in the fertility rate in Canada means that it is highly unlikely that Canada will have the capacity to replace its population by natural increases in the near future.

There are other demographic changes in Canada. Besides the trend of declining fertility, the most notable change is the aging tendency of Canada's population. Data on the age composition of the Canadian population between 1921 and 1991 show that the decline in the proportion of the population under 15 years of age

Figure 4.1 Total Fertility Rate, Canada, 1921–96

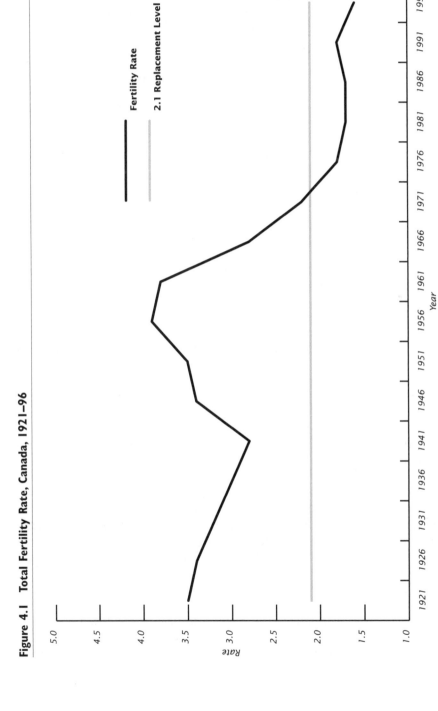

Source: Table A.3 in the appendix to this book.

also corresponded with the rise in the proportion of those 65 years and over (Li, 1996: 76–85). Prior to 1941, the elderly people constituted less than 6 per cent of the total population, and the youth population accounted for over 30 per cent. By 1941, the segment of the youth population under 15 years of age was 28 per cent of the total population; however, it rose to 34 per cent in 1961, mainly as a result of the increase in fertility during the postwar baby boom period. Since 1961, the youth population has been declining steadily; by 1971, it was down to 30 per cent, and in 1991, further to 21 per cent. As the proportion of the youth population shrank, there was a corresponding increase in the proportion of the elderly people. From 1941 to 1961, the elderly population—people 65 years of age and over—hovered around 7 per cent to 8 per cent of the total population. However, by 1981 it climbed to 10 per cent, and by 1991 to 12 per cent. In absolute numbers, the segment of the population 65 years and over had grown three times in the 40-year period, from 1.1 million people in 1951 to 3.2 million people in 1991, while the total population of Canada had expanded only about two times (Li, 1996: 78).

The aging trend of the Canadian population will likely continue, even assuming that the population will undergo an optimistic growth scenario.[3] For example, using a projection based on a medium-growth scenario that assumes a constant fertility rate of 1.7 births per woman, a constant annual immigration level of 250,000, and a life expectancy of 78.5 for men and 84 for women by 2016, the segment of the population reaching 65 years of age or over is expected to reach 16 per cent of the total Canadian population by the year 2016, 20 per cent by 2026, and 23 per cent by 2041 (George et al., 1994).

The aging of the Canadian population is also reflected in the projected decline of the youth population in the twenty-first century. When the census was taken in 1991, the group under 15 years of age was about 21 per cent of the total population. By the end of the first decade of the twenty-first century, the youth population is estimated to be 17 per cent. The decline is expected to continue into the 2030s, before the youth population will stabilize at around 15 to 16 per cent of the total population (George et al., 1994).

As the proportion of succeeding youth cohorts declines, there is a cumulative impact on the working population, which can be roughly defined as those between 15 and 64 years of age. In 1991, the population between 15 and 64 years of age was about 68 per cent (Li, 1996: 77). This segment of the population is expected to continue to grow slightly in proportion by the first decade of the twenty-first century. However, as the declining youth cohorts successively move into the adult population, the working population will decline in proportion. By 2021, the group between 15 and 64 years of age is expected to drop to 66 per cent, and by 2031, to 63 per cent. The decline is expected to continue into the 2030s before the proportion of the working-age population will stabilize at around 62 per cent of the total population (Li, 1996: 77).

Another way to look at the aging process is to compare the projected median age at various time points to the known median age of the population. In 1991, the median age of Canada's population was 34, whereas in 1981, it was 30 (Li, 1996:

77). In other words, half of the population was over 30 years of age in 1981, but by 1991, half was over 34 years of age. Using the scenario of medium population growth, the median age of Canadians is expected to be 40 by 2011. The aging of the Canadian population will continue in the decades after 2011. By 2026, the median age will reach 42; and by 2041, it is estimated to be 44. In short, by the middle of the second decade of the twenty-first century, more than half the Canadian population would be over 42 years of age.

There are further implications that can be drawn from declining fertility and the aging of the population. Over time, these two trends will bring an expansion of the elderly population and a decline in the proportion of people in the working ages, since the succeeding cohorts would be proportionately smaller. When this happens, there would be a smaller proportion of people in the working ages to support a tax system to finance the publicly funded health and income security programs; at the same time, there would be a substantial cost increase in maintaining these programs because of a rising number of users that results from the growing elderly population. For example, again using the scenario of medium population growth, by 2021 there would be 3.7 persons in the working-age population compared to one elderly person, and by 2041, only 2.7 persons in the working-age population to one elderly person (Li, 1996: 77). This represents a substantial decline from the ratio of 5.8 persons in the working ages to one elderly person in 1991 (Li, 1996: 77). In short, whereas 5.8 persons in the working ages in 1991 could potentially share the tax burden to provide the services for one elderly person, that same tax burden would have to be shared by 3.7 persons in the working ages in 2021, and by only 2.7 persons in the working ages in 2041.

The above demographic trends suggest that the decline in fertility will result not only in a decline in population size, but also in a reduction in the work force because smaller successive cohorts will move into the working ages and an increasing elderly population will require public support services.

Projections of Population Change

In view of the aging process and declining fertility in Canada, Canada's population will be unable to sustain a continuous growth in the twenty-first century, unless the gain in net migration can compensate for the loss in natural increase. Statistics Canada has used different assumptions to project the future of Canada's population, and the results show that Canada will have more deaths than births as early as 2016 under the scenario of low growth, and as late as 2036 under the scenario of high growth (George et al., 2001: 64).[4] Sometime between 2016 and 2036, Canada would have to rely exclusively on net migration in order to prevent its population from shrinking because of its inability to replace itself naturally.

Table 4.2 shows the projections of Canada's population change into the first half of the twenty-first century, using the scenario of medium growth. This scenario assumes a constant fertility of 1.48 births per woman by 2001, a constant annual immigration of 225,000 by 2001 to 2002, and life expectancy of 80 years for males and 84 years for females by 2026 (George et al., 2001: 59). The projection

Table 4.2 Components of Projected Population Change Based on a Medium-Growth Scenario, Canada, Selected Years, 2000–1 to 2050–1

Year	Natural Increase	Net Migration	Annual Total Growth	Total Population at Beginning of Period
	[1]	[2]	[3]	[4]
		(in thousands)		
2000–1	99.3	152.5	251.7	30,750.1
2005–6	75.7	160.6	236.2	31,992.1
2010–11	60.2	160.0	220.2	33,141.2
2015–16	45.9	159.0	204.9	34,214.6
2020–21	24.4	157.5	182.0	35,199.5
2025–26	-10.6	156.8	146.2	36,044.1
2030–31	-68.8	157.1	88.3	36,660.2
2035–36	-120.3	157.9	37.6	36,996.8
2040–41	-158.9	158.7	-0.3	37,104.9
2045–46	-183.7	159.0	-24.8	37,050.7
2050–51	-196.9	159.0	-37.9	36,897.6

Note: Assumptions of medium-growth scenario are: total fertility rate of 1.48 by 2001, life expectancy of 80 years for men and 84 years for women by 2026, and a constant annual immigration of 225,000 by 2001–2; assumptions of high-growth scenario are: total fertility rate of 1.8 by 2002, life expectancy of 81.5 years for men and 85 years for women by 2026, and annual immigration to reach 270,000 by 2005–6 (George et al., 2001: 59).

Source: M.V. George, Shirley Loh, Ravi B.P. Verma, and Y. Edward Shin, *Population Projections for Canada, Provinces and Territories 2000–2026*, Statistics Canada, Catalogue 91-520-XPB, pp. 64, 118 (Ottawa: Minister of Industry, 2001).

shows that Canada will experience a net annual loss in population in the magnitude of about 10,000 persons by 2025 to 2026 because of more deaths over births (Table 4.2, column 1). Such a population loss will intensify, reaching about 120,000 persons by 2035 to 2036, and about 197,000 by 2050 to 2051.

Under the assumption of a constant annual immigration of 225,000, Canada is expected to be able to maintain a net migration gain in the range of 152,000 to 160,000 persons per year (Table 4.2, column 2). In other words, the 225,000 immigrants assumed to come to Canada every year will more than offset the people leaving Canada to produce a net gain in the first half of the twenty-first century. It is this net migration gain that will progressively account for a larger proportion of Canada's population increase in the first two decades of the twenty-first century, ranging from 61 per cent in 2000 to 2001 to 87 per cent in 2020 to 2021. From 2025 to 2036, all of the population increases in Canada would have to come from the net gain in migration, since natural increase would only produce a net loss. In other words, after the first quarter of the twenty-first century, Canada would have more deaths over births, and the gain of in-migration over out-migration would be the only source from which such a decline can be slowed down.

Even assuming an annual flow of 225,000 new immigrants to Canada and assuming this number continues to exceed those leaving the country, Canada's population will still begin to shrink by the year 2040, because of the fact that the population gain in net migration would be insufficient to make up for the loss because of more deaths over births (Table 4.2, column 3). The magnitude of population decline is estimated to be around 3,000 persons a year by 2040 to 2041, 25,000 by 2045 to 2046, and 38,000 by the middle of the twenty-first century.

The last column of Table 4.2 shows that Canada's population will likely continue to grow slowly from 2001 to 2036 because of immigration. From then on, the population is likely to stay at around 37 million people until 2046, after which Canada's population will begin a slow decline. The projections make it clear that in the twenty-first century, annual immigration will be the main factor that contributes to Canada's population growth until some time in the third decade, and thereafter immigration will be the only source that slows down Canada's population decline.

Thus far, the projections have focused on the components of change in determining the size of Canada's population. However, there are also corresponding changes in the aging process and in the working age segment of the population. As noted before, Canada's population has been aging rapidly in the latter half of the twentieth century. In 1976, the median age of Canada's population was 27.7, but it quickly rose to 36.8 in 2000 (George et al., 2001: 66). This trend is expected to continue in the projection scenarios of slow growth, medium growth, and high growth. For example, under the scenario of medium growth, the median age of Canada's population is expected to reach 39 by 2006, 42.5 by 2021, and 46.2 by 2051. At the same time, the working-age segment of the population, defined as those 15 to 64 years of age, will continue to decline by proportion. Again under the medium-growth scenario, the group defined with the working ages will decline from 69.5 per cent of Canada's population in 2006 to 61.5 per cent in 2035, and to 60.9 per cent in 2051 (George et al., 2001: 76).

It appears that under all scenarios of projection, Canada will have an increasingly 'older' population as well as a smaller proportion in the working ages. However, the rate of aging and the rate of proportional decrease in the working-age population tend to be slower in a high-growth scenario than in a low-growth one (George et al., 2001: 66–76).

Population Size and Absorptive Capacity

In view of Canada's projected decline in population expected to occur in the fourth decade of the twenty-first century, the challenge for Canada is to adopt a sound immigration policy taking into account the long-term demographic profile of the country. The obvious choice is between maintaining the ongoing level of around 250,000 new immigrants a year, or embarking on an expansionist program to increase substantially the annual intake of newcomers. The choice is critical since the effect of immigration is cumulative but only apparent over an extended period of time.

The argument that questions the wisdom of increasing the immigration level is generally premised on two grounds. The first one has to do with the idea that an advanced industrial society needs a skilled labour force but does not necessarily need an expanding population to increase its productivity, and the second one is related to Canada's absorptive capacity and sustainability.

It is difficult to determine the optimal size of population or of the skilled labour force that is 'needed' for Canada's technology-based economy. As discussed earlier, attempts to use artificially constrained models to predict an optimal population size only produce highly contrived results. For example, using the criterion of maximizing the per capita income of Canadians, the Economic Council of Canada (1991: 25) estimated that the optimal population size for Canada would be 100 million, assuming that production technology and capital investment remained the same. However, it also suggested what it called a 'more realistic perspective' of raising the population by increments of one million people, as, for example, through immigration over 10 years, to generate a per capita income increase of 0.3 per cent. Other projections have also produced results that support the merits of increasing the volume of annual immigration. For example, using the benchmark of the labour force growth rate between 1986 and 1996, which was 1.154 per cent annually or 12.2 per cent over the decade, researchers discovered the following results:

> An immigration level of 227,000 a year, or 0.72 per cent of the population, would achieve the desired rate of labour force growth in 1996–2006. . . . In the following decade, though, immigration would have to be increased to 414,000 a year, or 1.16 per cent of the population, and in the two decades after that it would have to be increased again—to 568,000 (1.37 per cent) in 2016–26 and 591,000 (1.23 per cent) in 2026–36 (Denton, Feaver, and Spencer, 1999: 50).

The researchers also indicated that with no immigration, Canada's labour force would decline in about 10 years, and by 2036 it would shrink by 17 per cent. However, with an annual immigration level of 200,000, the labour force would remain constant from 2016 to 2036, and with 500,000 annual new arrivals, the labour force would be 66 per cent greater and the population 80 per cent larger than what was the case in 1996 (Denton, Feaver, and Spencer, 1999: 48). All these projections suggest if Canada were to maintain the growth of its labour force at the same rate as its immediate past, it would have to substantially increase the volume of annual immigration.

The objection to expanding the annual immigration intake is largely premised on the argument that Canada's productivity can be maintained or increased through production technology and not necessarily through increasing the size of the labour force or population. In short, the argument suggests that Canada can maintain its relative economy position and standard of living by relying on innovation and technological change, rather than increasing the number of people. However, in his analysis of immigration in the United States, Isbister (1996) suggests that both the size of the US economy and its ability to continue to grow are important to protect its world economic stature.

As Isbister (1996: 166–7) argues: 'The sheer size of the US economy makes it the largest in the world and means that the country is a leader not only in the economy but in much else besides—in international politics, diplomacy and military affairs and perhaps also cultural influence.' Accordingly, America may jeopardize its supremacy if it were to adopt a policy of zero population growth when the world population is continuously growing (Isbister, 1996: 167). The reason that the American economy is powerful and influential is not only because it is technologically advanced, but also because it is sizable. Furthermore, even if the productivity of a country can be maintained through technological innovation, allowing the size of its population and labour force to shrink when other countries' economies are expanding in size and in technological improvement would mean an eventual erosion of the economic standing of the country relative to others. This argument is particularly pertinent for Canada in that if the United States continues to expand in size and in production technology whereas Canada only grows in technological innovations but shrinks in population, Canada's economic standing relative to the United States would likely deteriorate, in terms of its ability to attract investment capital, to protect a domestic market, and to maintain a skilled labour force.

Even softening the argument in favour of economies of scale—the larger the population, the larger the scale, and the more efficient the economic production—it is hard to see how Canada can maintain its technological advancement and market advantage over other countries if its population and labour force continue to decline and to age. In view of the demographic challenges of the future, Canada probably stands a better chance to maintain its economic advantage as a technologically advanced society by having a larger flow in immigration than a smaller one; besides adding more people to Canada, immigrants can also contribute to Canada's economy and society in a variety of ways.

The argument about Canada's absorptive capacity—that its capacity to absorb newcomers is relative to its resources and ecological sustainability—is difficult to counteract because the concept is hard to quantify. But an equally imprecise response can be formulated based on the population size in the United States, which is roughly 9 or 10 times the size of Canada. The American economy is certainly powerful, and there is nothing to suggest that the American society is not viable. On such grounds, it would be difficult to argue that Canada has reached its limits of absorptive capacity when its population is only a small fraction of that of the United States. Furthermore, Canada has a population density of 3 people per square kilometre, compared to 29 in the United States (World Bank, 2000: 230–1).

Another loose way to think of Canada's 'capacity' to absorb immigrants is to review the ratio of immigrants to the native-born population. Throughout the twentieth century, the ratio of immigrants to the native-born population has declined. In the first three decades, there was one immigrant to four native-born

Canadians, but that ratio declined to about one immigrant to five native-born Canadians toward the latter half of the twentieth century (see Table 2.1). Putting it in another perspective, the volume of annual immigration in the latter half of the twentieth century only constitutes less than 1 per cent of Canada's population for most years, which is low by the historical standard (see Figure 2.1). These statistics suggest that even if incoming immigrants do incur certain 'costs' to native-born Canadians, by the end of the twentieth century, Canada had a greater capacity to absorb immigrants because the proportion of immigrants relative to the native-born population was relatively smaller than earlier times.

It is equally difficult to establish the relationship between immigration and sustainable development in Canada, in part because the notion of sustainable development is a complex one that incorporates social, economic, and environmental concerns (see World Committee on Environment and Development, 1987).[5] Even if the debate is restricted to one component of sustainable development regarding the environment, it is not clear that there is compelling evidence linking immigration to environmental degradation. However, there are controversial arguments for or against population control. On the one hand, some neo-Malthusians assert that the world population has increased beyond the capacity of the Earth to sustain its population, and that there is little guarantee that future technological advances can accommodate further population growth (Ehrlich and Ehrlich, 1990). On the other hand, skeptics of the Malthusian perspective note that population growth promotes technological advances and creates economies of scale that encourage economic expansions, which in turn can help to eradicate poverty and improve living standards (Harrison, 1992; Simon, 1981). As well, the skeptics argue that a larger and wealthier population is more likely to demand a healthier environment, and a more productive and efficient economy is also more likely to produce the technology needed to improve the environment; thus, a larger population may be less environmentally damaging than a smaller one.

The evidence available is tenuous at best. Proponents of the neo-Malthusian argument have used data on energy consumption to illustrate that excessive consumption in the North has disproportionately contributed to environmental deterioration (Daily and Ehrlich, 1992; Ehrlich and Ehrlich, 1991). Since each resident in a developed country on average is estimated to produce roughly 7.5 times more damage to the Earth's life-support system than a resident in a developing nation (Holdren, 1991), Ehrlich and Ehrlich (1990) argue that migration from the South to the North will eventually result in an increase in per capita waste production, since immigrants tend to adopt the higher consumption patterns of the receiving countries. Critics of the neo-Malthusian perspective argue that despite the increase in per capita consumption and production of waste, population increase has been shown to correlate positively with environmental improvement (Johnson and Nurick, 1995; Lockwood, 1995). It should be added that international migration does not impact on the world population size since the gain of population in the receiving country is the loss of population in the sending country. In terms of the argument that immigrants from less-developed countries would converge to a higher consumption lifestyle after immigration, it is unclear how this behavioural change would necessarily produce a net negative impact on the environment. Over time, as immigrants from less-developed countries adopt the higher consumption level of a country like Canada, they also exhibit a lower fertility rate typical of the receiving society. Halli et al. (1996) have confirmed the latter observation in their study of changing fertility of visible minorities in Canada, and have concluded that over time, the fertility of immigrants from countries of higher fertility converges with that of their adopted country. Thus, immigrants' convergence to a lower fertility would offset, at least globally, the negative environmental impact associated with higher levels of consumption that they may acquire as a result of moving from less developed to more developed countries.

Despite the absence of convincing evidence to substantiate the negative impact of immigration on sustainable development, anti-immigration groups in several industrially advanced countries have used the issue of environmental protection as a pretext to oppose international migration (see Norton et al., 1993; Isbister, 1996). In Canada, oppositions to immigration based on environmental issues have not been strong, although concerns were sometimes expressed in opinion surveys regarding the negative consequences of immigration, including their undesirable environmental impacts (see Ekos Research Associates, 1992).

Conclusion

Data on Canada's population and on components of demographic change suggest that immigration has contributed to population expansion in the history of Canada, in particular, during periods of high economic growth. However, in reviewing this demographic history, it is clear that net migration has not contributed consistently to Canada's population increase, such as in the first half of the twentieth century when the effect of net migration fluctuated substantially, but its contribution tends to be more consistent in the latter part of the century.

Throughout the twentieth century, natural increases have a larger impact on Canada's population expansion than net migration. For example, in the second half of the twentieth century, natural increases were responsible for 76 to 78 per cent of the population increases every decade, and the remaining growth can be attributed to net migration. However, with a higher level of annual immigration after the mid-1980s and with the continuing low level of fertility in Canada, net immigration has been playing a larger role in accounting for about 47 per cent of the population increase in Canada in the 1990s. The actual role of immigration in influencing Canada's population growth also tends to be underestimated because the effect of immigration is typically assessed in terms of net migration; thus, the full impact of immigration is discounted by emigration. If the full force of immigration were estimated in terms of the potential reduction in population gain, then over half of Canada's decennial population increases in the last quarter of the twentieth century would have been eliminated without immigration.

Canada's continuous decline in fertility to a point well below the replacement level and the corresponding aging process of the population suggest that in the near future Canada will be unable to replace itself naturally through births. At the same time, the ratio of the working-age population to the elderly population will probably decrease, resulting in a likely higher tax burden for the working population in the future. These demographic trends also suggest that Canada's natural increases in population in the twenty-first century will continue to decline and eventually produce a net loss because of more deaths than births. The reduction in population as a result of negative natural increases will begin after the first quarter of the twenty-first century, assuming a medium-growth scenario in fertility and immigration. From then on, immigration would be the only factor that would contribute to Canada's population increase until around the year 2036, after which point even a constant annual flow of 225,000 new immigrants a year would be insufficient to counteract the growing decline in population that results from an increasingly larger number of deaths over births. Under such a scenario, Canada's population is likely to peak at 37 million around 2041 before it begins a slow but steady decline.

The analysis of demographic data and population projections only suggests that should Canada wish to stabilize its population level to prevent it from declining in the twenty-first century, it would have to rely on immigration as a source, since fertility is not going to generate large enough birth cohorts to make up for the increasingly larger death cohorts. Thus far, the projections are mainly based on the scenario of medium growth, which assumes an annual immigration level of 225,000 new immigrants. In view of the demographic changes, an interesting question is whether it would be to Canada's interest to maintain a relatively constant level of annual immigration similar to its recent past, or to accept a larger volume of annual immigration for the future. It is difficult to establish what the optimal population size should be for Canada. If Canada were to maximize per capita income or to maintain a steady growth in labour force, all the analyses indicate that Canada would have to substantially increase the current level of immigration.

Two arguments are sometimes used to counteract the expansionist view of immigration. The first one is premised on the idea that in the knowledge-based economy, productivity can be increased through technological innovations, and not necessarily population increase. The second argument has to do with the limited absorptive capacity of Canada, and the potential negative impact of immigration on environmental sustainability. Using the population size of the United States as a comparison, it is difficult to argue that Canada has reached its absorptive capacity when Canada with a lower population density has only a fraction of American's population. It has also been recognized that the reason that the United States is so powerful economically, politically, and culturally is precisely because of its size and technological advantage. Thus, if Canada's population begins to decrease, technological change alone will not be able to maintain its economic position relative to the United States, which is expanding in technology and growing in population. In short, Canada will have an even smaller economy by comparison, even if Canada's technological innovation can keep up with that of the United States. Canada's absorptive capacity is difficult to quantify, but using the ratio of annual immigration to the native-born population as a benchmark, it can be shown that the ratio of annual arrivals to native-born Canadians in fact has declined in the second half of the twentieth century relative to its historical trend.

The argument and evidence on immigration and population change indicate that the future of Canada's population growth, and indeed Canada's future, will be increasingly affected by its immigration policy. The government of Canada sets the annual target levels of immigration as ceilings for admitting new immigrants. In the short term, a fluctuating annual immigration level is not likely to produce a large demographic effect. However, over a long period, the impact of immigration levels on the future of Canada's population can be profound. In view of Canada's history and future, and considering the dubious link between immigration and absorptive capacity, it would be difficult to justify a policy to reduce the size of annual immigration, or for that matter, to just maintain it at the level of about 250,000 a year. Such a policy may economize the short-term cost of settling new immigrants, but it represents a short-sighted view of Canada's future. In light of the well-established demographic trends of Canadian society, it would be a rational choice for Canada to expand the annual intake of immigrants, since immigration would be the only source from which Canada's population and labour force can continue to grow. After all, enlarging the volume of immigration does not just mean Canada's population and labour force; immigrants can also enrich Canada economically and culturally by bringing technical skills, linguistic diversity, international experiences, as well as investment capital and entrepreneurship. The ultimate question perhaps has less to do with whether Canada has much to gain in expanding immigration than whether Canada can afford the loss in not increasing immigration and in continuing a path of population decline. The full impact of such a loss probably won't be realized until several decades later, when even the most aggressive policy to expand immigration may be too late and too slow to alter the demographic future of Canada.

Chapter 5

Economic Benefit of Immigration

In the last chapter, arguments for and against expanding immigration have been discussed in light of the population changes in Canada and its future demographic profile. This chapter reviews arguments and prevailing research findings regarding the cost and benefit of immigration to Canada, and assesses how immigrants have contributed to its economic growth and vitality. As noted before, the immigration discourse is primarily articulated from the vantage point of Canada's self-interest, and the debate mainly concerns assessing whether immigrants bring benefits to the resident population. Naturally, economic benefits represent only one of many considerations of immigration, since immigrants bring diverse cultures and languages that impact the receiving society in many ways. These other topics are discussed in later chapters.

A contentious debate of immigration has to do with assessing the merits of immigration in terms of how much immigrants have benefited or cost the resident population of the receiving society. The debate assumes that the worth of immigrants depends on their ability to generate more benefits than costs to the receiving society, and at the very least, that immigrants should not be an economic or financial burden to the resident population. The underlying thinking is that Canada should admit immigrants who can enrich the existing population and not those who would be a tax burden. It is understandable that such a utilitarian view has become a centrepiece in the immigration debate; Canada enjoys a high living standard and a robust economy that give its citizens reasons to be complacent about its ability to maintain its privileged position in the world, as well as its future capacity. From this vantage point, it is easy to see why immigrants are seen as superfluous to Canada, and why immigrants are deemed worthwhile only if they can bring additional benefits to an already well-endowed nation.

Objectives of the Immigration Program

In the immigration discourse, there is a prevailing expectation that immigrants' worth is measured by their level of human capital and by the net economic benefits they produce for the resident population. This expectation is premised on two assumptions. First, immigrants are deemed unworthy unless they can generate an obvious gain to the existing population, and such a gain is typically gauged in economic terms. Second, the higher the human capital of immigrants, the more they are considered to be productive, and thus the greater the capacity to contribute to the receiving society.

Such assumptions have guided much of the research on the economic performance of immigrants, with most of the efforts going into estimating whether immigrants produce a net gain for the receiving society, or whether the resident population enjoys a higher earning level or a lighter tax load as a result of having immigrants. To the extent that the economic performance of immigrants can result in measurable gains for the native-born population, immigrants are seen as producing a benefit for Canada. Policy discussions have made implicit and explicit reference to the need of having immigrants that benefit Canada. As an example, a document entitled *Managing Immigration: A Framework for the 1990s* that was published by the Department of Employment and Immigration in 1992 made this point clear:

> This (immigration) framework is based on two principles which may seem self-evident, but are worth stating clearly. First, an effective immigration program must allow us to make effective choices. . . . Second, those choices must be made to benefit the people of Canada. This does not mean that we should ignore the personal needs of potential immigrants, or that we should not be mindful of the concerns of the international community. It means that we should attend to those needs and concerns in the context of Canadian interests (Employment and Immigration Canada, 1992b: 1–2).

The above message places substantial emphasis on Canada's interests in the immigration program, and provides only a nominal support for humanitarian concerns. It may seem obvious that Canada should stress the importance of benefits from immigration. However, the objectives of immigration, as described in the *Immigration Act* of 1977 and the *Immigration and Refugee Protection Act* of 2001, tend to be much broader and more visionary than what are typically presumed in academic research and policy debates (S.C. 1976–7, c. 52; S.C. 2001, c. 27). The 1977 *Immigration Act* lists 10 objectives of immigration, including recognizing the need to enrich the cultural and social fabric of Canada, to facilitate Canadians and permanent residents to reunite with their family and relatives abroad, to fulfill Canada's international legal obligations and humanitarian tradition regarding refugees and displaced persons, as well as to foster the development of a strong and prosperity economy (S.C. 1976–7, c. 52, s. 3). The 2001 *Immigration and Refugee Protection Act* also provides 10 objectives for the immigration program, and another 8 objectives for the refugee program. The fact that there are two sets of objectives in the new Act indicates the two programs are intended to accomplish different purposes. Among the objectives for the immigration program are to allow Canada to maximize social, cultural, and benefits of immigration, to enrich the country's social and cultural fabric, to support minority official languages communities, and to reunite families (S.C. 2001, c. 27, s. 3.1). In contrast, the objectives of the refugee program are silent about benefits to Canada, but they stress the primary importance of saving lives and offering protection to those displaced and persecuted, as well as the need for Canada to fulfill its international legal obligations and to express its humanitarian ideals (S.C. 2001, c. 27, s. 3.2). Canada's immigration policy has been structured to admit different types of immigrants, under the family class, the refugee class, and the economic class, in order to fulfill the statutory objectives of immigration. The new Act goes further in actually specifying the selection of permanent residents to include the family class, the economic class, and the refugee class (S.C. 2001, c. 27, s. 12). Despite the clarity in the statutory specifications of the immigration and refugee program, the immigration discourse often overlooks the fact that different objectives are served in admitting immigrants under various admission classes. Furthermore, studies of immigrants in Canada typically treat them as a homogeneous group when compared to the native-born, and assess immigrants' contributions largely on the basis on their economic and educational worth even though some have not been admitted on those grounds.

Statistics on the immigrants admitted to Canada in recent years indicate that there has been a shifting emphasis to admit a larger intake of immigrants in the economic class. The shift is a response to what was seen as too many unsolicited immigrants coming to Canada in the late 1980s and early 1990s. This concern was described in a 1993 government publication as follows:

> There is evidence to suggest that control over the volume and composition of immigration has been eroding. Instead, immigration flows have come to be dominated by persons who are essentially self-selected. This shift has brought with it a concern that the educational and skill advantages formerly enjoyed by immigrants are declining. Only a very small percentage (11 per cent or 24,000 principal applicants) of the immigrants admitted to Canada in 1991 were selected purely on the basis of economic and settlement criteria (Employment and Immigration Canada, 1993b: 2).

It is obvious that 'self-selected' immigrants include those who were admitted on the grounds of family relations or humanitarian considerations and not on selection criteria based on human capital and labour market needs. To highlight the problem of having too many 'self-selected' immigrants, the report quoted statistics pertaining only to principal applicants of the economic class, rather than the entire economic class, which includes principal applicants and their spouse and dependant if they immigrate together.[1] The report then discussed the need to rebalance the humanitarian, family, and economic interests of the immigration program by applying limits (Employment and Immigration Canada, 1993b: 7).

Between 1980 and 2000, Canada admitted about 3.7 million immigrants, 36 per cent of whom were admitted under the family class, 46 per cent under the economic class, and 16 per cent under the refugee class (see Table 5.1). The composition of the admission class varies from time to time, depending on the volume of immigrants the government deems appropriate to admit and the type of immigrants that the government wishes to balance in the program. Such official expectations are tabled in the annual report to Parliament by the minister in charge of immigration.[2] Throughout the 1980s, immigrants admitted under the economic class made up about one-third to one-half of the total volume of immigration to Canada. The shifting emphasis to rebalance the program in the early 1990s resulted in a larger share of immigration being allotted to the economic class. By the mid-1990s, over half of all immigrants admitted every year belonged to the economic class (see Table 5.1). In 2000, the economic class reached as high as 58 per cent of the total number of immigrants admitted that year. Naturally, for a given level of immigration, increasing the relative size of the economic class implies decreasing proportionally the intake of other classes, and vice versa. For example, the family class made up about 55 per cent of the total immigration in 1983, 50 per cent in 1984, but declined to 42 per cent in 1994, and to 27 per cent in 2000, as the proportion of the economic class increased (see Table 5.1). Green and Green (1995) applied this understanding to analyze the effectiveness of the immigration point system in selecting immigrants, and concluded that increasing the proportion of the family class and refugee class reduces the proportion of the economic class that is selected mainly on skills, which in turn causes reductions in the overall skill level of the inflows.

There is no doubt that increasing the proportion of the economic-class immigrants and decreasing that of other admission classes would maximize Canada's interests, if economic gain is the only objective of immigration. However, the very fact that the Immigration Act and the immigration program discuss admissions under different classes is itself an indication that there are other national interests to be maintained besides economic gains. This point is sometimes forgotten in immigration debates and academic research in that immigrants, irrespective of the class under which they are admitted, are uniformly expected to match the economic performance of the resident population and to produce an economic gain for Canada in order to earn their place in Canadian society. Indeed, public debates tend to maintain the same expectation for all immigrants, and academic research tends to apply the same economic benchmark to them, irrespective of the class and therefore the program objective under which immigrants are admitted.

It is rather obvious that if the objective to rebalance the immigration program is to maximize the human capital content of new immigrants to Canada, then placing a strong emphasis on selection would produce such a desirable outcome. The rationale for such a policy change is premised on the concern over the rise of 'self-selected' immigrants and the corresponding decline of economic-class immigrants. It also seems to be justified by several studies that show that recent entry cohorts of immigrants have lower relative earning levels than earlier cohorts of immigrants,

Table 5.1   Immigrants Admitted to Canada by Class of Admission, 1980–2000

Year	Family Class %	Economic %	Refugee %	Other %	Total N	%
1980	35.7	35.1	28.2	1.1	143,131	100
1981	39.7	47.1	11.6	1.6	128,632	100
1982	41.3	42.9	14.0	1.9	121,166	100
1983	54.6	27.4	15.7	2.3	89,177	100
1984	49.7	30.3	17.4	2.6	88,239	100
1985	45.7	31.9	19.9	2.5	84,302	100
1986	42.5	36.3	19.3	1.8	99,219	100
1987	35.2	48.8	14.2	1.8	152,098	100
1988	31.7	49.8	16.6	2.0	161,929	100
1989	31.7	47.2	19.3	1.9	192,001	100
1990	34.3	45.5	18.5	1.6	214,230	100
1991	37.4	37.6	23.1	1.8	230,781	100
1992	39.5	37.8	20.5	2.2	252,842	100
1993	43.9	40.0	11.9	4.2	254,321	100
1994	41.9	43.1	8.8	6.2	223,875	100
1995	36.3	47.4	13.0	3.3	212,869	100
1996	30.2	53.2	12.5	4.0	226,050	100
1997	27.8	58.1	11.2	3.0	216,014	100
1998	29.2	54.5	13.0	3.2	174,162	100
1999	29.1	55.5	12.8	2.5	189,911	100
2000	26.6	58.1	13.2	2.0	227,209	100
1980–2000	36.1	45.6	15.6	2.7	3,682,158	100

Note: Economic class includes business immigrant, assisted relative, and other independants; Refugee class includes refugees and designated class; Other includes retirees, live-in caregivers, backlog, and not stated.

Source: Data for 1980 to 1983 are from Employment and Immigration Canada, *Immigration Statistics 1984*, Catalogue MP22-1/1984, Table IM14, p. 48 (Ottawa: Minister of Supply and Services Canada, 1986); for 1984–7, *Employment and Immigration Canada, Immigration Statistics, 1988*, Catalogue MP22-1/1988, Table IM14, p. 50 (Ottawa: Minister of Supply and Services Canada, 1990); for 1988–91, Citizenship and Immigration Canada, *Immigration Statistics 1992*, Catalogue MP22-1/1992, Table IM14, p. 54 (Ottawa: Public Works and Government Services Canada, 1994); for 1992 –3, Citizenship and Immigration Canada, *Facts and Figures 1994*, Catalogue MP43-333/1994E, p. 8 (Ottawa: Minister of Supply and Services Canada, 1994); for 1994, Citizenship and Immigration Canada, *Facts and Figures 1996*, Catalogue MP43-333/1996E, p. 4 (Ottawa: Minister of Supply and Services Canada, 1997); for 1995, Citizenship and Immigration Canada, *Facts and Figures 1997*, Catalogue MP43-333/1998E, p. 3 (Ottawa: Minister of Public Works and Government Services Canada, 1998); for 1996, Citizenship and Immigration Canada, *Facts and Figures 1998*, Catalogue MP43-333/1999E, p. 4 (Ottawa: Minister of Public Works and Government Services Canada, 1999); for 1997, Citizenship and Immigration Canada, *Facts and Figures 1999*, Catalogue MP43-333/2000E, p. 4 (Ottawa: Minister of Public Works and Government Services Canada, 2000); and for 1998–2000, Citizenship and Immigration Canada, *Facts and Figures 2000*, Catalogue 43-333/2001E, p. 5 (Ottawa: Minister of Public Works and Government Services Canada, 2001).

and that because of the declining human capital content of recent immigrants, they cannot be expected to catch up with the earnings of the native-born within a reasonable timeframe (Abbott and Beach, 1993; Bloom, Grenier, and Gunderson, 1995). However, McDonald and Worswick (1998) and Grant (1999) have come up with divergent results that do not indicate declining relative earnings of recent immigrant cohorts. Although these studies are controversial regarding whether recent immigrants have performed less well or equally well as native-born Canadians in earnings, they have not questioned the fundamental assumption about gauging the worth of immigrants in terms of their earning capacity and the implied benefit to Canada. Using a different argument, Green and Green (1999) have come to the conclusion that immigration policy is not a particularly effective tool to meet economic goals, and that many potential benefits, both cultural and economic, may be realized in generations following the original immigrants. In other words, Green and Green are also suggesting that rather than just focusing on economic goals, there are other objectives of the immigration program that should be considered.

Difficulties in Estimating Benefit of Immigration

Although the question about immigrants' net economic benefit appears to be straightforward, research to date has only produced speculative and imprecise answers. Several reasons explain why estimating the costs and benefits of immigration is difficult and often inconclusive. First, the cost of immigrants to the resident population, if any, is usually short term, whereas the net benefit of immigrants to the receiving society tends to be long-term. For example, whatever public financial costs are associated with immigrants' initial settlement, such costs usually apply to the first few years of arrival. Over time, immigrants work, consume, and pay taxes, and they and their children continue to contribute to the economy indefinitely. Thus, performing a balance sheet calculation based on the first few years of immigration may yield a net cost for the resident population, whereas a long-term perspective would yield a net gain.

Second, tracking the costs and benefits over time is complex since an economic impact in one area is likely to produce a chain effect; as well, costs and benefits affect different segments of the resident population unequally. For example, immigrants willing to fill low-paying jobs may create a benefit for employers by expanding the labour pool and thus by economizing the cost of labour, but they may also create an income loss to those resident workers competing for such jobs. However, the same resident workers may benefit in the long run by moving to higher-paying jobs as a result of an expanded market prompted by higher consumer demands triggered by immigrant spending and the corresponding larger inflows of capital.

Third, a complete accounting of costs and benefits requires developing a theoretical framework to capture all relevant items as well as measuring tools to gauge them accurately. Immigrants pay various kinds of taxes and user fees to the receiving society, and they and their family members receive services and benefit in return. Take public education as a case in point. Should the cost in educating immigrants' children be factored into the equation? If so, should the cost be balanced by the benefit of having properly educated immigrant children, the majority of whom would eventually join the labour force? Should immigrant children's educational costs be discounted by the human capital which their immigrant parents bring with them when they immigrate, since the latter represents a cost to the sending country and a gain of the receiving country? How should the cost of education be estimated, using real cost or marginal cost, that is, the cost in educating one more child since a given cost is already incurred in having schools to service an existing school-aged population? Even if all these conceptual and measurement problems could be resolved, and even if it could be shown that the cost in educating immigrant children could not be recuperated by these children becoming productive members in the labour force when they grow up, such a net cost must be assessed in relation to the net cost of educating the children of the resident population. In other words, immigrant children are entitled to an education in the same way as other children, even if public education produces a net loss for society. To argue that immigrant children should be responsible for whatever higher costs are required to educate them than to educate the resident children on average is equivalent to saying that the right to education and other essential services is not universally based. Similar technical and ethnical difficulties plague efforts to estimate the costs and benefits of practically every area of consideration.

Fourth, systematic data over time regarding immigrants and their economic performance are difficult to obtain, and researchers often have to resort to partial data, usually at one point in time to make their estimates. Depending on the type of data available and the specific items used in estimating costs and benefits, studies can produce different and at times conflicting conclusions regarding whether immigrants represent a net benefit or a net cost to the receiving society.

Despite the many conceptual and technical difficulties involved, researchers have posed three general questions with regard to costs and benefits of immigration. First, what is the relationship between the level of immigration and aggregate economic benefits? Second, do immigrants take more than they contribute to the public purse? Third, are immigrants as productive as the resident population and are they able to earn as much within a predictable period of time? The answers to these questions are complex and often inconclusive. Studies about the economic performance of immigrants in Canada are reviewed in the following sections to see what conclusions can be drawn regarding the economic benefits of immigration.

Immigration and Aggregate Productivity

Canadian economists have tried to calculate the aggregate economic effects of immigration by estimating the effect of different levels of net immigration on Canada's per capita income or employment rate, but have come to different conclusions, depending on the type of simulation model used and assumptions made (see Economic Council of Canada, 1991; Marr and Percy, 1985; Samuel and Conyers, 1987). Samuel and Conyers (1987) cited several studies conducted in the 1970s to show that on the one hand, higher unemployment rates were predicted from hypothetically higher levels of immigration using some simulation models, and that on the other hand, improved unemployment rates were estimated from higher immigration based on other models. These studies were unable to provide a conclusive answer regarding the effect of raising the level of immigration on Canada's unemployment rate.

There were also attempts to determine how different levels of immigration affect economic aggregates such as per capita gross national product or per capita income. Davies (1977) used different econometric models to estimate the effect of raising the immigration level from 100,000 to 200,000 a year for the period 1961 to 1974, and found that such a hypothetical increase would have produced negligible negative effects on per capita gross national expenditure. Rao and Kapsalis (1982) used an improved simulation model to estimate the effect of elevating the immigration level from 50,000 to 100,000 every year from 1980 to 1990, and concluded that the real per capita gross national product would decline marginally by 0.24 per cent in 1980, and drop in the magnitude of 1.5 per cent in 1990. However, Marr and Percy (1985) cautioned the use of such results from simulation models on the grounds that they tend to estimate only short-term economic effects, and that such hypothetical models have to make many assumptions that may be biased or unrealistic.

A study by Clark and Smith (1996) analyzed the volume of annual immigration and capital flows in Australia, Canada, and the United States over an extended period of time, and found that there is a positive relationship even though it is difficult to say whether immigration is a cause of capital flows. In the case of Canada, the study shows that there is a strong correlation in the magnitude of 0.72 between annual immigration and annual flow of capital to Canada, using data from 1870 to 1991. Even though the causal role of immigration is not clear, the authors concluded that there is some evidence to suggest that capital follows labour.

In a 1991 publication entitled *Economic and Social Impacts of Immigration,* the Economic Council of Canada attempted to answer the question as to whether immigration has an effect on the economic efficiency of the host community, in terms of improving the per capita income of the resident population, as well as adding to their tax burden or worsening the unemployment rate (Economic Council of Canada, 1991: 21). It made assumptions about the size of Canada's population to see at which hypothetical population level the per capita income of Canadians would be the highest, and, on the basis of Canada's current production technology and capital investment, concluded that a population of 100 million people would maximize the per capita gross domestic product. Using this hypothetical scenario, the Council indicated that an increase of one million people from Canada's current population would increase the per capita gross domestic product by 0.3 per cent. The Council suggested that enlarging Canada's population through increasing immigration level by 100,000 a year would, over 10 years, produce an increase of $71 per capita yearly for the resident population forever (Economic Council of Canada, 1991: 25). On the basis of such calculations, the Council came to the conclusion that immigration would likely produce a small but positive gross benefit for the present resident population (Economic Council of Canada, 1991: 26).

The Economic Council of Canada has used a highly contrived and restricted model to estimate the economic effects of immigration (Li, 1992). In the model, the economic effects of immigration are only gauged in terms of how it enlarges Canada's population, which in turn, produces a larger work force that brings an expected higher per capita income. The study by the Economic Council of Canada is no more convincing or conclusive than previous research in clarifying the question regarding the economic benefits of immigration. However, based on a review of existing studies and evidence, Foster, Gruen, and Swan (1994) concluded that immigration has had a moderate positive or neutral economic effect on Canada in the postwar period.

Immigrants' Tax Contribution and Tax Burden

Several studies have used different methods to determine whether Canadian immigrants contribute more in taxes than they take in benefits, or whether they draw disproportionately from public assistance programs (Akbari, 1989, 1995; Baker and Benjamin, 1995a; Samuel and Conyers, 1987; Wang and Lo, 2000). Samuel and Conyers (1987) reviewed studies and arguments about the supply and demand of immigrants in Canada to come up with what they called 'a balance sheet approach'. They summarized their findings as follows: 'During 1983–85, it is possible that immigrants may have generated more employment than they took in Canada. And if the composition of immigration . . . remain(s) the same, the employment generation potential of immigration could be true for even higher levels of immigration' (Samuel and Conyers, 1987: 288). On balance, according to Samuel and Conyers, immigrants in the mid-1980s produced a positive economic effect by creating jobs through their demands of goods and services, and this effect was great enough to offset the economic costs of admitting immigrants.

Akbari (1989) compared the consumption of major government funded services and payments of major taxes by immigrants and non-immigrants using the 1981 Census data. The study found that immigrants who had been in Canada for less than 15 years on average consumed fewer government-funded services than non-immigrants, but immigrants who stayed in Canada for more than 15 years consumed more; further, immigrants who had been in Canada for more than 3 years on average paid more taxes than non-immigrants. Extrapolating from the 1981 Census data over the lifetime performance of a typical immigrant, Akbari concluded that a typical immigrant household is a source of public fund transfers to non-immigrant household for at least 35 years after arrival. Similar findings were reported based on data from the 1991 Survey of Consumer Finances that show the average native-born household receiving a transfer of public funds from the average immigrant household that has been in Canada for 11 to 45 years (Akbari, 1995).

Wang and Lo (2000) used aggregate income tax data of immigrants in Toronto to show that immigrants who arrived in Canada between 1980 and 1995 were not a public burden, since the social assistance and employment insurance benefits they received were lower than the taxes they paid. According to the authors, in 1995, immigrants in Toronto were estimated to contribute to the treasury of

Canada and Ontario a sum of $578.2 million—the difference between income taxes paid by immigrants and social assistance in welfare and employment insurance received by them. Furthermore, immigrants admitted under the family class also made a positive but lower contribution than those admitted under the economic class; however, those admitted under the refugee class collected more benefits than taxes in the first 10 years, but paid marginally more taxes than benefits received after 10 years.

Few other studies have taken the 'balance sheet approach' to estimate whether immigrants contribute more than they receive. But there are several studies that have assessed whether immigrants rely more on transfer payments such as unemployment insurance or social assistance than native-born Canadians (Baker and Benjamin, 1995a; Sweetman, 2001). The Economic Council of Canada (1991) used a simulation model described earlier to estimate how an increase in population through immigration would increase the tax gains and tax costs, and concluded that raising the net immigration level from 0.4 per cent to 0.8 per cent of the population would produce a marginal saving for the average Canadian in financing expenditures on health, education, and income security.

Baker and Benjamin (1995a, 1995b) analyzed data from the 1986 and 1991 Survey of Consumer Finances, and found that immigrants have lower participation rates in unemployment insurance and social assistance than native-born Canadians, although over time, immigrants' participation rates increase. Immigrant women also have typically lower participation rates in these two transfer payment programs than native-born women. The authors concluded that there is no evidence to indicate that 'immigrants pose an excess burden on Canada's transfer payment' (Baker and Benjamin, 1995a: 671).

McDonald and Worswick (1997) used data from 11 cross-sectional surveys to study the unemployment incidence among immigrant men, as compared to native-born Canadians, and found that except for one year, unemployment rates were lower for immigrants than non-immigrants between 1982 and 1993. In recession periods, recent immigrant arrival cohorts had higher unemployment probabilities than similar non-immigrants, but with more years in Canada, immigrants' unemployment probabilities converged with that of non-immigrants. The study indicates that the economic condition at the time of immigrants' arrival, in terms of labour demand, has a significant effect on the difference in unemployment rate between immigrants and non-immigrants, but that with more years in Canada, even immigrants who arrive in recession years are able to catch up with non-immigrants. In a subsequent study that compares the unemployment insurance claims of immigrants admitted under different classes in 1980, 1985, and 1989, Marr and Siklos (1999) found that the claims rose in the first few years after arrival, but declined thereafter for all classes after three or four years.

Sweetman (2001) also compared the use of unemployment insurance (called employment insurance after July 1996) by immigrants and native-born Canadians, using data from the 1996 Census and data from the 1998 Survey on Repeat Use of Employment Insurance conducted by Statistics Canada, and confirmed that immigrants were much less likely than native-born Canadians to use the program. Furthermore, immigrant users of the program collected fewer weeks of unemployment insurance and lower amounts than users born in Canada. Sweetman also discovered that native-born Canadians were inclined to use unemployment insurance in temporary layoffs whereas immigrants were more likely to use it after a permanent separation from employment. Furthermore, recent immigrants used more unemployment insurance than earlier arrivals, but not to the same extent as native-born Canadians; however, recent immigrants who were unemployed used more techniques to search jobs and were willing to accept lower wages.

Another approach has been used to assess whether immigrants are a burden to Canada; essentially, it examines whether immigrants displace native-born Canadians from jobs they hold. In a study that examines the effect of immigrant workers on the employment of native-born Canadian workers across 125 Canadian industries in 1980, Akbari and DeVoretz (1992) found that there was no economy-wide displacement of Canadian-born workers by immigrants, although displacements were found in a portion of Canada's economy where a relatively large foreign-born labour content was present and where a large share of value added was attributed to physical capital. A more recent study by Roy (1997) indicates that job displacement effects vary by immigrants' country of origin, and that: (1) immigrants from the United States and native-born Canadians are substitute groups or competing groups in the labour market; (2) immigrants from Europe and native-born Canadians are competing in certain occupations; and (3) Third World immigrants are least likely to compete with native-born Canadians.

The studies suggest that over time immigrants contribute more than what they receive from public assistance. The cumulative difference between what immigrants contribute in taxes and what they receive in benefits represents a net benefit to native-born Canadians. Other studies also show that immigrants rely less than native-born Canadians on unemployment insurance or social assistance. On the basis of the existing studies and available evidence, it is fair to conclude that immigrants have created a saving and not a burden for Canada's transfer payment program, and that the potential adverse economic effect of expanding immigration is nil or small while the predicted economic benefit of increased immigration is modest.

Immigrants' Earnings

Studies comparing immigrants' and native-born Canadians' economic performance indicate differences and similarities, although the direction and magnitude of difference vary depending on the measurement used and the population being analyzed. Researchers also differ in their interpretation of economic disparities between immigrants and native-born Canadians.

Using data from a 1973 mobility survey, Boyd (1985) found that native-born and foreign-born males had similar occupational statuses, but education had a greater influence on occupational outcomes for men born in Canada than immigrant men, and that immigrant women had the lowest occupational status compared to other gender and nativity groups. Boyd (1984, 1985: 440–1) suggests that immigrants are handicapped because the education they received outside of Canada tends to be valued less in Canada, and immigrant women are particularly disadvantaged in their double-negative status.

Beach and Worswick (1993) used the same data and found that immigrant working women had a slightly higher level of working experience, a smaller number of children and higher earnings than native-born women; although immigrant women had lower returns to their education than native-born women, the double-negative effect seemed to adversely affect immigrant women with higher education more than those with less education.[3] Beach and Worswick also found that the number of years since immigration did not significantly change immigrant women's earnings. They argued that immigrants follow a family investment strategy; accordingly, immigrant wives work hard to maximize earnings for a few years after arrival to subsidize their husbands' human capital investment that increases their husbands' long-term market value.

An analysis of the 1971 and 1981 censuses indicated that immigrants earned 7 per cent less than non-immigrants in 1971 when variations in other variables had been adjusted, but the earning profiles crossed after 12.8 years; however, immigrants in the 1981 Census earned about 17 per cent less than native-born Canadians after adjusting for other differences, but their earning profiles crossed after 22 years (Bloom and Gunderson, 1991). Bloom and Gunderson suggested that since immigrant cohorts in 1981 took longer than those in 1971 to catch up the average earnings of non-immigrants, it could be imputed that as a result of changes in Canada's immigration policies in 1974 to increase the admission of family-class immigrants, those arriving after 1974 had lower skill levels than their predecessors. This latter point was reiterated by Coulson and DeVoretz (1993) who showed that immigrants' total human capital flows from all countries to Canada had declined since the 1967 to 1973 period, although there was no significant change in the average educational content of highly trained immigrants for the periods 1967 to 1973, 1974 to 1979, and 1979 to 1987.

Another study of immigrant cohorts in the 1961 to 1986 censuses showed that immigrant men arriving since 1975 and immigrant women arriving since 1970 had lower income than native-born Canadians of the same sex and age group, but that earlier immigrants tended to have higher income levels than their Canadian-born counterparts (Beaujot and Rappak, 1990). Furthermore, in 1986 immigrant cohorts arriving between 1980 and 1984 had lower income, education, and labour force participation than those of the same sex and age born in Canada. Beaujot and Rappak (1990: 138) attributed these disadvantages to the immigrant cohorts being 'less selective on characteristics of education, labour force status and income'.

Using pooled regression estimates based on the 1971, 1981, and 1986 censuses, Bloom, Grenier, and Gunderson (1995) found that immigrant men and women of more recent entry cohorts were estimated to take much longer than those of earlier cohorts to reach income parity with their Canadian-born counterparts, and that 'complete assimilation', as the authors called it (1995: 999), would be 'out of reach for post-1970 immigrants'. Their measurement of 'assimilation' is the regression coefficient of 'the number of years since immigration to Canada', so that a positive value indicates the percentage by which immigrants are able to narrow their income disparity with their Canadian counterparts each year (Bloom, Grenier, and Gunderson, 1995: 993–4).[4] The point about more recent immigrants having a lower earning than native-born Canadians and a lower rate of earning improvement over time was also reported by Abbott and Beach (1993) who showed that immigrants from the mid-1960s to the early 1970s would take longer than earlier immigrants to catch up with the earnings of native-born Canadians.

The finding about recent immigrants having lower relative earnings than their predecessors when compared to the earnings of native-born Canadians has been challenged by several studies. McDonald and Worswick (1998) used pooled cross-sectional survey data for 1981 to 1992 to estimate the relative earnings of immigrant men, and found that when job tenure and macroeconomic conditions are taken into account, recent immigrant cohorts suffered a smaller earnings disadvantage on entry than earlier cohorts. In short, the study suggests that poor economic conditions adversely affect the entry earnings of immigrants and their job tenure, which in turn, affect their earnings. On the basis of the findings, the authors argued that policy adjustment aimed at changing the immigration mix of economic class and other classes in the hope of raising the human capital content is unwarranted (McDonald and Worswick, 1998: 481). Another study, using the 1991 Census, also indicated that immigrants arriving in the early 1980s were improving their earnings at a faster rate than their predecessors, and that those arriving in the late 1980s had similar entry earnings to those who came in the early 1980s (Grant, 1999).

There is further evidence to suggest that even though more recent immigrant entry cohorts may have lower relative earnings than earlier ones, the capacity of more recent immigrants to catch up with native-born Canadians has in fact improved. The earnings of immigrants who landed in Canada between 1980 and 1997 have been tracked by Citizenship and Immigration Canada and used to develop the Longitudinal Immigration Data Base (Langlois and Dougherty, 1997). The data of the 1980 to 1995 immigrant landing cohorts indicate that recent immigrants' earnings one year after landing, relative to average Canadian employment earnings of the same year and the same sex, have indeed declined as compared to immigrants who came earlier (Citizenship and Immigration Canada, 1998). This is true for those admitted under the economic class, as well as those who came under the family class and refugee class, although the decline is more pronounced among the economic class immigrants. For example, male and female principal applicants of the economic class who came to Canada in the early 1980s earned more than the average Canadian, but those came in the early 1990s earned about 10 per cent to 20 per cent less than the average Canadian depending on the gender of the immigrant and the landing year. However, over time, immigrants tend to improve their earnings and eventually reach a level equivalent to the average Canadian earnings. Economic-class principal applicants who landed in Canada in the mid-1980s took over 10 years to reach earnings parity, but more recent immigrant cohorts tend to have a higher catch-up rate than earlier ones, and are expected to take less than 10 years to close the initial earnings difference (see Table 5.2). The pattern of more recent entry cohorts taking a shorter timeframe to reach earnings parity is evident among immigrants in all admission classes. In particular, the data show that refugees who came to Canada in 1995 and 1996, despite their lower relative entry earnings, are expected to catch up with the average Canadian in about 7 years, as compared to refugee arrivals throughout the 1980s who took much longer to catch up (see Table 5.3). As well, recent arrivals of family-class immigrants are also expected to take fewer years to catch up with the average Canadian earnings level than their predecessors. On the basis of these initial findings, it is difficult to claim that the relative economic performance of recent immigrant cohorts over time has eroded, compared to that of earlier arrivals. Using an early version of the same data set, deSilva (1997) concluded that the earnings of male immigrants admitted under the independent class (or economic class), the assisted-relative class, and the refugee class converged rapidly over time, and that age at entry is probably more important than other attributes reported at landing in explaining earnings performance. The findings reported in Tables 5.2 and 5.3, and the study by deSilva (suggest that considerations of immigrants' economic contribution should take into account immigrants' capacity to improve their earnings over time, and not just their initial earnings shortly after landing.

Studies that compare the earnings of immigrants and native-born Canadians have produced findings to suggest that some immigrants have lower earnings that can be attributed to race, gender, and other features not related to education and marketable skills. Consequently, earnings differentials and disparities reflect not only productivity of individuals but also unequal opportunities of society. Shamsuddin (1998) made this point clear in his analysis of immigrants' earnings. Using a 1983 data set, Shamsuddin found that a typical female or male immigrant had a significantly greater endowment of productivity characteristics than their native-born counterpart, but because immigrant women were subject to gender discrimination and immigrant men were subject to discrimination by birthplace, their actual earnings were lower than what they were entitled or expected to earn.

An analysis of income levels of immigrants and native-born Canadians based on the 1981 Census revealed that both immigrant men and women had an average total income higher than Canadian-born men and women respectively (Beaujot, Basavarajappa, and Verma, 1988). However, after adjusting for age and education, only male immigrant cohorts arriving before 1960 and female immigrant cohorts arriving before 1970 had higher incomes than native-born Canadians of the same gender group. As well, immigrant men had higher employment income than native-born men, and immigrant women earned slightly less than native-born women; however, after differences in age and education were considered, the employment income of immigrant men and women fell below that of their Canadian counterparts.

Based on a literature review and an analysis of the 1986 Census, Reitz and Breton (1994: 90–124) concluded that immigrants of European origin earned as much as English Canadians, after adjusting for differences in education and other

Table 5.2 **Years in Canada Needed for Immigrants to Reach Earnings Parity with Average Canadian Male and Female with Employment Earnings, for Economic Class Immigrants, by Sex and Landing Year, 1980–96**

		Male			Female		
Admission Class	Landing Year	Catch Up Initially %	Never Catch Up %	Years Required to Reach Earnings Parity (Excluding Those Who Never Catch Up)	Catch Up Initially %	Never Catch Up %	Years Required to Reach Earnings Parity (Excluding Those Who Never Catch Up)
Economic Class:							
Principal							
applicant	1980	66.6	3.9	8.7	59.0	14.0	5.4
	1981	55.5	0.3	9.9	48.8	1.3	11.0
	1982	53.1	0.2	6.7	54.9	1.4	6.7
	1983	33.1	2.6	10.7	20.4	3.0	11.3
	1984	28.3	1.2	16.6	14.6	1.1	19.0
	1985	21.5	9.5	12.5	22.5	2.7	12.3
	1986	32.0	5.7	10.8	29.9	5.9	12.7
	1987	35.1	5.7	11.3	55.0	3.4	6.4
	1988	27.7	4.0	6.4	80.9	2.0	3.9
	1989	10.0	0.3	8.1	52.7	1.2	4.2
	1990	4.4	0.6	16.9	39.3	1.0	4.9
	1991	2.4	0.9	9.3	5.6	3.8	5.1
	1992	3.0	0.6	10.5	5.7	3.6	5.0
	1993	3.3	0.5	15.8	4.3	0.6	5.3
	1994	3.0	0.7	7.7	3.7	1.0	4.8
	1995	1.3	0.4	4.3	3.5	4.1	3.1
	1996	4.0	0.4	3.3	3.8	0.5	2.8
Economic Class:							
Spouse and							
dependant	1980	7.9	4.1	11.1	7.3	2.9	11.7
	1981	7.8	0.7	14.1	7.9	3.6	11.1
	1982	2.4	1.9	13.6	8.4	2.2	10.7
	1983	7.8	5.1	13.6	4.6	1.2	12.0
	1984	8.1	6.8	14.2	4.7	3.2	25.4
	1985	2.8	12.8	13.4	9.2	0.3	13.6
	1986	7.0	4.0	11.4	7.4	3.7	10.8
	1987	4.3	5.2	10.3	5.3	1.7	10.5
	1988	4.6	3.0	10.9	2.6	0.3	10.6
	1989	2.3	1.0	10.4	2.8	0.3	9.4
	1990	0.6	0.7	9.9	1.2	0.0	9.3

Table 5.2   *(continued)*

Admission Class	Landing Year	Male Catch Up Initially %	Male Never Catch Up %	Male Years Required to Reach Earnings Parity (Excluding Those Who Never Catch Up)	Female Catch Up Initially %	Female Never Catch Up %	Female Years Required to Reach Earnings Parity (Excluding Those Who Never Catch Up)
	1991	0.2	2.0	11.5	0.4	0.1	9.1
	1992	0.3	1.2	9.1	0.4	0.2	9.4
	1993	0.0	1.3	9.3	1.2	0.3	9.1
	1994	0.3	1.2	8.9	0.1	1.6	8.5
	1995	0.7	0.5	8.0	0.0	0.7	6.2
	1996	0.6	3.5	5.2	1.6	0.7	4.5

Source: Author's calculations using data from IMDB (Longitudinal Immigration Data Base) custom-made compendium tables, 1980–97, based on immigrants with employment earnings. The IMDB is developed by Citizenship and Immigration Canada and Statistics Canada.

Table 5.3   Years in Canada Needed for Immigrants to Reach Earnings Parity with Average Canadian Male and Female with Employment Earnings, for Family Class and Refugee Class Immigrants, by Sex and Landing Year, 1980–96

Admission Class	Landing Year	Male Catch Up Initially %	Male Never Catch Up %	Male Years Required to Reach Earnings Parity (Excluding Those Who Never Catch Up)	Female Catch Up Initially %	Female Never Catch Up %	Female Years Required to Reach Earnings Parity (Excluding Those Who Never Catch Up)
Family Class:							
	1980	6.3	1.7	16.6	8.0	2.5	16.3
	1981	5.0	3.4	14.7	7.8	0.7	16.2
	1982	1.1	2.1	14.8	7.0	1.8	13.6
	1983	1.1	0.7	23.2	6.9	1.3	14.5
	1984	2.8	3.3	22.7	6.3	0.3	15.9
	1985	1.7	2.9	14.1	5.3	2.8	13.3
	1986	2.2	2.2	14.6	6.2	2.1	14.8
	1987	1.0	5.5	20.8	3.4	1.5	16.3
	1988	0.5	3.9	15.2	3.9	2.0	17.9
	1989	0.8	3.0	13.7	2.1	2.8	13.4
	1990	0.2	1.9	12.8	2.6	0.9	12.8

Table 5.3 *(continued)*

		Male			Female		
Admission Class	Landing Year	Catch Up Initially %	Never Catch Up %	Years Required to Reach Earnings Parity (Excluding Those Who Never Catch Up)	Catch Up Initially %	Never Catch Up %	Years Required to Reach Earnings Parity (Excluding Those Who Never Catch Up)
	1991	0.0	1.0	13.2	1.0	0.5	12.7
	1992	0.1	0.9	10.5	0.3	1.0	10.4
	1993	0.1	0.9	10.4	1.3	0.8	10.7
	1994	0.0	1.1	9.8	1.5	1.6	11.1
	1995	0.1	1.4	8.3	1.5	1.0	8.0
	1996	0.5	0.5	6.8	2.3	1.1	5.8
Refugee Class:							
	1980	2.9	0.4	18.9	4.6	0.6	16.3
	1981	2.4	0.6	13.0	1.1	0.2	15.0
	1982	2.1	0.2	11.6	1.5	0.7	11.8
	1983	1.9	0.1	13.8	1.3	0.1	13.2
	1984	1.4	0.8	14.0	0.7	1.9	14.0
	1985	2.4	0.1	14.0	2.0	0.7	13.4
	1986	0.2	0.3	13.5	2.2	0.9	13.1
	1987	0.1	0.6	13.8	0.4	0.9	12.6
	1988	0.2	0.4	13.5	0.6	0.7	12.9
	1989	0.1	0.3	12.1	0.1	0.5	16.5
	1990	0.0	0.4	10.7	0.1	0.2	10.3
	1991	0.0	0.8	10.3	0.6	0.7	9.9
	1992	0.0	1.9	10.5	0.1	1.4	10.0
	1993	0.2	0.9	10.7	0.2	2.7	10.7
	1994	0.3	1.2	7.2	0.1	3.7	14.1
	1995	0.0	0.7	7.8	0.8	6.1	6.9
	1996	0.0	2.4	7.0	0.7	9.1	6.5

Source: Author's calculations using data from IMDB (Longitudinal Immigration Data Base) custom-made compendium tables, 1980–97, based on immigrants with employment earnings. The IMDB is developed by Citizenship and Immigration Canada and Statistics Canada.

demographic factors; however, non-European immigrant men and women, mainly blacks and Asians, had an income disadvantage relative to European immigrant men and women respectively. Also using the 1986 Census, Boyd (1992) showed that native-born racial minorities were less disadvantaged than foreign-born minority immigrants in earnings, as compared to native-born European Canadians. Pendakur and Pendakur (1998, 2000) used data from the 1991 Census to show that visible minority immigrants suffered larger earnings differentials than white immigrants after controlling for occupation, industry of work, education, potential experience, knowledge of official languages and other factors, and that for immigrants, earnings penalties that can be attributed to visible minority status are greater for men than for women.

The studies comparing economic performance show that immigrants have an average earnings level similar to or higher than non-immigrants, but immigrants, especially visible minorities, have lower earnings after accounting for differences in education and other variables. The studies also indicate that although returns to schooling are lower for immigrants than native-born Canadians, this disparity narrows the longer immigrants stay in Canada. Several studies have pointed out that more recent immigrant cohorts, probably because they have less human capital, did not earn as much as those who came earlier when compared to native-born Canadians, and that it would take them longer to catch up. However, more recent data indicate that recent cohorts, irrespective of the class of admission, are expected to take fewer years to catch up with the earnings of the average Canadian than earlier cohorts.

Immigrants' Costs and Benefits

What can be concluded from the vast body of literature that attempts to determine the costs or benefits of immigration? The answer depends on the specific empirical question posed, the method used, and the theoretical interpretation adopted. If the net benefit of immigration is defined as the ability of new immigrants to augment the national aggregate production and to improve the per capita income of the resident population, then the available studies have produced mixed results—some show immigration bringing a small gain in per capita income and others show a marginal loss. The prevailing conclusion is that an increase in immigration would increase marginally the per capita income. However, the findings are based on studies using simulation models that make assumptions that may be unrealistic.

If the net benefits of immigrants are gauged in terms of whether they contribute more taxes than social benefits they receive, then the few available studies indicate that over the course of their life, immigrants contribute taxes that exceed the costs of social assistance and social benefits they receive through transfer payments. Other studies also show that immigrants rely less on social assistance than native-born Canadians. Thus, native-born Canadians can be said to benefit from immigrants in that the savings from immigrants can be considered as a source of public fund transfers to non-immigrants. However, estimates based on a balance-sheet approach are sensitive to the items included as costs and benefits, as well as on the timeframe used.

If immigrants' benefits to Canada are measured in terms of individual productivity or earnings, then the literature indicates that immigrants have earnings similar to or higher than native-born Canadians; but there are substantial variations among immigrants depending on the entry cohort, length of residence in Canada, gender, country of origin, and other characteristics. Furthermore, some immigrants are disadvantaged in that their earnings are lower than native-born Canadians' once variations in education and other social and economic features are taken into account. Thus, if gross earnings are used as a measurement of individual productivity, immigrants are as productive as native-born Canadians. If net earnings—that is, earnings that would result if immigrants and native-born Canadians had similar characteristics—were used as a proxy of productivity, then many immigrants would earn less than native-born Canadians. However, such earnings differentials can also be interpreted as the result of social inequality and not individual productivity.[5]

The findings of some studies suggest that recent immigrants are less productive than earlier ones, on the grounds that the relative earnings of more recent immigrant entry cohorts are lower than that of earlier ones. However, other studies have challenged this conclusion and suggested that macroeconomic conditions affect the job opportunity and therefore earnings opportunity of immigrants. There is also evidence to indicate that recent immigrants are expected to improve their relative entry earnings faster than their predecessors, and on this basis, it is difficult to claim that more recent immigrants are less productive than earlier arrivals.

Immigrants and Canada's Labour Force

Thus far, economic costs and benefits of immigrants have been evaluated in a framework that contains two segments of the labour force—immigrants and native-born Canadians—to see whether the former benefits the latter. Immigrants and native-born Canadians are cast as opposites in that the economic loss of one group is the gain of the other. This narrow framework views the contributions of immigrants in terms of their capacity to increase Canada's economic efficiency, which is measured by increments in the per capita earnings of native-born Canadians as a result of immigration. In this way, the mere ability of immigrants to enlarge the economy is seen as only increasing the economic scale and not its efficiency.

The value of immigrants to Canada can be seen in a different light—the reliance on immigrants to fill industries' additional demands of labour during postwar economic booms, especially when emigration levels were high. Parai (1965) studied immigration and emigration of Canada between 1950 and 1963, and found that in the two decades prior to 1967, Canada was losing professional and technical workers to the United States. However, Canada was able to compensate for the loss and in fact enjoyed a net gain in professional and skilled labour because of immigration to Canada from around the world.

Census data from 1961 to 1981 indicate that immigrants made up a progressively larger share of the workforce of Canada in the fields of engineering, teaching, and medicine and health. For example, immigrants made up about 26 per cent of those who engaged in work in natural sciences, engineering, and mathematics in 1961, 31 per cent in 1971, and 28 per cent in 1981 (Li, 1992). In the teaching profession, immigrants accounted for 7 per cent of those engaged in this sector in 1961, and 18 per cent in 1971 and 1981; and in the medicine and health field, immigrant workers made up 14 per cent in 1961, 21 per cent in 1971 and 20 per cent in 1981. In short, if immigrant workers were not available in Canada, the workforce in 1981 would have shrunk by 28 per cent in the fields of natural sciences, engineering, and mathematics, 18 per cent in the field of teaching, and 20 per cent in the field of medicine and health.

Li (1992) argued that the professional and skilled immigrants to Canada in the

1970s helped to make up a large part of the much-needed human capital in the 1970s that Canadian universities were unable to produce. For example, between 1961 and 1974, Canadian universities graduated 180,382 students in science, engineering, and mathematics, but Canada admitted 91,079 immigrants in these fields (Li, 1992). The number of immigrants admitted in some professions exceeded the number of Canadian university graduates in the same profession. For example, between 1961 and 1974, Canadian universities produced 50,311 graduates in medicine, but Canada admitted 64,510 immigrants in the same field. Canada benefits from not having to pay for the educational costs to secure the human capital that professional and technical immigrants bring with them.[6] DeVoretz and Laryea (1998) estimated that between 1967 and 1987, Canada benefited from the postsecondary educational training of immigrants equivalent to the value of $42.9 billion.

The immigration of skilled labour to Canada is particularly critical in light of Canada's loss of highly trained workers to the United States. Research on brain drain from Canada to the US indicates that there are enduring structural conditions that prompt the emigration of skilled labour from Canada, and that the negative impact of such an outflow would have been more severe for Canada had it not been for the fact that Canada receives substantial skilled inflows from the rest of the world (DeVoretz, 1999; DeVoretz and Laryea, 1998).

Data from the 1996 Census indicate that immigrants made up 19 per cent of the workforce in all occupational groups, even though immigrants only account for 17.4 per cent of Canada's population (see Table 5.4). The presence of immigrants in certain occupational groups is particularly conspicuous. For example, among men, immigrants accounted for 22 per cent of those in managerial occupations, 23 per cent of those in professional occupations, and 32 per cent of those engaged in food and beverage services. Among women, immigrants made up 20 per cent of those in managerial occupations, 39 per cent of those in manufacturing and processing, and 22 per cent of those in travel- and recreation-related services. Although these statistics in themselves do not indicate the precise benefits of immigrants to Canada, they show that Canada's workforce would have been reduced by about one-fifth in the absence of immigrant labour.

Immigration has contributed to the growth of Canada's labour market, even though the magnitude of contribution varies depending on the period. Based on data from 1951 to 1996, Denton, Feaver, and Spencer (1999) estimated that net immigration accounted for about 22 per cent of the growth in Canada's labour force for 1966 to 1971, 16 per cent for 1971 to 1976, before dropping to 10 per cent for 1976 to 1981. However, since the mid-1980s, net immigration has accounted for a larger share of Canada's growth in the labour force; between 1986 and 1991, net immigration was responsible for 46 per cent of Canada's expansion in labour force, and between 1991 and 1996, 71 per cent.

Conclusion

In the immigration discourse, there is a prevailing bias in assessing immigrants' worth mainly in terms of their ability to benefit and to enrich native-born Canadi-

Table 5.4   Immigrants in Occupational Groups, Canada, 1996 Census (%)

Occupation	Immigrants in Male and Female Labour Force	Immigrants in Male Labour Force	Immigrants in Female Labour Force
Managerial	21	22	20
Professional	20	23	18
Financial, secretarial, and administrative	17	21	16
Clerical	18	19	17
Wholesale	19	19	19
Retail trade and sales	16	17	15
Food and beverage services	20	32	14
Protective services	11	11	9
Childcare and home support workers	20	15	20
Travel and accommodation, recreation, and sport services	21	20	22
Construction, transportation, and trade	17	17	18
Occupations unique to primary industries	11	9	16
Manufacturing and Processing	29	24	39
Total (all occupational groups)	19	19	19

Source: Compiled from 1996 Census of Canada, Public Use Microdata File (PUMF) on Individuals.

ans. Thus, immigrants who are selected on the basis of educational and occupational skills are deemed to be more productive than those admitted for family relations or humanitarian considerations. This utilitarian perspective is widely accepted in the official and popular discourse as well as in academic research, despite the fact that Canada's immigration program is designed by law to serve different purposes.

The debate as to whether immigrants benefit Canada is controversial. The problem has to do with conceptual limitations and measurement difficulties in gauging the economic value of immigration. The conventional approach has cast immigrants and the native-born as opposites in that the former is only valuable to Canada if the former benefits the latter. As well, the costs and benefits of immigration are difficult to assess because there are complicated chain effects beyond what a simple balance-sheet approach can capture, and because the costs of immigration to Canada are mainly short-term in the first few years of settlement but the benefits tend to be long-term.

Even using a narrowly framed utilitarian perspective to gauge the value of immigration, there is no evidence to suggest that immigrants have been harmful to Canada or its economy. On the contrary, most studies indicate that immigrants have contributed to Canada in a variety of ways, and the weight of evidence suggests that Canada has benefited from immigration.

Simulation models attempting to estimate the effects of immigration on aggregate production have generated mixed findings, but the general conclusion is that immigration brings a small but positive effect in terms of expanding Canada's labour force and increasing the per capita income. Studies that use a balance-sheet approach to calculate the net cost or net benefit of immigration show that immigrants contribute more taxes than social benefits they receive, and that immigrants do not pose a burden in the transfer payments of Canada. Studies that compare the earnings of immigrants and native-born Canadians have produced rather clear results, but there are disagreements as to whether net earnings disparities between the two groups should be interpreted as differences in individual productivity or as inequalities of opportunities. The general findings indicate that immigrants earn as much or more than native-born Canadians, but when differences in schooling, occupational, and other individual and work features are taken into account, immigrant men and women typically earn less than their native-born counterparts. There is little support of the belief that immigrants are less productive than the native-born, but there are solid findings that suggest that immigrants, especially women and visible minorities, encounter unequal opportunities in Canada. Finally, census statistics indicate that by 1996 immigrants made up about one-fifth of Canada's workforce. Other data show that net immigration accounted for a large share of the labour force increase in Canada in recent years. For 1991 to 1996, about 71 per cent of the growth in the labour force can be attributed to net immigration.

The review of the arguments and evidence about the economic benefits of immigration suggests that Canada has much to gain and little to lose from immigration. Immigrants earn as much or more than native-born Canadians, despite the fact that immigrants' net earnings are often lower. On the basis of income data and economic analyses, there is little to suggest that immigrants are less productive than native-born Canadians; however, there are strong grounds to indicate that immigrants encounter unequal opportunities based on gender, race, and other features. The evidence is also clear that Canada's labour force would have decreased by 20 per cent without immigration, and its future growth would be severely curtailed without new immigrants. In short, immigrants have now made up a substantial portion of Canada's active labour force, and on balance, all the evidence suggests that immigrants have not created a financial burden for Canada but have contributed to Canada even if contributions are only considered in economic terms.

Chapter 6

Human Capital of Immigrants

In the immigration discourse, it is taken for granted that immigrants who come to Canada with higher educational levels have more to offer, since higher education is equated with higher earnings or productivity. This economic view considers a person's education as a form of human capital that requires an investment and that yields a return in the labour market. The immigration program favours selecting immigrants endowed with this type of human capital, on the grounds that such immigrants have more to contribute to the knowledge-based economy of Canada. In this chapter, we see how Canada has stressed human capital as a criterion for selecting immigrants and has admitted an increasingly larger proportion of immigrants with substantial educational qualifications in recent years. As well, the chapter uses the most recent census data to see how immigrants' credentials are being rewarded in Canada.

Human Capital and Other Forms of Capital

Economists typically refer to a person's education as human capital. It represents a form of investment, usually made in the formative years of a person's life, that brings a return that can be realized when the person joins the labour force and earns an income commensurate with the amount of schooling.[1] The empirical relationship that associates higher earnings with higher education is interpreted as returns to investments in schooling. According to this economic perspective, the decision to invest or not to invest in education is an individual rational choice, after taking into account the cost of education, both direct and indirect, with its anticipated benefit (Becker, 1993: 18–19). The explanation why people with more education earn more is based on the assumption that higher education equals higher capital investment, and the larger the investment, the greater the output, subject to the rule of diminishing return (that is, up to a certain level, after which the rate of return diminishes). This theoretical framework that links earnings to human capital has been adopted to evaluate the productivity and potential economic contribution to Canada of immigrants.[2]

The human capital theory, like the status attainment model developed by sociologists to study how prior acquired educational status positively affects later occupational status, views the capitalist economy as an open market in which individuals compete freely and fairly for earnings or social status based on their level of human capital.[3] It follows that individuals who invest more in human capital have more to offer in the market, for which they are rewarded a higher income because of higher productivity. The thrust is on individual self-effort and open market competition, rather than structural constraints, as key determinants of economic outcomes. Consequently, factors such as discrimination and unequal treatments are seldom considered in the framework of the human capital theory.

Critics of the human capital theory stress structural opportunity, and not rational choice, as a source of differential investment in human capital. Furthermore, social inequality gives rise not only to unequal resource levels or capacities in the pursuit of human capital, but also produces differences in cultural and social capital that can be converted into financial or economic capital (Bourdieu, 1986). The point about how a structure of inequality can reproduce itself is skillfully made by Bourdieu (1986: 241–2) as follows: 'Capital, which in its objectified or embodied forms, takes time to accumulate and which, as a potential capacity to produce profits and to reproduce itself in identical or expanded form, contains a tendency to persist in its being, is a force inscribed in the objectivity of things so that everything is not equally possible or impossible.' In other words, individuals are not subjected to the same conditions of competition in the free market, and individuals' capacity to reproduce future capital depends on how capital is distributed.

Bourdieu's analysis shows that besides economic capital, there is non-economic capital, and these are cultural capital and social capital; the latter can be converted to the former and vice versa. Bourdieu (1986) further subdivides cultural capital into three types: the embodied state in the form of a person's dispositions; the objectified state in the form of cultural goods; and the institutionalized state in the form of educational qualifications and credentials. Bourdieu criticizes the narrow economic model that only considers the social rate of return or the social gain of education as measured by productivity, and which ignores the fact that the acquisition of educational credentials is contingent on the capital already possessed by the family.

The work of Bourdieu (1986) and later that of Coleman (1988) and Portes (1998) point to the importance of social capital. Bourdieu (1986: 248–9) defines social capital as 'the aggregate of the actual or potential resources which are linked to possession of a durable network of more or less institutionalized relationships of mutual acquaintance and recognition'. Social capital refers to a network of social relationships, which is socially constructed and is a product of what Bourdieu (1986: 249) calls 'investment strategies, individual or collective'. The development of social capital requires the cultivation of actors. As Coleman (1988: S105) puts it:

'[A]ctors establish relations purposefully and continue them when they continue to provide benefits.' Coleman argues that social capital is productive in that it can facilitate certain actions of actors within a social structure; he further shows that social capital in the family and in the community helps the formation of human capital.

This debate on human capital suggests that the neoclassical economic model of human capital puts too much emphasis on competition and the free market, and ignores the influence of structured inequality. It further shows that besides human capital, there are other forms of capital that can be productive and can be converted to economic capital.

Human Capital as Immigrant Selection Criterion

As discussed in Chapter 2, the 1960s' changes in immigration regulations were meant to modernize the immigration system to enable Canada to broaden the intake of immigrants based on educational and occupational qualifications rather than country or racial origin. Recent changes in the immigration Act and regulations further support the selection of economic immigrants based on human capital. The point system developed in 1967 for selecting immigrants allocated substantial weight to education and occupational experience as criteria for selecting independent or economic immigrants. Under the original point system, of the total 100 points used in evaluating prospective economic immigrants, 20 points were assigned to the category 'education and training', and another 10 points to 'occupational skill' (P.C. 1967–1616). Subsequent amendments resulted in modifications of the point system to allow even greater weight being allocated to formal credentials and training. Under the new immigration regulations announced in June 2002, as much as 70 points can be given to economic immigrant workers and 84 points to investors and entrepreneurs on the basis of formal education, official language capacity, and work experience (see Table 3.1). A significant aspect of the change has to do with moving away from a selection system of skilled workers based on estimated occupational demands in Canada and intended occupation of immigrants to one based on flexible skills. Another important change involves raising the maximum points allowed for formal educational from 16 to 25, and allocating points for educational credentials earned (see *Canada Gazette*, Part II, vol. 136, no. 9, pp. 1–449).

As in the past, the new regulations announced in 2002 only recognize the merits of formal educational training, and not social capital, in the selection of immigrants. The formal selection system does not place much value on immigrants' family and ethnic networks in Canada, and does not recognize that social networks or social capital can be productive in assisting immigrants economically and socially.[4] There is little research in Canada that has demonstrated empirically the economic value of social capital for immigrants. However, a study that compares the economic performance of skilled immigrants and 'family unification' immigrants in the United States suggests that access to kinship network probably explains why kinship immigrants were able to upgrade their occupational performance over time (Jasso and Rosenzweig, 1995). In Canada, deSilva (1997) also shows that the earnings of male immigrants admitted under different admission classes converged over time. Furthermore, the findings reported in Chapter 5 regarding the catch-up rates of family-class immigrants and refugee-class immigrants also raise the interesting question as to why such immigrants, who, being less endowed with human capital, demonstrate such a strong capacity to catch up with the earnings of the native-born over time (see Table 5.3). A possible answer lies in the ability of immigrants to mobilize kinship and ethnic networks to improve economic outcomes in the labour market, especially to compensate for the absence of human capital; but much research is needed in this area.

Even before the announcement of the Immigration and Refugee Protection Regulations in 2002, there had been a shifting emphasis in increasing the intake of economic immigrants since the mid-1990s (see Table 5.1). The result is that immigrants with university education have made up a greater proportion of annual immigration to Canada since 1995. For example, about one-quarter of all new immigrants 15 years of age or older coming to Canada in 1995 had a least one university degree, and by 1998, immigrants with university degrees made up 35 per cent of all adult arrivals in that year (see Table 6.1). By 2000, 44 per cent of new adult immigrants came with at least one university degree.

The point system has been devised as a means to screen economic immigrants applying to immigrate to Canada in order to select the ones with substantial human capital. Recent statistics indicate that Canada has succeeded in admitting a greater share of the annual intake of immigrants with substantial educational credentials. The emphasis on immigrants' human capital also results in a high expectation being placed on economic immigrants; in particular, they are expected to be as productive as native-born Canadians and to generate an income level comparable to that of the native-born.

For example, the policy concerns that economic-class immigrants admitted in the 1990s did not catch up with the average earnings of Canadians one year after landing, compared to the more superior earning levels of economic-class immigrants who entered Canada in the early 1980s, is based on an expectation that economic immigrants should have average Canadian earnings after arrival since they are selected because of their human capital (Human Resources Development Canada, 2001: 8–9). As mentioned in Chapter 5, the decrease in entry earnings of recent immigrant cohorts is interpreted as the result of declining human capital content and not structural forces in the labour market. McDonald and Worswick (1998) pointed out that macroeconomic conditions—economic forces at the time of the immigrants' arrival—significantly influence the probability of job tenure for immigrants and the native-born, which in turn affects their earnings.

There are many other reasons that would explain why immigrants do not earn as much as native-born Canadians shortly after arrival. For example, immigrants may not have the same level of human capital as native-born Canadians, and their lower earnings simply reflect this. Human capital theory suggests this sort of income difference. However, immigrants' educational level may be comparable to

Table 6.1   Immigrants 15 Years of Age or Older Admitted to Canada, by Level of Education, 1995–2000 (%)

Education Level	1995	1996	1997	1998	1999	2000
0 to 9 years of schooling	20.6	19.2	18.3	15.7	15.3	15.1
10 to 12 years of schooling	28.8	26.1	23.1	21.8	18.9	17.9
13 or more years of schooling	9.6	8.7	14.1	8.5	8.5	9.0
Trade certificate	9.1	9.5	8.3	9.1	7.6	5.5
Non-university diploma	7.3	7.8	7.3	9.5	9.1	8.6
University degree	24.7	28.7	29.0	35.4	40.7	44.0
Total	100.1	100.0	100.1	100.0	100.1	100.1
[Number of cases]	[167,753]	[175,807]	[166,803]	[134,145]	[147,361]	[176,097]

Source: Citizenship and Immigration Canada, *Facts and Figures 1997*, Catalogue MP43-333/1998E, p. 6 (Ottawa: Minister of Public Works and Government Services Canada, 1998); Citizenship and Immigration Canada, *Facts and Figures 2000*, Catalogue MP43-333/2001E, p. 9 (Ottawa: Minister of Public Works and Government Services Canada, 2001).

that of the native-born, and they still earn less. Again, there are many reasons to account for this disparity. Immigrants may not speak the official languages as well as native-born Canadians, and consequently they are penalized in pay for their language deficiency despite their educational level. Immigrants, too, may be unfamiliar with the Canadian labour market when they first arrive, in terms of job information, social connections, and work styles. One may argue that new immigrants have a disadvantage in some of the areas relevant to job competition, and therefore they end up earning less than the native-born. However, one can take the relevant factors into account by statistically adjusting for differences between immigrants and the native-born, and if immigrants still earn less than the native-born, there must be other factors not related to human capital, language capacity, experience about Canada, and other identifiable individual features that produce the difference in earnings. Essentially, this is the logic being used in the subsequent analysis to compare the earnings of immigrants and native-born Canadians.

Earnings Disparities

Earnings disparities between immigrants and non-immigrants are typically seen as resulting from immigrants having less human capital than the native-born, in terms of marketable skills and credentials, Canadian experiences as well as language capacity.[5] If these factors are responsible for immigrants' initial lower level of earnings, then as immigrants acquire such human capital, they can be expected to catch up with native-born Canadians in earnings. From this vantage point, if immigrants fail to narrow the income gap over time, it is tempting to attribute such persistent disparity to immigrants' coming to Canada with lower human capital, or to immigrants' inability to acquire the necessary skills and experiences needed to compete in the Canadian labour market. Such reasoning assumes a rather perfect competitive system in which immigrants and native-born citizens are rewarded in the same way in the labour market except for differences in human capital and marketable skills.

As discussed in Chapter 5, the findings that show differential economic returns for immigrants and native-born Canadians, after taking into account differences in human capital, can also suggest that some immigrants encounter market barriers that penalize them in earnings. The type of barriers may vary depending on the gender and racial origin of immigrants. But the major barriers have to do with immigrants' foreign credentials not being fully recognized in Canada (Basavarajappa and Verma, 1985; Basran and Zong, 1998; McDade, 1988; Rajagopal, 1990), as well as employment discrimination against those with identifiable linguistic characteristics and racial features (Henry, 1989; Henry and Ginzberg, 1985; Scassa, 1994). Earnings disparities not only reflect differences in human capital, but also how human capital and its holders are evaluated based on socially constructed characteristics. These considerations suggest that a simple comparison of immigrants and native-born Canadians camouflages important differences of gender and race, factors that interact with immigrant status to produce complicated effects on earnings.

Furthermore, earnings disparities reflect unequal opportunities available to immigrants and native-born Canadians in urban markets of different sizes (Boyd, 1985: 407). Several measurable features of the metropolitan market can be taken into account. For example, the American literature has suggested that immigrants who work in areas with large immigrant concentrations can benefit from the presence of enclave businesses, although the precise effect of the immigrant enclave economy on the earning capacity of immigrants' remains contentious (Portes and Jensen, 1989; Sanders and Nee, 1987; Wilson and Martin, 1982; Wilson and Portes, 1980; Zhou, 1992). Urban locations also differ in unemployment rates, which can adversely affect opportunities of job seekers, especially recent immigrants (Richmond, 1984).

The following analysis employs data from the 1996 Census to see how earnings differ for various immigrant groups as compared with native-born Canadians of similar gender and race, while taking into account both human capital and other individual characteristics, as well as urban size and selective market features. The purpose of the analysis is to see if there are empirical grounds to attribute earning differences between immigrants and native-born Canadians to unequal opportunities in different labour markets.

Data from the 1996 Census (see Table 6.2) show that about 44 per cent of

Table 6.2   Number of Immigrants and Native-Born Canadians in the Labour Market, by Gender and Visible Minority Status, for Four Census Metropolitan Areas (CMA) Levels, 1996 Census

		Native-Born Canadian	Immigrant	Immigrants as % of Labour Market	Mean Earnings
Not CMA:					
White:	Male	2,808,216	180,324		
	Female	2,295,612	142,164		
Visible minority:	Male	16,452	37,764		
	Female	14,040	31,248		
Total Not CMA		5,134,320	391,500	7.1	$23,435
Small CMA (<500,000):					
White:	Male	745,164	105,048		
	Female	684,180	85,716		
Visible minority:	Male	11,016	35,352		
	Female	9,756	28,620		
Total Small CMA		1,450,116	254,736	14.9	$27,166
Medium CMA (500,000–999,999):					
White:	Male	829,188	110,808		
	Female	732,564	89,316		
Visible minority:	Male	14,112	78,804		
	Female	12,852	71,244		
Total Medium CMA		1,588,716	350,172	18.1	$26,964
Large CMA (1,000,000+):					
White:	Male	1,803,384	446,364		
	Female	1,644,228	350,460		
Visible minority:	Male	64,260	484,128		
	Female	62,748	434,772		
Total Large CMA		3,574,620	1,715,724	32.4	$29,374
Canada (All CMA and non-CMA Levels)		11,747,772	2,712,132	18.8	$26,521

Source: Compiled from 1996 Census of Canada, Public Use Microdata File on Individuals, based on a 2.8 per cent probability sample of the population, excluding persons under 15 years of age, persons not in the labour force, and non-permanent residents. Cell frequencies have been weighted to population size.

native-born Canadians in the labour market, compared with only 14 per cent of immigrants, resided in non-Census Metropolitan Areas (CMAs). In contrast, about 63 per cent of immigrants and 30 per cent of native-born Canadians in the labour market lived in large CMAs with one million people or more. As a result, immigrants accounted for 32 per cent of the labour market of large CMAs, and only 7 per cent of that of non-CMAs. Thus, immigrants are more likely than native-born Canadians to reside in larger CMAs. Table 6.2 also indicates that large CMAs had the highest earnings, and non-CMAs, the lowest.

The gross earnings of immigrants and native-born Canadians at four CMA levels for male and female as well as for white Canadians and visible minorities are shown in columns 1 and 2 of Table 6.3. Gross earnings are actual earnings before individual variations in human capital and other market and individual features have been taken into account. These earnings are given in deviations from national mean earnings such that a positive sign indicates earnings above the mean, and a negative sign, earnings below the mean. The data show that before differences in human capital and in other factors between immigrants and native-born Canadians have been adjusted, immigrant men earned annually more than their native-born counterparts at all CMA levels, whereas immigrant women made about the same or more than their native-born counterparts. Thus, based on the 1996 Census data, immigrants did not earn less than native-born Canadians.

The magnitude of gross earnings difference (column 3) between immigrants and native-born Canadians varies, depending on the CMA level, but also on racial origin and gender. For example, white immigrant men in non-CMAs and small CMAs earned over $6,000 more than their native-born counterparts, but immigrant men of the same racial origin in large CMAs only earned about $2,300 more per year. Immigrant men of visible minority origin earned $8,143 more than native-born men of the same origin in non-CMAs, but at all other CMA levels, the earnings advantage was between $5,000 to $5,500 a year. Women, irrespective of racial origin or nativity, earned below the national level at all CMA levels, although immigrant women, like immigrant men, earned more than their native-born counterparts. However, the magnitude of difference between immigrant women and native-born women varies, contingent on the CMA level and racial origin.

When variations in individual human capital and other individual and market work-related variations are taken into account (columns 4 and 5), all immigrant groups earned substantially less than their native-born counterparts of the same gender, racial origin and CMA level.[6] These findings suggest that immigrants of various gender and racial groups had higher earnings than their counterparts originally in part because of differences in human capital, occupation, the industry of work, experiences, and other work-related variations. Once educational advantage and other variations are removed, the initial earnings advantage of immigrants over native-born Canadians disappears in all comparative groups.

In terms of net earnings levels (columns 4 and 5), immigrant women irrespective of racial origin had the lowest earnings, followed by the earnings of visible minority immigrant men, except for those in non-CMAs. In contrast, the only group in large, medium, and small CMAs that had an income level close to or above the national average was immigrant men who were white, even though the earnings of this group still lagged behind those of their native-born counterparts.

The magnitude of earnings disadvantage ranged from $3,115 a year below the

Table 6.3 Gross and Net Earnings of Immigrants and Native-Born Canadians as Deviations from National Mean Earnings ($26,521), for Four Census Metropolitan Areas (CMA) Levels, 1996 Census

| | | Gross Earnings | | | Net Earnings After Adjusting for Individual & Market Characteristics | | |
		[1] Native-Born Canadian	[2] Immigrant	[3] Difference [1] - [2]	[4] Native-Born Canadian	[5] Immigrant	[6] Difference [4] - [5]
Not CMA:							
White:	Male	$1,601	$7,661	-$6,060	$5,136	$1,258	$3,878
	Female	-$9,384	-$6,888	-$2,496	-$2,901	-$8,645	$5,744
Visible minority:	Male	-$4,737	$3,406	-$8,143	$4,801	$1,686	$3,115
	Female	-$11,918	-$9,375	-$2,543	$336	-$5,768	$6,104
Small CMA (<500,000):							
White:	Male	$6,300	$12,702	-$6,402	$6,044	$2,432	$3,612
	Female	-$6,096	-$4,974	-$1,122	-$3,238	-$9,578	$6,340
Visible minority:	Male	-$3,218	$1,845	-$5,063	$4,764	-$2,151	$6,915
	Female	-$9,691	-$9,352	-$339	-$1,517	-$8,250	$6,733

Table 6.3 *(continued)*

	Gross Earnings			Net Earnings After Adjusting for Individual & Market Characteristics		
	[1]	[2]	[3]	[4]	[5]	[6]
	Native-Born Canadian	Immigrant	Difference [1]-[2]	Native-Born Canadian	Immigrant	Difference [4]-[5]
Medium CMA (500,000-999,999):						
White: Male	$6,661	$11,447	-$4,786	$5,136	$1,349	$3,787
Female	-$5,873	-$5,702	-$171	-$3,813	-$10,578	$6,765
Visible minority: Male	-$7,885	-$2,380	-$5,505	$61	-$6,372	$6,433
Female	-$11,304	-$9,511	-$1,793	-$1,588	-$9,823	$8,235
Large CMA (1,000,000+):						
White: Male	$9,561	$11,876	-$2,315	$5,392	-$314	$5,706
Female	-$1,998	-$1,919	-$79	-$3,508	-$10,188	$6,680
Visible minority: Male	-$4,840	$493	-$5,333	$479	-$6,654	$7,133
Female	-$10,158	-$6,400	-$3,758	-$2,722	-$10,372	$7,650

Note: Net earnings are adjusted earnings after differences in individual characteristics and differences in market characteristics have been taken into account. Individual characteristics include: industry of work, occupation, full-time or part-time work, years of schooling, years of work experience, experience squared, number of weeks worked, official languages ability, and number of years since immigrated to Canada for immigrants (native-born=0); market characteristics include the level of unemployment in the person's region of residence, and the size of immigrants' population as a per cent of the region's total population.

Source: Compiled from 1996 Census of Canada, Public Use Microdata File on Individuals, based on a 2.8 per cent probability sample of the population, excluding persons under 15 years of age, persons not in the labour force, and non-permanent residents.

average income for immigrant men of visible minority origin in non-CMAs to $8,235 below the average for immigrant women of visible minority origin in medium CMAs. The pattern appears to be similar for large, medium, and small CMAs where visible minority immigrant men and women were generally most disadvantaged compared to their native-born counterparts; immigrant women not of visible minority origin at these urban levels also suffered an income disadvantage that is only marginally less severe. Thus, if the net earnings of native-born Canadians are used as benchmarks to gauge immigrants of the same gender and racial origin, then column 6 of Table 6.3 suggests that white immigrant women, and immigrant men and women of visible minority origin were similarly disadvantaged in small, medium, and large CMAs. Only in non-CMAs was their earnings disadvantage less pronounced. In contrast, white immigrant men had earnings gaps that were smaller in non-CMAs and medium and small CMAs than in large CMAs.

To be expected, schooling and work experience bring positive returns to earnings; an increment of one year in either variable increases the net annual earnings by about $840. For immigrants, the number of years in Canada since landing also increases their earning capacity, with each additional year raising the net earnings by $181. Knowledge of the official languages also affects earnings, and being bilingual in both official languages brings a net earnings advantage, about $838 a year, whereas being unilingual in French only or speaking neither official language results in a net penalty of about $1,500 a year. These findings confirm that human capital does make a difference in earnings, but at the same time, the persistence of earnings disparity suggests that there are other market forces that affect the opportunities of immigrants, especially women and visible minorities.

Social Inequality

The analysis of microdata from the 1996 Census indicates that immigrant men at different CMA levels earned more than native-born men of the same racial origin, and immigrant women earned either the same or more than their native-born counterparts of the same racial background and CMA level. However, the earnings advantage of various immigrant groups over their native-born counterparts disappears once differences in human capital, experience, and other work-related individual variations are taken into account. Substantial earnings disparities between immigrants and native-born Canadians remain once variations in individual features and market characteristics pertaining to immigrant size and unemployment rate of CMA are also controlled.

Comparisons of the immigrant groups of the same gender and racial origin at various CMA levels with their native-born counterparts indicate that the net earnings disadvantage for immigrants vary, depending on gender and racial origin, but less so on the CMA level. In general, income disparities between immigrants and native-born Canadians of the same gender and racial origin are similar at all CMA levels, except for those in non-CMA areas. The noted exception is for white immigrant men, whose income disadvantage as compared with their native-born counterparts increases in large CMAs. Within the various immigrant groups, immigrant women of visible minority origin at all CMA levels suffer the greatest net earnings disadvantage, in the magnitude of about $6,100 to $8,200 a year. White immigrant women suffer only marginally less, in the amount of about $5,700 to $6,800 a year depending on the CMA level. The income disadvantage for immigrant men of visible minority origin ranges from $3,100 to $7,100 a year at various CMA levels. In contrast, white immigrant men suffer the smallest income disadvantage, from $3,600 to $5,700 a year.

The analysis further indicates that many factors affect the earnings of immigrants and native-born Canadians. Beside human capital, experience, and work-related variations as identified in the literature, official language ability, the number of years immigrants are estimated to have spent in Canada, the size of the immigrant population and the unemployment rate of the local market are found to influence earnings. However, the fact that immigrants earned either the same or more than native-born Canadians, but suffer an income disadvantage once other variations have been controlled suggests that the earnings opportunities are not the same for immigrant groups as for native-born Canadians in different urban markets of Canada.

Gender and racial origin interact with immigrant status to produce complex interactive effects on earnings. Immigrant women, especially those of visible minority origin, suffer the most income disadvantage as compared with other immigrant groups, although white immigrant women only suffer marginally less. These findings are persistent at all CMA levels, and they suggest that even though larger immigrant communities and lower unemployment rates in larger urban markets do increase the earnings of immigrant women, they remain at the bottom of the income hierarchy among all immigrant and native-born groups. Thus, being female and being immigrant seem to produce a double penalty in net earnings for immigrant women, although the additional effect of racial origin appears to be less apparent at this low level of earnings. Immigrant men of visible minority origin earned less than native-born men of the same origin, as well as less than white immigrant men at all CMA levels. The disparities show that being non-white and being immigrant disadvantage immigrant men of visible minority origin. In contrast, white immigrant men had earnings levels closest to that of native-born men at all CMA levels, indicating that this group suffers net income disadvantage arising from immigrant status, but not gender or race.

Finally, the relative earnings opportunities of immigrants are generally similar in different CMA levels and slightly better in non-CMAs, when comparisons are made with their native-born counterparts of the same gender and racial origin. However, compared with the earnings of native-born white men at each CMA level, the relative earnings opportunities of various immigrant groups are better in smaller CMAs than in larger ones.

The findings strongly suggest that interpreting earning disparities between immigrants and native-born Canadians mainly as a result of differences in human capital or productivity is tenuous and simplistic. At the very least, it is not just the level of human capital that matters, but racial, gender, and nativity characteristics of holders of human capital also affect how such capital is evaluated or devalu-ated. In short, if the work world undervalues or overvalues the human capital of its holders on the basis of their racial, gender, and nativity characteristics, then the penalties and rewards associated with such evaluation should be interpreted as features of the labour market, and not results of individual efforts. In the case of immigrants in the Canadian labour market, how well they perform relative to the native-born population is not only a function of immigrants' human capital, but also a function of how prepared Canadian society is to reward them in the same manner as native-born Canadians, irrespective of superficial differences in gender, race, and nativity.

Devaluation of Immigrants' Educational Credentials

Much has been written about the problem of discounting immigrants' credentials in Canada.[7] Immigrants' educational experiences acquired outside Canada are often not fully recognized as equal to those of native-born Canadians, in terms of human capital quality and accreditation standing. However, differences in the quality of credentials between immigrants and native-born Canadians are often presumed. Thus, the earnings for some immigrants in the Canadian labour market are less than those of native-born Canadians, not necessarily because they have less human capital, but because a lower market value is given to their educational qualifications.

The literature suggests that the life chances for immigrants and native-born Canadians are not the same, especially for non-white immigrants from Asian and African countries whose earnings are lower than white immigrants from Europe (Canada, Royal Commission on Equality in Employment; 1984; Li, 2000; Reitz and Breton, 1994; Satzewich and Li, 1987). Several studies using different data have made this claim. An analysis of longitudinal data collected by the Department of Manpower and Immigration on new immigrants arriving in Canada between 1969 and 1971 found the rankings of immigrant groups by occupational status and employment income persisted over a three-year period, with immigrants from European countries and the United States having an advantage and with immi-grants from non-white source countries having a disadvantage that can be attributed to immigrants' origin. Furthermore, despite a narrowing of occupational status over time among immigrants from different countries of origin, the income disparity widened even after adjusting for differences in other variables (Satzewich and Li, 1987). A study based on the 1981 Census revealed that after adjusting for differences in age and education, immigrant men and women from Europe and the US had higher employment income than immigrants of the same gender group from Asia and Africa (Beaujot, Basavarajappa, and Verma, 1988). Similar findings were reported by Reitz and Breton (1994: 114), whose analysis of the 1986 Census showed that black and Asian immigrant men and women earned less than white male and female immigrants respectively, after differences in education and occu-pation were taken into account. Finally, the analysis presented in the earlier sec-tion, based on data from the 1996 Census, indicates that immigrant men and women had net earnings lower than native-born men after controlling for urban size and other individual and market characteristics, and that immigrants of visible minority origin tended to be further disadvantaged than immigrants not of visible minority origin.

Several factors have been identified as creating barriers of employment and social mobility for immigrants, especially for those from non-European origins. Trovato and Grindstaff (1986) studied immigrant women who were 30 years old in the 1981 Census, and compared the economic status of those who came to Canada as children, adolescents, and adults to that of Canadian-born women of the same age. The findings indicate that among the 'ever married' women—those who immigrated to Canada as adults and were therefore most likely to have completed their education outside Canada—were more likely to have completed university, but were less likely to be in the higher income group and more likely to be in the lower end of the occupational structure. Trovato and Grindstaff suggested three factors to explain the findings: the problem of full recognition of foreign credentials, the short residency of fewer than 10 years in Canada, and the problem of possible discrimination in the job market.

The point about foreign credentials was also made by Basavarajappa and Verma (1985), who, based on their analysis of Asian immigrants in Canada in the 1981 Census, argued that the insistence by employers on having Canadian experience as a condition of employment and the problem of foreign credentials not being fully recognized would explain why Asian immigrants were less likely to be in professional and managerial jobs, despite their relatively high educational attainment. Rajagopal (1990) produced data from the 1986 Census to indicate that Indo-Canadians in Ontario were more likely to have completed university than the general population in Toronto, but Indo-Canadians in Toronto had a lower annual income than immigrants and non-immigrants in Toronto. Rajagopal also suggested that one of the barriers had to do with Indo-Canadians' foreign credentials being highly discounted or not recognized by business and educational institutions, and with evaluators using prejudicial opinions and not objective criteria in assessing Indian applicants.

McDade (1988) has identified several barriers of employment for immigrants related to their credentials and training not being fully recognized in Canada. For example, in Ontario foreign-trained persons in trades were routinely required to have more experience than those trained in the province before examination, and immigrants' training in their home countries were often discounted (McDade, 1988: 10–11). In many professional fields, those with foreign credentials often had to meet more stringent standards than those trained in Canada before professional certification was given; for example, in engineering, foreign-trained engineers were required to complete a longer period of satisfactory practice experience, in addition to fulfilling all examination requirements (McDade, 1988: 12–19). A 1992 Task Force to examine the recognition of foreign qualifications in Alberta also identified several obstacles for immigrants, including the absence of an agency to evaluate immigrants' qualification, the arbitrary standards used by licensing bodies, and their insistence on having Canadian experience as a criterion for registration qualification (Alberta Task Force on the Recognition of Foreign Qualifications, 1992).

Even though foreign credentials of immigrants can adversely affect their earnings, earning disadvantage can in fact derive from several confounding sources. When holders of foreign credentials experience differential treatments in the Canadian labour market, it is often not clear whether it is credentials, or racial origin, or other features that are being disadvantaged. For example, Scassa (1994) has argued that non-native speakers of the dominant language encounter discrimination in employment and in access to services on the basis of their language characteristics, and that their lack of fluency, their accents, and their idiosyncratic language use that deviates from the usual practice of the dominant group can be used as bases of unfavourable treatment and as surrogates of racial discrimination. Ethnographic accounts by immigrant women also indicate that their accents and colour set them apart from mainstream society, despite their ability to speak English (Miedema and Nason-Clark, 1989). Several empirical studies of hiring practices have also indicated that minority job seekers have less chance of being employed than white Canadians (Billingsley and Muszynski, 1985; Henry, 1989; Henry and Ginzberg, 1985). Therefore, the racial and gender characteristics of foreign credential holders are often assessed in the labour market along with foreign credentials.

In a field study in Toronto, Henry and Ginzberg (1985) used matched black and white job seekers to apply for entry positions advertised in a newspaper, and found that white applicants received job offers three times more often than black applicants. Furthermore, telephone callers with Asian or Caribbean accents were often screened out when they called about a job vacancy. A follow-up study of employers and personnel managers of large businesses and corporations in Toronto revealed that 28 per cent of the respondents felt that racial minorities had less ability than white Canadians to meet performance criteria (Billingsley and Muszynski, 1985).

Henry (1989) replicated the 1984 study in 1989 and reported results of discriminatory practices in hiring; however, the findings also produced controversial interpretations by other researchers. Swan and colleagues (Economic Council of Canada, 1991) accepted the smaller difference in the likelihood of black and white job seekers being hired in 1989 as an indication of no racial discrimination. However, Reitz and Breton (1994: 84) argued that the demand for workers was greater in 1989 than in 1984, and when the effect of labour demand was removed, more jobs were offered to whites than blacks; they further argued that the results also showed that 'no statistically significant change had occurred since 1984'.

Academic writings reported incidents and perceptions of racial discrimination in many facets of Canadian life, as did testimonies by members of visible minorities. For example, Nodwell and Guppy (1992) analyzed self-reported experiences of discrimination collected from 294 Indo-Canadians residing in South Vancouver in 1983 and found that half the men and women had experienced some form of racial hostility that ranged from verbal abuse and physical harm to workplace discrimination; the frequency of racial incidents was not related to the victims' personal attributes or their public practices of ethnicity. Foschi and Buchan (1990) studied perceptions of task competence in an experiment setting, and found that university male subjects accepted more influence from a partner portrayed as white than from one portrayed as East Indian. Basran and Zong (1998) surveyed immigrants of Chinese and East Indian background who were in professional jobs and residing in BC. Their study showed that many foreign-trained non-white immigrants in professional fields experienced downward mobility in Canada, and that an overwhelming majority of respondents attributed their occupational disadvantage to the problem of foreign credential devaluation, as well as to discrimination based on colour or racial origin. Shamsuddin (1998) analyzed data on income and assets collected in the mid-1980s and found that immigrant women in Canada suffered a double-negative effect that was due more to gender earnings discrimination than birthplace discrimination; birthplace discrimination was more pronounced for immigrant men. Shamsuddin cautioned that research on immigrant quality should take into account the potential role of labour market discrimination.

The testimonies of members of racial minorities before the House of Commons Special Committee on Participation of Visible Minorities in Canada in 1983 also revealed many accounts of differential treatment (Canada, House of Commons, 1983). These materials, together with the foregoing studies cited, suggest that racial minority immigrants do not have the same life chances as other Canadians, and that unfavourable evaluation of foreign credentials and racial discrimination are some of the main obstacles identified as affecting their opportunities.

Gauging the Market Worth of Immigrants' Credentials

Despite the rich literature on immigrants' credentials and qualifications, there has been little attempt to actually estimate their precise market worth. The noted exception is a study by deSilva (1992: 28–35), which used the 1986 Census data to construct models to test earnings differences between immigrants who immigrated before six years of age, and therefore had to obtain all of their education and work experience in Canada, and immigrants who had fewer 'years of residence in Canada' than 'years of total estimated work experience', and therefore had acquired education and some work experiences before immigration. The study found lower returns for immigrants' foreign experience and education, but comparable returns for immigrants' Canadian experience and education, when compared to match age groups of native-born Canadians. However, deSilva's study combines both experience and education in his estimation, and makes no distinction between those with university degrees and those without. Boyd (1992) also used the 1986 Census to compare the earnings of four groups of men: native-born Canadians, immigrants who immigrated before age 15, and immigrants who immigrated at age 25 or older, which were further subdivided into those who were born in the US, the UK, and Europe, and others born outside of these regions. The study found that postsecondary credentials were devalued for immigrant men born outside of the US, the UK, and Europe, but not for those born in these regions, nor for men who immigrated early in life. Boyd's preliminary study did not include immigrant men who arrived between the ages of 15 and 24, but the comparison with native-born Canadians may be skewed because of the inclusion of an age cohort among native-born Canadians that was left out of immigrants. Furthermore, deSilva did not consider the likely interaction effects between credentials and characteristics of holders, especially pertaining to racial origin and gender, although Boyd did try to address this problem by focusing her analysis only on men.

It is often not clear whether it is immigrants' racial origin, gender, or postsecondary degree that is being undervalued because of the difficulty in distinguishing the credentials from the holders. Using data from the 1996 Census, the following analysis estimates the type of university credentials held by immigrants based on their age of immigration and educational degrees, and assesses its market worth relative to that of native-born Canadians. The analysis takes into account interaction with gender and race and controls for variations in other features. The purpose is to set up typologies to compare the net market worth of different types of immigrant credentials and those of native-born Canadians, and to hold gender and race constant while adjusting for other variations.

Types of Degree Holders and Their Gross Earnings

According to the 1996 Census, 2.3 million Canadians outside the Atlantic provinces and the Territories had at least one degree, and immigrants accounted for 26 per cent of all degree holders (column 3, Table 6.4). Based on the fact that immigrants made up 17.4 per cent of Canada's population in 1996 (see Table 2.1), they can be said to have contributed a larger share to the pool of university-degree holders in Canada. Several types of degree holders among immigrants can be estimated based on the age of immigration.[8] Table 6.4 shows that 'immigrant foreign degree holders' made up about 14 per cent of all degree holders, 'immigrant Canadian degree holders', 6 per cent, and 'immigrant mixed education degree holders', 7 per cent. Thus, among immigrants, about half of the degree holders can be estimated to have obtained their first degree from outside Canada, slightly less than one-quarter received their degree in Canada, and about a quarter had a mixture of foreign and Canadian educational experience that made it difficult to say whether their degree was from a Canadian or foreign university (column 4). Table 6.4 (column 5) also shows the proportion of degree holders is highest (27 per cent) among those who immigrated at the age of 25 or older, followed by those who immigrated before age 13 (22 per cent); in contrast, degree holders made up 16 per cent of those born in Canada.

The average gross annual earnings of degree holders, by gender and visible minority status, are given in Table 6.5. The data indicate that for all types of degree holders, white males had the highest earnings, followed by visible minority men and then white females. Visible minority women had the lowest earnings. These data clearly indicate that gender and racial origin make a difference in earnings for both native-born Canadians and immigrants before other factors are taken in to account.

Among white males (Table 6.5, column 1), immigrants with any type of degree

Table 6.4   Types of Degree Holders, by Nativity, for Canada, Excluding Atlantic Provinces and Territories, 1996 Census

Nativity/Age of Immigration	Estimated Type of Degree Holders	Estimated Number in 2.8% Sample	Estimated Number in Total Population	% of All Degree Holders	% of Immigrant Degree Holders	% Degree Holders Among Each Group Defined by Nativity and Age of Immigration
		[1]	[2]	[3]	[4]	[5]
Native-born:	Canadian	48,364	1,727,286	73.7	—	16.1
Foreign-born:						
Immigrated between ages 0–12	Canadian	3,872	138,286	5.9	22.5	21.8
Immigrated between ages 13–24	Mixed Education	4,436	158,429	6.8	25.7	16.9
Immigrated age 25 and over	Foreign	8,928	318,857	13.6	51.8	26.9
Total (native–born and foreign–born degree holders)		65,600	2,342,857	100	100	17.4

Source: Compiled from 1996 Census of Canada, Public Use Microdata File on Individuals, based on a 2.8 per cent probability sample of the population, excluding persons under 15 years of age, persons not in the labour force, non-permanent residents, and those in the Atlantic Provinces and Territories where information on age of immigration is not available.

Table 6.5   Actual Annual Earnings for Holders of Different Types of Degree, by Gender and Visible Minority Status, 1996 Census

Nativity/Age of Immigration	Estimated Type of Degree Holders	Male		Female	
		White	Visible Minority	White	Visible Minority
		[1]	[2]	[3]	[4]
Native-born:	Canadian	$51,903	$39,099	$33,567	$26,628
Foreign-born: Immigrated between ages 0–12	Canadian	$56,139	$36,261	$35,705	$27,015
Immigrated between ages 13–24	Mixed Education	$55,931	$43,080	$36,430	$28,733
Immigrated age 25 and over	Foreign	$54,320	$38,273	$31,372	$25,571

Source: Compiled from 1996 Census of Canada, Public Use Microdata File on Individuals, based on a 2.8 per cent probability sample of the population, excluding persons under 15 years of age, persons not in the labour force, non-permanent residents, and those in the Atlantic Provinces and Territories where nformation on age of immigration is not available.

earned about $54,000 to $56,000 a year, compared to $52,000 a year for native-born Canadian degree holders. Similarly, native-born visible minority men with degrees did not have an obvious earnings advantage over their counterparts born outside of Canada (column 2). In fact, immigrants with mixed-education degree earned more than native-born Canadian degree holders, and other immigrant degree holders only earned marginally less their native-born counterparts.

Among female white Canadians, native-born Canadian degree holders also did not have an advantage over immigrant degree holders of the same gender and origin, except over white women who immigrated at age 25 or older. Similarly, native-born visible minority female degree holders (column 4) had no clear income advantage over their foreign-born counterparts. When gender and racial origin are taken into account but before variations in other factors are controlled, Table 6.5 shows that immigrant holders of any type of degree had earnings levels that were the same or higher than native-born degree holders.

Net Market Worth of Immigrant Degree Holders

The net effects of various types of degree holders on earnings are given as adjusted earning levels in Table 6.6. In other words, these were expected earnings, expressed as deviations from the average earnings, after variations in other factors have been taken into consideration.[9]

Table 6.6 shows a rather different picture than Table 6.5 before adjusting for other variables. For all four gender and racial groups, native-born Canadian degree

Table 6.6 **Adjusted Annual Earnings for Holders of Different Types of Degree, by Gender and Visible Minority Status, Expressed as Deviations Above (+) or Below (−) Mean Annual Earnings ($44,298) of All Degree Holders, 1996 Census**

Nativity/Age of Immigration	Estimated Type of Degree Holders	Male		Female	
		White	Visible Minority	White	Visible Minority
		[1]	[2]	[3]	[4]
Native-born:	Canadian	$7,480	$1,668	-$1,849	-$1,319
Foreign-born: Immigrated between ages 0–12	Canadian	-$1,344	-$5,908	-$11,129	-$8,395
Immigrated between ages 13–24	Mixed Education	-$1,084	-$6,184	-$11,854	-$11,538
Immigrated age 25 and over	Foreign	-$1,696	-$12,520	-$13,528	-$17,501

Source: Compiled from 1996 Census of Canada, Public Use Microdata File on Individuals, based on a 2.8 per cent probability sample of the population, excluding persons under 15 years of age, persons not in the labour force, non-permanent residents, and those in the Atlantic Provinces and Territories where information on age of immigration is not available.

holders had higher net earnings than immigrant degree holders. In general, native-born Canadian degree holders had the highest earnings, followed by immigrant Canadian degree holders and immigrant mixed-education degree holders, who had rather comparable earnings. In contrast, immigrant foreign-degree holders had the lowest earnings.

Foreign degree and nativity affect immigrants differently, depending on gender and racial origin. For example, native-born white men earned about $9,000 a year more than each of the three groups of immigrant degree holders (Table 6.6, column 1). However, native-born visible minority men earned about $8,000 more than immigrant Canadian degree holders and immigrant mixed-education degree holders of the same gender and origin, but $14,000 more than immigrant foreign-degree holders (column 2). Thus, compared to white males, foreign credentials have a more severe net adverse effect on visible minority men.

The pattern is similar for women. Native-born white women earned $42,449 a year after adjusting for other differences, but immigrant Canadian degree holders and immigrant mixed-education degree holders earned about $33,000 a year (column 3). By comparison, white female immigrants with foreign degrees earned about $30,770 a year. Native-born visible minority women also had the highest earnings ($42,979) compared to immigrants of the same gender and origin (column 4). In contrast, female immigrant Canadian degree holders of visible minority origin earned $35,903 a year, followed by mixed-education degree holders ($32,760); those with foreign degrees earned the least ($26,797). Foreign credentials also are a disadvantage to visible minority women more than female white Canadians. For example, white women born in Canada earned about $12,000 more than immigrant foreign-degree holders of the same gender and origin, but visible minority women born in Canada earned $16,000 more than their counterparts who were immigrant foreign-degree holders.

Table 6.6 also shows that the hierarchy of earnings for various gender and racial groups found in Table 6.5 is generally maintained, although the advantage of white women over visible minority women disappears. For all types of degree holders, white men had the highest earnings level, followed by visible minority men who had an advantage over white women, as well as visible minority women. In short, Table 6.6 clearly suggests that gender, racial origin, and foreign credentials tend to interact to produce complex outcomes for various groups of degree holders. But as confirmed in previous research (Li, 1992), racial differences are more pronounced among higher income earners (men) than lower income earners (women).

The precise effects of foreign credentials on earnings for various gender and racial groups are further decomposed into two parts (see Table 6.7). Using the

Table 6.7 Decomposing Net Earnings Disadvantage of Immigrants' Educational Credentials as Deriving from Immigrant Status and/or Foreign Degree

Market Disadvantage (-) Measured by Earning Difference Between	Disadvantage Due to	Male		Female	
		White	Visible Minority	White	Visible Minority
		[1]	[2]	[3]	[4]
Native-born Canadian degree holders and immigrant Canadian degree holders	Immigrant Status	-$8,824	-$7,576	-$9,280	-$7,076
Immigrant Canadian degree holders and immigrant foreign degree holders	Foreign Degree	-$352	-$6,612	-$2,399	-$9,106
Native-born Canadian degree holders and immigrant foreign degree holders	Both	-$9,176	-$14,188	-$11,679	-$16,182

Source: Compiled from 1996 Census of Canada, Public Use Microdata File on Individuals, based on a 2.8 per cent probability sample of the population, excluding persons under 15 years of age, persons not in the labour force, non-permanent residents, and those in the Atlantic Provinces and Territories where information on age of immigration is not available.

earnings level of native-born Canadians as a benchmark, and controlling for gender and racial origin, part of the net earnings disadvantage of immigrants may be attributed to their immigrant status, and part to foreign credentials. The last row of Table 6.7 shows that the net difference between native-born Canadian degree holders and immigrant foreign-degree holders, controlling for gender and racial origin. The difference is largest among visible minority women (–$16,182), followed by visible minority men (–$14,188), and then white women (–$11,679). The net difference is smallest among white men. The joint negative effects of immigrant status and foreign degree are most severe for visible minority women and men, and less so for white women and men.

Table 6.7 also shows that for white men (column 1) and women (column 3), much of the net income disparity between native-born Canadian degree holders and immigrant foreign-degree holders arises from immigrant status. But about 47 per cent of the net income disparity between native-born Canadian degree holders and immigrant foreign-degree holders can be attributed to foreign credentials for visible minority men, and 56 per cent, in the case of visible women. If foreign degrees were to be recognized as equivalent to Canadian degrees in the Canadian labour market, visible minority women and men would stand to benefit the most in terms of achieving income parity with their native-born counterparts.

Human Capital and Earnings

The above analysis of earnings indicates that there are major income disparities that cannot be attributed to differences of human capital alone. In fact, data from the 1996 Census clearly show that immigrants tend to earn as much or more than native-born Canadians, but their income falls behind once differences in other factors have been taken into account.

The analysis of data from the 1996 Census also shows that immigrants are more likely than native-born Canadians to be degree holders, and that only about half of immigrant degree holders have a foreign degree. The other half can be assumed to have either a Canadian degree or mixed-education degree. A comparison of gross earnings of different types of degree holders while controlling for gender and visible minority status indicates that credentials have only marginal effects on the earnings of immigrants in that the earnings of immigrant and native-born degree holders are rather similar, irrespective of whether immigrants' degrees are obtained from a foreign institution. However, when variations of individual and work-related characteristics have been taken into account and when gender and racial origin are controlled, immigrants' credentials tend to substantially disadvantage their net earnings. In general, immigrants' credentials adversely affect the earnings of visible minority women and men more than white women and men. In particular, for visible minority women and men, about half of the income disparity between native-born Canadian degree holders and immigrant foreign-degree holders can be attributed to foreign credentials. These findings clearly suggest that foreign credentials of immigrants are being disadvantaged in the Canadian labour market. At the same time, there is an earnings disadvantage for immigrant foreign-degree holders who are women of visible minority origin. Thus, as other studies have shown, there is a multiple-negative effect of gender and race on the earnings of immigrant women of visible minority origin (Beach and Worswick, 1993; Boyd, 1984; Shamsuddin, 1998). It also becomes clear that gender and racial characteristics of holders of credentials cannot be separated from the credentials themselves, since they produce complicated interaction effects on earnings.

The large body of sociological literature on immigrants' earnings, as well as the analysis of the 1996 Census, indicate that there are many sources of income inequality arising from differences in gender, race, immigrant status, and type of credentials. Thus, it would be simplistic to attribute earnings difference between immigrants and native-born Canadians to differences in human capital or quality of credentials. Reitz (2001) has made bold estimates of how different sources contribute to what he calls 'immigrant earnings deficit', that is, the amount of additional income that immigrants would have earned if they were rewarded in the same rate as native-born Canadians in the labour market. Reitz's calculations, based on the 1996 Census, show that of the total $55.5 billion annual immigrant earnings deficit, $10.9 billion can be attributed to skill underutilization, and $44.5 billion to pay inequity.

Immigrants do face obstacles in the Canadian labour market. There is no doubt that immigrants with human capital stand a better chance to do well in the labour market, but to eradicate social barriers that are premised on race and gender requires not only immigrants making efforts to improve their qualifications, but also policy change that addresses structural features of society. Policies that help to recognize foreign credentials being equivalent to Canadian credentials in the labour market would contribute to bridging some of the income gap. However, the labour market may continue to devalue foreign credentials of job seekers in jobs that do not require formal certification. This is because recognition of foreign credentials involves formal certification by licensing bodies and regulatory agencies in jobs that require such certification as well as social recognition by employers, colleagues, and co-workers in the workplace even if certification is not required. Finally, it should be stressed that pre-existing racial and gender pay inequity are features of Canadian society and not of immigrants. It would be incorrect to attribute earnings disparity arising from these sources to immigrants, their human capital level, or other individual characteristics.

Conclusion

In the official and public immigration discourse, there is a prevailing assumption that Canada would receive a greater value from economic immigrants than from family-class immigrants or from refugee-class immigrants, on the assumption that economic immigrants are more educated and therefore more productive. This expectation has been reinforced by the neoclassical economic model of human capital that attributes individual earnings differences to variations in individual productivity that, in turn, is determined by the level of human capital individuals possess. Critics of the human capital theory caution that the undue emphasis on individual qualification and productivity undermines the importance of structured inequality as a source to account for earnings differentials. Furthermore, there is a strong relationship between economic capital and other forms of capital such that wealthy families can further transfer advantages to future generations by endowing them with all forms of capital, including privileged schooling.

Recent changes in the immigration selection system have placed an even greater emphasis on human capital as a key criterion in selecting economic immigrants. Even in the mid-1990s, before the new immigration regulations were announced in 2002, there had been a strong emphasis on human capital in the immigration selection system. Such an emphasis has produced an expectation that immigrants perform economically as well as the native-born, and has prompted policy concerns on the first sign that recent immigrant entry cohorts may not be doing as well economically as their predecessors in terms of their earnings relative to Canadians.

There is a substantial literature to suggest that many factors influence the earnings of immigrants—human capital, gender, race, place of origin, and others. Many studies indicate that various forms of discrimination against immigrants can affect their life chances. As well, marcoeconomic forces play a role in affecting the earnings of immigrants. These studies suggest that earnings differentials should not be simply interpreted as individual differences in productivity or in investment strategies in human capital, but should take into account larger structural forces of inequality.

Data from the 1996 Census indicate that immigrant men and women often earn as much as native-born Canadians, but when variations in human capital and other job-related features are taken into account, immigrants, especially women and visible minorities, are often disadvantaged in the labour market. Such findings, along with other findings reported in the literature, suggest the need to consider structured inequality as a source that affects the economic opportunities of immigrants, and the need to abandon the circular logic in equating what may well be consequences of structured inequality with individual productivity.

Chapter 7

Immigration and Diversity

In previous chapters, the cost and benefit of immigration have been analyzed in relation to Canadian demographic trends and in terms of human capital and labour market outcomes. In this chapter, the focus is on the cost and benefit of diversity as articulated in the immigration debate. It is a widely held belief that immigration has altered the racial composition of Canada and increased its diversity. The increased number of immigrants of visible minority origin has prompted some strong reactions in Canada and added a new dimension to the immigration debate. One aspect of the debate assesses the effect of non-white immigrants on the Canadian population from the perspective of European tradition and culture. In the process, a discourse of diversity is constructed; such a discourse entails a codified language, an implied rationale, normative concepts, and accepted syntax, with which the problem of diversity is articulated (Li, 2001b).

Two rather obvious points are sometimes overlooked in the immigration debate. The first is that Canada is an immigrant society because its principal population has been shaped by the arrival of immigrants at different times (see Chapter 2); each wave of immigrants brought new, sometimes incompatible, cultural features from the standpoint of those already well entrenched in Canada. The second point is simply that Canadian society is always changing;[1] immigration is one of the many factors that affect Canadian society, and in turn, immigrants are affected by it. As Hiebert (2000: 28) put it, '[E]ven if immigration would somehow have stopped in the 1990s, Canadian cities would still have experienced fundamental change.' In other words, the history of Canada has been shaped by immigration, and Canadian society has continually changed, with desirable and undesirable outcomes that may not be related to the arrival of new immigrants.

There is a common perception that Canada has become more diverse as a result of large numbers of immigrants from different cultural and racial backgrounds coming to Canada since the late 1960s, and that such increased diversity is challenging, if not undermining, the cultural security and social cohesion of traditional Canada. This perception is at least partially correct with respect to the 1967 immigration regulations that adopted a universal system to assess prospective immigrants, and as a result, facilitated the admission of immigrants from outside Europe and the United States, notably those from Asia and Africa who were historically unwelcome in Canada. However, it is unclear whether recent Asian, African, and non-European immigrants have produced more diversity in Canadian society, if diversity is broadly conceptualized in reference to the charter groups. Equally uncertain is whether the cultural diversity that non-European immigrants supposedly have brought is weakening the cultural tradition and social cohesion deemed by long-time Canadians to have prevailed in Canada. Nevertheless, the tone of the debate clearly suggests that recent immigrants are seen as mainly responsible for some of the undesirable social changes in Canadian society, and that cultural diversity is at best viewed with suspicion. Consequently, diversity becomes a codified concept to refer to unbridgeable differences of people and to injurious consequences that such differences have created. Rarely is diversity cast in an objective light, nor is it considered as a possible resource or advantage for Canada in a global age.

The Demographic Reality of Ethnic Diversity

Despite the popular belief that the recent arrival of immigrants from 'non-traditional' sources has greatly increased the diversity of Canada, census data show that the degree of ethnic diversity in Canada is stable in the postwar period, when diversity is measured in terms of the segment of the population not of British and French origin. At the same time, there has been increased racial differentiation within the non-British and non-French segment of the population.

There are different ways to describe the diversity of Canada. Historically, Canada has considered the British and the French as the charter groups, and measured Canada's diversity in relationship to the two founding groups of the confederation. It was in this spirit that the 1963 Royal Commission on Bilingualism and Biculturalism adopted a relatively simple trichotomy to characterize a multicultural Canada, one that was made up of the British, the French, and the other Canadians.[2] When the 1963 Royal Commission wrote about the 'Third Force' of Canada in 1965, it referred to Canadians not of British and French origin, but whose ethnic backgrounds collectively made up another force after the two charter groups (Canada, Royal Commission on Bilingualism and Biculturalism, 1965: 52). This framework has been widely adopted as the way to discuss the composition of Canada's population and the nature of its diversity.

Without doubt, the mosaic of Canada to which the 1963 Royal Commission referred was overwhelmingly European in origin. The 1961 Census, taken just two years earlier, clearly showed that of 18.2 million people in Canada, 97 per cent were of British, French, and other European origin (see Table 7.1). In fact, the percentage of Canadians of European origin had not changed much between 1921 and

1961, accounting for 97 per cent to 98 per cent of Canada's total population. Even in 1971, the British, the French, and other European Canadians still made up 96.3 per cent of the total population. However, within those of European origin, the British had declined in proportion from over 50 per cent in the 1920s and 1930s to about 44 per cent in 1961; at the same time, Canadians of European origin other than British and French had grown from 14 per cent to 17 per cent in the 1920s and 1930s to about 23 per cent in 1961 (see Table 7.1). Thus, the rise of ethnic or cultural pluralism in this period was synonymous with the growth of European pluralities, since those of non-European origin only made up 2.5 per cent of the total population in 1921, and 3.2 per cent in 1961.

In 1961, the Third Force was predominately composed of those of European origin. Table 7.2 shows that in 1961, about 88 per cent of those not of British or French origin were of European origin. This Canadian mosaic of British, French, and other Europeans dated back to the late nineteenth century, and it persisted for much of the twentieth century. Changes in the mosaic before the 1970s were mainly in the direction of having more European diversities other than the British and the French in the Canadian population.

By 1971, Canadians of European origin continued to account for 96 per cent of the 21.5 million people in the total population. Even within the Third Force, European origin dominated. Table 7.2 clearly indicates that European-Canadians other than British and French accounted for 86 per cent of the 5.8 million people who declared a non-British and non-French ethnic origin in the 1971 Census. However, by 1981, this group had declined to 75.8 per cent of those not of British or French origin. By 1991, despite the growth of the non-British and non-French origin to 7.4 million people, the European component of the Third Force had further declined to 55.7 per cent.

Table 7.1   Population by Ethnic Origin, Canada, 1921–71 (%)

Ethnic Origin	1921	1931	1941	1951	1961	1971
British	55.4	51.9	49.7	47.9	43.8	44.6
French	27.9	28.2	30.3	30.8	30.4	28.7
Other European	14.2	17.6	17.8	18.2	22.6	23.0
Asian	0.8	0.8	0.6	0.5	0.7	1.3
Aboriginal	1.3	1.2	1.1	1.2	1.2	1.5
Black	0.2	0.2	0.2	0.1	0.2	0.2
Other	0.2	0.1	0.4	1.2	1.2	0.8
Total %	100.0	100.0	100.0	100.0	100.0	100.0
Total Number	8,787,949	10,376,786	11,506,655	14,009,429	18,238,247	21,568,310

Source: Compiled from Statistics Canada, 1971 Census of Canada, *Population: Ethnic Groups,* Catalogue 92-723, Vol. 1, Part 3, Bulletin 1.3, Table 1 (Ottawa: Minister of Industry, Trade and Commerce, 1973).

Table 7.2 Composition of Non-British and Non-French Ethnic Origins in Canada, 1961–91

Non-British and Non-French Single Ethnic Origin	1961 N	1961 %	1971 N	1971 %	1981 N	1981 %	1991 N	1991 %
European (non-British and non-French)	4,116,849	87.6	4,959,680	86.0	4,648,675	75.8	4,146,065	55.7
Aboriginal	220,121	4.7	312,760	5.4	413,380	6.7	470,615	6.3
Asian	121,753	2.6	285,540	5.0	694,830	11.3	1,607,230	21.6
African*	32,127	0.7	34,445	0.6	55,760	0.9	251,050	3.4
Latin, Central and South American**	—		—		117,550	1.9	179,930	2.4
Pacific Islanders	—		—		80,340	1.3	7,215	0.1
Other single origin	210,382	4.5	171,645	3.0	120,990	2.0	780,035	10.5
Total number of people of non-British and non-French single origin	4,701,232	100.0	5,764,070	100.0	6,131,525	100.0	7,442,140	100.0
Non-British and non-French single origins as % of total population		25.8		26.7		25.5		27.6
Total Population	18,238,247		21,568,310		24,083,495		26,994,045	

Notes: *Includes 'Negro' for 1961 and 1971, 'North African Arab' for 1981, and 'Black origins' for 1991.
**Includes 'North American origins' (excluding 'Native peoples') for 1981 and 'Caribbean origins' for 1991.

Source: Compiled from Dominion Bureau of Statistics, 1961 Census of Canada, *Population: Ethnic Origins*, Vol. 1, Catalogue 92-911 (Ottawa: Minister of Trade and Commerce, 1962); Statistics Canada, *Population: Ethnic Groups*, Catalogue 92-723, Vol. 1, Part 3, Bulletin 1.3, Table 1 (Ottawa: Minister of Industry, Trade and Commerce, 1973); Statistics Canada, 1981 Census of Canada, *Population: Ethnic Origin*, Vol. 1, Catalogue 92-911, Table 1 (Ottawa: Minister of Supply and Services Canada, 1984); Statistics Canada, 1991 Census of Canada, *Ethnic Origin: The Nation*, Catalogue 93-315, Table 1A (Ottawa: Minister of Industry, Science and Technology, 1993).

Thus, between 1961 and 1991, those not of British or French origin made up slightly more than one-quarter of Canada's population, around 26 to 28 per cent.[3] Using the charter groups as the reference point, Canada in 1991 was no more diverse than it was in 1961. However, there were changes in the ethnic and racial differentiation in the Third Force to include a growing segment of non-European origin. For example, in 1971, those of Asian origin accounted for only 5 per cent of those not of British or French origin; by 1981, this had grown to 11.3 per cent, and by 1991 to 21.6 per cent. Similarly, those of African origin rose from less than 1 per cent of those not of British or French origin in 1971 to 3.4 per cent in 1991 (see Table 7.2).

By the time the 1991 Census was taken, 55 per cent of the Third Force was still made up of Europeans, but Asians and Africans accounted for about one-quarter of it. Those originated from Pacific Islands and Latin America accounted for another 2.5 per cent of those not of British or French origin. Therefore, it is not so much the increase in the proportion of the Third Force in the total population as it is the growth of racial minorities within the Third Force that makes ethnic diversity more noticeable in Canada in the 1980s. This point is also evident in the 1996 Census, despite a substantial number of Canadians choosing the 'multiple origins' and 'Canadian origins'.[4] On the surface, it would appear that the non-British and non-French segment of Canada's population had grown to 49 per cent in 1996 (see Table 7.3). In reality, about one-fifth of the total population chose 'Canadian origins'. However, Pendakur and Mata (1998) showed that people reporting 'Canadian' as an origin were similar to those who reported British or French origins, and that despite the growth of people reporting Canadian origin, it did not have a measurable impact on the reporting of ethnic minorities. Thus, the segment of the population that was non-British, non-French, and not Canadian origins made up 28.5 per cent in 1996 (see Table 7.3), which is comparable to the proportion of non-British and non-French reported in the censuses between 1961 and 1991 (Table 7.2). Even within the more broadly defined category of non-British and non-French origins, 'other European origins' and 'Canadian origins' accounted for about two-thirds of this group in 1996.[5]

The growth of visible minorities within the Third Force creates the impression that there has been more cultural diversity in the Canadian population, even though the Canadian population continues to consist overwhelmingly of British, French, or other European origins. Undoubtedly, the increased immigration from Third World countries since the 1970s has contributed to the increase of Asians, Africans, and other visible minorities in Canada. The tendency of recent immigrants to settle in metropolitan areas also reinforces the impression that there have been dramatic changes in diversity. For example, even though nationally visible minorities made up 11.2 per cent of Canada's population in 1996, they accounted for 32 per cent of the population of the Toronto CMA (Census Metropolitan Area) and 31 per cent of the Vancouver CMA (Statistics Canada, 1998b). Thus, the growth of visible minorities in Canadian society and their concentration in major urban centres convey the impression that Canada has become more culturally diverse. In reality, the recent arrival of non-white immigrants has not altered the numeric

Table 7.3   Composition of Ethnic Origins in Canada, 1996

	Number	%
British single origin	3,267,520	11.5
French single origin	2,683,840	9.4
British/French multiple origins	8,547,145	30.0
Non-British and non-French single and multiple origins	14,029,610	49.2

	Number	%
Other European	*3,742,890*	*13.1*
Canadian origins (single and multiple)	*5,906,045*	*20.7*
Aboriginal	*477,630*	*1.7*
Asian	*1,968,465*	*6.9*
Arab origins	*188,435*	*0.7*
African	*137,315*	*0.5*
Latin, Central and South American	*423,930*	*1.5*
Pacific Islanders	*5,765*	*0.0*
Other (single and multiple origins)	*1,179,135*	*4.1*
Total non-British and non-French	*14,029,610*	*49.2*
Total Population	28,528,115	100.0

Source: Statistics Canada, 1996 Census of Canada, *Total Population by Ethnic Categories (36) and Sex (3), For Canada, Provinces, Territories and Census Metropolitan Areas, 1996* (Census 20% Sample Data), 93F0026XDB96002, released 17 Feb. 1998, available at <http://library.usask.ca/data/social/census96/nation/ethnic.html>.

supremacy of those of European origin in the total population, and non-whites, including those born in Canada, remain a numeric minority in Canadian society.

It appears that much of the reservation towards diversity being expressed in the immigration discourse is based on race and on the perception of some long-time Canadians that non-white immigrants mean unbridgeable differences. It is not the growing number of non-white immigrants in Canadian cities that is challenging the social cohesion. Rather, it is the ideological interpretation of 'race' and 'colour' as implying fundamental and undesirable differences that is seen as challenging the normative tradition of Canada, one that is based on the cultural balance between the British and the French, and one that is characteristically European in flavour. As Breton (1984, 1999) argues, the tensions related to changing linguistic and ethnocultural diversity in Canada may be seen as arising from the resistance by members of the dominant group who perceived such diversity as a contestation to restructure the symbolic and cultural order of Canada.

Cultural Diversity and Social Cohesion

In the public discourse of immigration, concerns have been routinely expressed over the increased diversity brought about by recent immigrants from non-European countries, often referred to as non-traditional sources, and over the tensions and problems that diversity has created for Canadian society (Li, 2001b).⁶ Typical examples cited include immigrants' tendency to congregate in ethnic neighbour-hoods, the undue demands placed on the school system as a result of large num-bers of immigrant children not speaking the official languages, the social segregation and urban congestion created by the development of ethno-specific immigrant malls and concentrated ethnic businesses, as well as the confrontations in established neighbourhoods where the heritage and traditional values of Canada are deemed to have been undermined by new immigrants' disregard of architec-tural preservation and environmental protection (Li, 1994a). Some of the problems identified are typical problems of urban development that may have been aggra-vated by more immigrants concentrated in urban centres, but the nature and the severity of the problems are sometimes inflated to give the appearance that diver-sity is the root cause. A 1989 discussion paper produced by Employment and Immigration Canada and intended to 'stimulate an informed and frank debate' is rather blatant about the public's increasing concern over diversity and over its injurious effect on the national identity.

> More and more in public discussions of immigration issues people are drawing atten-tion to the fact that Canada's immigration is coming increasingly from 'non-tradi-tional' parts of the world. Thirty years ago, more than 80 per cent of Canada's immigrants came from Europe or countries of European heritage, whereas 70 per cent now come from Asia, Africa, and Latin America, with 43 per cent coming from Asia alone. . . . As a result, many Canadians are concerned that the country is in danger of losing a sense of national identity. . . . Unfortunately, some of the opposition to immi-gration which has been expressed in Canada is rooted in racism and we must vigi-lantly ensure that this destructive force does not spread. People's fears must be confronted and misinformation must be dispelled. . . . Yet it would be wrong to dis-miss most Canadians' concerns on these grounds. Many Canadians, who have always been proud of Canada's humanitarian and tolerant traditions, are also feeling uneasy (Employment and Immigration Canada, 1989b: 8–9).

The report goes on to describe other adverse effects of diversity on large urban centres that are 'experiencing adjustment strains as their social services and schools endeavor to meet the diverse needs of these concentrated numbers of new immigrants' (Employment and Immigration Canada, 1989b: 11). In other words, it is not just the increase in the number of immigrants in urban Canada that is strain-ing the public service, but along with such an increase is the pressure for service delivering agencies to have to respond to 'diverse needs', that is, the needs of peo-ple from a different racial and cultural background than majority Canadians.

The above viewpoint, its language, and its logic are rather revealing. Terms such as *diverse* or *diversity* have been used as surrogates to refer to 'non-white' immigrants, and these terms provide a neutral appearance to conceal the fact that such social signification is based on 'race'. The 'problem of diversity' has been presented as being triggered by large numbers of immigrants from non-traditional source countries, mainly those from Asia and Africa. This line of argument is increasingly evident in government discussion papers on immigration throughout the 1990s. For example, in a 1994 discussion document circulated by Citizenship and Immigration Canada, it repeats under the heading of 'immigration and diversity' the fact that large numbers of immigrants now come from Asia, and concludes that 'while there may be increasing concerns about the number of immigrants coming to Canada, there is evidence to suggest that these concerns are linked as much to issues of unemployment and the economy as they are to issues of diversity' (Citizenship and Immigration Canada, 1994c: 10). In other words, not only is the 'problem of diversity' caused by large numbers of 'non-white' immigrants concentrated in urban centres, but citizens' concerns over too many immigrants are really prompted by their uneasiness over 'non-whites', as much as by issues pertaining to unemployment and the economy. Thus, citizens' concerns over 'diversity' have been elevated to the same magnitude and seriousness as concerns over the economy and jobs. Over time, as the concept of 'diversity' is repeatedly used in immigration discourse in the above context, it becomes a coded word to designate 'non-white immigrants' and their problems they have brought to urban Canada, as well as the grounds for citizens' concerns.[7]

The message of citizens' concerns over 'diversity' is unmistakable about how a sudden increase in 'diversity' over a short period of time can create tensions and divisions, since 'diversity' is cast as different from, and sometimes opposed to, Canadian values and traditions. More specifically, the concerns are based on the presumed truism that, unlike native-born Canadians or European immigrants who came earlier, the recent Third-World type of 'non-white' immigrants bring with them different values and behaviours that are incompatible with those in traditional Canada, and their large concentrated presence in Canada's cities undermines Canada's unity. In reality, the view about 'diversity' causing divisiveness is not based on solid scientific findings, but premised on the mere fact that 'non-white' immigrants have a different skin colour and look different from European Canadians, and on the rhetoric that immigrants must respect core Canadian values. Thus, it remains a yet-to-be proven claim that 'non-white' immigrants possess such different cultural beliefs that they would undermine Canadian values, traditions, institutions, and in short, its cohesiveness. There is no evidence that immigrants from 'non-traditional source' countries do not respect core Canadian values, such as those articulated in the *Charter of Rights and Freedoms*, since equality, freedom, and liberty are universal values. Yet in the immigration discourse, the linkage between 'diversity' and 'fragmentation' is unmistakable. For example, this message is reiterated in another 1994 report as follows:

A number of Canadians expressed concerns about the impact which immigration and citizenship policies are having upon the values and traditions that form the foundation of Canadian society. This is not to say that Canadians are becoming intolerant. In fact, when describing the most cherished characteristics of their society, Canadians usually mentioned tolerance among the first. Many people agreed with the Standing Committee on Citizenship and Immigration which reported that '*Diversity is one of Canada's great strengths* . . . ' [emphasis in original]. But they are also worried that their country is becoming fragmented, that it is becoming a loose collection of parts each pursuing its own agenda, rather than a cohesive entity striving for the collective good of Canada (Citizenship and Immigration Canada, 1994b: 10).

The message on 'the problem of diversity' is always presented as legitimate concerns of Canadians who support the 'humanitarian and tolerant traditions' and are proud of Canada's diversity, but who nevertheless worry about Canada losing its national identity because of too many immigrants from different cultures and origins. In short, the message makes it clear that racism is unacceptable to Canada, and Canadians remain tolerant and are not being racists when they voice their concerns over too much 'diversity'. This is accomplished by reiterating Canada's long-standing position of tolerance and anti-racism, every time Canadians pass judgment on the social worth of immigrants' 'race' or 'colour'.

Concerns over 'the problem of diversity' are often justified on the grounds that long-time Canadians are experiencing too rapid social changes within too short a time that are caused by too many 'non-traditional' immigrants. Obviously, what constitutes 'too many', 'too rapid', and 'too short' requires a normative assessment. There is no doubt that the immigration patterns of the 1980s and 1990s have changed the racial composition of immigrants. However, similar concerns over 'too many' non-white immigrants and the atmosphere of unease that they created were expressed in the 1970s even before the large arrival of immigrants from non-traditional source countries.[8] It would appear that it is not so much the actual number as the constructed image of hordes of immigrants of a different race or colour that has been seen as challenging the cultural complacency of Canada and its implied cohesiveness.

There are also other manners in which the coded messages in the immigration discourse are articulated. For example, a 1989 report indicates that some Canadians 'are uneasy or unsure about immigration's impact' and that 'close to one fifth of Canadians are quite opposed to many aspects of Canada's immigration program and an even greater number just do not know how many, or what kinds of immigrants, Canada should encourage in the next decade' (Employment and Immigration Canada, 1989b: 2). A 1994 report cites Canadians' worries about personal safety and about fiscal burdens because some immigrant sponsors fail to honour their financial obligations (Citizenship and Immigration Canada, 1994b: 11–12). Other typical concerns of a more specific nature have to do with Canadians 'losing a sense of national identity', Canadian society 'changing too fast', and the need to preserve Canada's 'core national values' (Employment and Immigration Canada, 1989b: 9).[9] It appears that the discourse of diversity is preoccupied with the idea of immigrants from diverse cultural backgrounds making it difficult for Canada to preserve its national values, as though such values do not change over time. In reality, Canada's values, in terms of attitudes towards authority in the family, attitudes to the workplace and to politics, are all changing in the direction of what

Nevitte (1996) calls the decline of deference, and such changes reflect features of postindustrial society not necessarily unique to Canada.

Since the destruction of the World Trade Center in New York by airplane hijackers on 11 September 2001, there has been heightened security in North America and an increased concern over the screening of immigrants. An opinion poll conducted by Leger Marketing in October 2001 shows that 8 out of 10 Canadians thought that Canada should be stricter in immigration (*Star Phoenix,* 2001). Another poll conducted by Ipsos Reid for the *Globe and Mail* in December 2001 indicates that 69 per cent of respondents said that Canada is not screening new immigrants carefully enough (*Globe and Mail,* 2001a). There is no doubt that concerns over security influenced these responses, but it is also likely that the image of hijackers as 'foreign-looking' and the reservation towards non-white immigrants and the diversity they represent might have prompted Canadians to be more draconian towards the screening of newcomers.

Canadians, however, did not have the same concern over border control between Canada and the United States, as 63 per cent of the respondents in the Ipsos Reid survey indicated that the federal government has done either enough or too much about Canada–US border control (*Globe and Mail,* 2001a). The strong views regarding stricter screening of immigrants is at least partly influenced by an ongoing concern over immigrants from different racial and cultural backgrounds. As one pollster put it, 'You've got people saying yes, we should be more strict . . . but also yes, we should remain true to how we've defined ourselves as Canadians' (*Star Phoenix,* 2001).

Taken together, these coded messages equate diversity with non-white immigrants, and attribute various problems in urban centres of Canada to the influx of recent immigrants from cultural and racial backgrounds different than European Canadians. Such a narrowly framed notion of diversity is also believed to be fragmenting the social cohesion of Canada, which is largely presumed. In her discussion of the limits of the concept 'social cohesion', Jenson (2000) argues that the focus on the term is often on the deterioration of conditions and processes of a properly functioning society even though there is no consensus on the concept. For those who have attempted to define 'social cohesion', the emphasis is on cultural sameness and shared values.[10] Yet, it is a loose understanding of social cohesion and an idealized Canada that sees the diversity brought by new immigrants as fragmenting an otherwise cohesive Canada.

Multiculturalism and Conformity

There is no evidence to indicate that recent immigrants from non-European sources have weakened Canada's social cohesion or its normative order. Yet, in the immigration discourse, cultural diversity and racial difference are often questioned on the grounds that they would fragmentize and even balkanize Canada. As well, public policies are sometimes seen as attending 'too much to the concerns of special interest groups, rather than to those of average Canadians' (Citizenship and Immigration Canada, 1994d: 10).[11] One such policy is the multiculturalism policy, which has been criticized for emphasizing ethnic differences too much and encouraging immigrants to pursue separate ways rather than to embrace the Canadian way of life.[12]

Despite Canada's adoption of the multiculturalism policy since 1971, the forces of cultural and linguistic conformity have remained strong in Canadian society, and little institutional support has been developed to enable cultural minorities to resist conformity. The policy and its evolution can be seen as the state's attempt to regulate diversity in providing a symbolic framework to incorporate and to interpret cultural differences. Over time, multiculturalism in Canada has become highly politicized, as competing interest groups attempt to redefine multiculturalism and attribute merits and woes to the policy to suit their political agenda (see Abu-Laban and Stasiulis, 1992; Howard-Hassmann, 1999).

When the federal multiculturalism policy was first announced in 1971, it was officially described as an enlightened policy to allow individuals to pursue a cultural life of their free choice (Li, 1999). The policy was designed as complementary to the policy of bilingualism in that although linguistically, only English and French would remain official languages of Canada, culturally everyone would be equal. The multiculturalism policy was launched, in part, to counteract Quebec nationalism, and, in part, to appease the 'Third Force' that was made up of mostly 'other Europeans' in the 1960s (see Breton, 1988; Hawkins, 1988). In reiterating the legal status of the English and French languages, and offering a symbolic endorsement of cultural diversity in Canada, the federal multiculturalism policy separated the question of language rights of the British and the French from that of individual cultural freedom. As Trudeau put it, '[A] policy of multiculturalism within a bilingual framework commends itself as the most suitable means of assuring the cultural freedom of Canadians' (Canada, House of Commons, 1971: 8545).

This differential approach to cultural diversity and official bilingualism is characterized by what Kallen (1982: 56) calls 'a clear division between private and public sectors', wherein members of ethnic groups would be expected to conform to Canada's official languages in public institutions, but would be encouraged to pursue an ethnic culture and lifestyle of their choice in their private life. In other words, whereas bilingualism constitutes linguistic rights and institutional obligations, multiculturalism represents personal cultural choices, and not a collective right. Thus, despite the multiculturalism policy, the norms and practices of the two charter groups prevail in the public sphere, and the policy does not provide a viable option for cultural minorities nor new immigrants to escape the forces of conformity in major institutions.

The symbolic recognition of cultural diversity explains why the federal policy only provided moderate financial assistance to ethnic groups for their pursuit of cultural expression, and why no political demand was placed on key cultural, educational, and political institutions to make fundamental changes to incorporate multiculturalism (Li, 1999). The government also chose to create separate programs under direct government administration to promote minority arts, cultures, and heritages that became subsumed under multiculturalism (Li, 1994b). Thus, multiculturalism did not transform key institutions of Canada in the same way as official bilingualism. Instead, the multiculturalism policy was to support what Fleras and Elliott (1992: 73) call 'a restructuring of the symbolic order to incorporate all identities on an equal basis', or what others characterize as token or symbolic pluralism (Brotz, 1980; Roberts and Clifton, 1982).

It is clear that the launching of the official policy of multiculturalism in 1971 had little to do with the growth of the visible minorities that was only conspicuous in the late 1970s and early 1980s. But the multiculturalism policy did produce an ideological framework for interpreting cultural diversity, and reinforced an institutional practice that reflected the legitimacy and dominance of the British and the French. Even though some segments of the Canadian public continues to view multiculturalism as serving the special interests of cultural minorities at the expense of the majority (see Li, 1999), the reality is that there are strong forces of conformity in Canadian society (Reitz and Breton, 1994). The end result is that new immigrants do conform to the institutional life of Canada and to the cultural and linguistic patterns of the dominant group. There is little support of the belief that the multiculturalism policy has provided new immigrants with the necessary resources and institutional basis to remain segregated in Canadian society.

Many studies comparing immigrants and native-born Canadians conclude that over time, immigrants resemble native-born Canadians in many social and economic aspects of life, and that children born in Canada of immigrant parents often display linguistic and social patterns different from their parents' generation but similar to the majority of Canadians. In addition to the studies of labour market performance discussed in Chapters 5 and 6, other studies have shown how the process of conformity extends to many facets of Canadian life (deVries, 1990; deVries and Vallee, 1980; Driedger, 1978; Kalbach and Richard, 1990; O'Brien, Reitz, and Kuplowska, 1976; Reitz, 1980; Richard, 1991a, 1991b; Richmond and Kalbach, 1980).

For example, Kalbach and Richard (1990) found, based on the 1981 Census, that for first-generation immigrants, ethnic church affiliation is associated with less acculturation and lower socioeconomic status, but that ethno-religious differences become minimal after the first generation. Linguistically, immigrants and native-born Canadians show marked differences in the ability of various ethnic groups to retain their ancestral language. Reitz and Breton (1994: 57–8) found that the variation is much larger among those born outside of Canada. Except for immigrants whose mother tongue is English, the ability of immigrant groups to retain their ethnic language declines drastically over the second and subsequent generations (deVries, 1990; deVries and Vallee, 1980; O'Brien, Reitz, and Kuplowska, 1976; Reitz, 1980; Reitz and Breton, 1994). Local studies of specific immigrant groups also report a substantial rate of ethnic language loss among children of immigrant parents (Aliaga, 1994; Basran, 1993). Socially, first-generation immigrants tend to maintain a higher degree of involvement in their ethnic social networks than second or subsequent generations (Isajiw, 1990; Reitz, 1980).

In terms of intermarriages, researchers have found that group size and generational composition of the group to be most important in determining the rate of exogamy, that is, the tendency to marry outside one's ethnic group; as of 1981, 29 per cent of native-born husbands and 22 per cent of foreign-born husbands in Canada were exogamous (Reitz and Breton, 1994; Richard, 1991a). However, an analysis of the 1971 Census shows that native-born husbands in the age groups 15 to 24 and 65 and over were less exogamous than foreign-born husbands in the same age groups (Richard, 1991b).

A study comparing charitable giving by immigrants and native-born Canadians shows that the average direct donations given in a year are almost identical between the two groups, although the propensity to give varies among immigrants depending on birthplace, socio-demographic, and residential characteristics (Mata and McRae, 2000). The study also reports that as the duration of residence in Canada lengthens, the average contribution of immigrants also increases. Another study that examines homeownership indicates that immigrants in Canada have higher rates of homeownership than the Canadian-born population, but there are substantial variations among immigrants depending on the country of origin, period of immigration, and other factors (Ray and Moore, 1991).

The foregoing studies clearly suggest that the process of adjustment for immigrants is also one of eventual conformity to the linguistic and social patterns of the native-born population. The duration of residence and generational status appear to account for many differences between immigrants and native-born Canadians. Eventually, however, immigrants and especially their children adopt the behavioural patterns similar to native-born Canadians.

Finally, a study by Reitz and Breton (1994) shows that Canada and the United States incorporate ethnic groups into society similarly, despite the popular belief that Canada supports multiculturalism and the United States endorses the ideology of a melting pot. The findings cast serious doubt on the view that immigrants and their superficial differences are fragmenting Canada, and that their cultures are undermining the traditions and institutions of Canada.

Linguistic Diversity and Language Loss

Thus far, the analysis has shown that the forces of conformity are strong in Canada; neither its institutions nor its culture is under siege as a result of immigrants from different racial and cultural backgrounds. New immigrants do bring diverse cultures and languages to Canada, but over time they—and to a greater degree their children—succumb to the overpowering influence of the dominant culture. The weakening of cultural diversity and the corresponding conversion to dominant cultural practices can be clearly seen in the changing linguistic diversity. Linguistic diversity in Canada can be measured by the extent to which Canadians adopt a non-official language as mother tongue or home language. Research on this question has come to two general conclusions: (1) linguistic diversity in Canada has increased in more recent censuses as a result of more immigrants coming to Canada from diverse cultural and linguistic backgrounds; and (2) the pull towards adopting English as mother tongue and home language has been strong over time. Richmond and Kalbach (1980: 435) showed from the data of the 1971

Census that recent immigrants were likely to speak a home language similar to their mother tongue, but as succeeding cohorts of immigrants increased their period of residence in Canada, there was a corresponding increase in the use of English as home language by those whose mother tongue was not English. Also using the 1971 Census, deVries and Vallee (1980: 109) found that there was a strong tendency for those not of British or French origin to shift to English mother tongue, especially among those born in Canada. An analysis of language data of the 1986 Census also indicates that Canada's linguistic diversity, most notable in metropolitan centres, has been increasing as a result of changing immigration patterns, but at the same time, there has been pressure to convert to English mother tongue and home language (Bourbeau, 1989). In short, all these studies confirm the fact that recent immigrants have brought substantial language diversity to Canada but that over time there is tendency for them and their children to convert to the use of official languages, particularly English.

Data from the 1996 Census reveal that there is substantial linguistic diversity among foreign-born Canadians, in terms of adopting a non-official language as mother tongue or home language, but the linguistic diversity declines dramatically among native-born Canadians. In other words, a large proportion of those born outside of Canada adopt a mother tongue or home language other than English or French, but this pattern is not sustained among those born in Canada. For example, 67 per cent of foreign-born Canadians spoke a non-official language mother tongue, and 45 per cent of them maintained a non-official home language (see Table 7.4). However, only 6.2 per cent of native-born Canadians speak a non-official language mother tongue and only 2.8 per cent speak a home language other than English or French. In short, there is a much smaller degree of language diversity among native-born Canadians than among those born outside of Canada.

When foreign-born Canadians are compared to native-born Canadians, the decline in percentage of people with a non-official language mother tongue or home language for the same ethnic group may be viewed as the rate of loss of minority language identity. Table 7.4 shows that the loss of minority language identity is more severe for those not of visible minority origin than those of visible minority origin. For example, 26 per cent of those of German origin born outside of Canada, compared with only 7.8 per cent of the same origin born in Canada, adopt a home language other than English or French. The rate of minority language loss in home language for those of Italian origin is from 60 per cent among those born outside of Canada to 12 per cent among those native born. In contrast, the decline is from 67 per cent among foreign-born Arab Canadians to 43 per cent among native-born Arab Canadians, and from 84 per cent for foreign-born Chinese Canadians to 38 per cent for native-born Chinese Canadians. These differences reflect partly the changing patterns of immigration.

There are many reasons that would explain why the rate of language loss is not the same among racial and ethnic groups. Europeans have been immigrating to Canada for a longer history because of the past policy that favoured European immigration. Immigrants from Asia, Africa, and other non-European source countries

Table 7.4 Non-Official Language Mother Tongue and Home Language of Racial and Ethnic Groups, Canada, 1996 Census

Racial and Ethnic Groups	Foreign-Born Non-Official Languages			Native-Born Non-Official Languages		
	Number	Mother Tongue (%)	Home Language (%)	Number	Mother Tongue (%)	Home Language (%)
Not Visible Minorities:						
British, British Isles, British and Canadian	703,800	1.0	0.2	5,295,276	0.1	0.1
French, French and Canadian	59,436	1.9	0.8	3,208,896	0.1	0.1
Dutch	118,944	90.0	11.6	180,936	13.5	2.1
German	213,444	89.5	25.9	506,340	27.0	7.8
Other West European	36,504	72.4	17.8	45,756	18.0	6.5
Hungarian	51,012	93.6	43.3	41,724	39.9	5.9
Polish	155,160	95.2	69.8	103,680	42.6	14.3
Ukrainian	42,804	91.7	56.3	283,392	37.0	4.8
Balkan	108,000	96.3	65.4	51,840	56.1	21.7
Greek	73,332	96.5	70.5	68,580	67.9	37.0
Italian	330,372	94.8	59.8	385,344	44.9	11.9
Portugal	158,472	94.0	64.2	80,568	60.9	31.5
Spanish	17,388	91.3	51.6	7,956	55.2	33.9
Jewish	62,640	63.6	33.4	128,916	9.5	3.2
Other European	166,896	87.9	38.6	219,528	24.0	3.7
Other British multiple origins	118,656	9.6	4.0	2,508,444	0.7	0.2
Other French multiple origins	30,168	35.4	13.1	441,792	1.4	0.5
British and French, British and French and other	36,288	3.4	1.2	1,645,344	0.2	0.1
Other single and multiple origins	260,028	71.5	37.8	1,274,148	10.1	3.1
Canadian	27,396	13.7	5.8	5,229,396	0.5	0.3

Table 7.4 *(continued)*

Racial and Ethnic Groups	Foreign-Born Non-Official Languages			Native-Born Non-Official Languages		
	Number	Mother Tongue (%)	Home Language (%)	Number	Mother Tongue (%)	Home Language (%)
Visible Minorities:						
Arab	97,380	91.5	67.4	28,548	59.5	42.9
West Asian	56,628	94.5	74.8	8,784	78.3	66.8
South Asian	458,172	76.1	61.3	188,496	51.7	40.4
Chinese	633,996	94.1	84.2	205,272	57.9	38.1
Filipino	155,772	88.1	62.3	37,476	23.7	17.4
Vietnamese	81,360	94.2	86.8	20,772	80.9	73.5
Other East/Southeast Asian	87,408	91.4	72.6	48,960	47.4	23.8
Latin/Central/South American	76,464	93.7	75.9	15,660	77.2	67.8
Black	314,928	30.0	19.9	246,708	5.3	4.8
Other single and multiple origins	213,624	66.0	47.7	121,248	27.0	20.2
Aboriginal People	5,364	12.1	7.4	782,676	26.1	18.3
Total	4,951,836	66.8	45.1	23,412,456	6.2	2.8

Source: Calculated from Statistics Canada, *1996 Census of Canada*, Public Use Microdata File on Individuals. The numbers have been weighted to population size.

only began to enter Canada in large numbers in the late 1960s. Thus, native-born Canadians of European origin are more likely to have been in Canada for several generations longer than native-born visible minorities. Consequently, European Canadians who don't speak English or French have had more time to lose their ethnic language identity and to convert to official languages than visible minority Canadians have. This explains why the rate of minority language identity loss varies among Canadians of different origins. No doubt, there are also other differences in ethnic groups in that some groups have developed a stronger sense of distinct community in enabling their members to preserve their identity. However, differences in these factors are insufficient to explain why over time, all non-official language groups tend to lose the ethnic language and convert to official languages.

The evidence on the demise of linguistic diversity beyond the immigrant generation and the conversion to official languages is compelling. Whatever linguistic diversity new immigrants bring to Canada, they give up their linguistic endowment over time in favour of the official languages, especially English. It's also clear that linguistic diversity does not weaken the official languages; on the contrary, there is a danger that Canada could lose its linguistic diversity because of insufficient institutional and social support to preserve non-official languages beyond the first generation of immigrants.

In a study based on the 1996 Census, Li (2001c) found that the adoption of a non-official language as mother tongue or home language brings no earnings advantage in the labour market—in fact, a net income penalty results except for a few language groups among women—whereas English as mother tongue or home language yields a consistent income gain for both men and women. Pendakur and Pendakur (forthcoming) found a similar pattern when they analyzed the market returns of official and non-official languages using the 1991 Census. Li (2001c) argued that over time the market incentives and disincentives encourage Canadians to abandon non-official languages as mother tongue and home language in favour of the English language. These market forces would explain why linguistic diversity is a social feature associated mainly with the immigrant population and why there is a substantial decline in minority language identity among native-born Canadians. The findings on the decline of language diversity in Canada further confirm that there are strong forces of conformity in Canada.

Cultural Diversity and Globalization

The foregoing analysis shows that there has been a rather biased interpretation towards diversity in the immigration debate. Diversity is seen as an undesirable social feature that recent non-white immigrants bring to Canada, and if left unchecked, would eventually undermine the institutions and culture of Canada. Such a view is unfounded. The negative approach also does not consider how diversity can be a social resource to better connect Canada with the rest of the world in global commerce, cultural exchanges, and political dialogues.

As discussed in Chapter 1, although the term *globalization* is a bit of a cliché, it does characterize a world in which nations have become more interdependent than before. Globalization may be viewed as a process brought about by the ubiquitous expansion of the market economy and the emergence of a homogenizing material culture. This process is characterized by an increased interdependence of nation-states and regional economies, a blurring of national borderlines, and a high degree of movement of people, capital, goods, services, and information across national boundaries. The rise of mercantilism in sixteenth-century Europe and the spread of a capitalist economy as a world system marked the advent of a global era; but it is only now, with the emergence of an interdependent world market and an information-based global economy, that unprecedented flows across nations are being witnessed.

There are strong indicators that countries of the world are becoming more integrated economically than before. For example in the 1990s, world trade in goods and services has grown twice as fast as global Gross Domestic Product (GDP), and in the early 1990s, about one-third of all manufacturing trade in the value of about US$800 billion had to do with parts and components that involved global production networks (World Bank, 2000: 33). From 1980 to 1995, the total foreign direct investment stock has increased from about US$500 billion to over US$2.5 trillion, which represents an increase from about 4.5 per cent of the world GDP to about 10 per cent (United Nations Conference on Trade and Development, 1996: 16).[13] Despite the 1998 Asian financial crisis, the international financial flows are on an upward trend (World Bank, 2000: 34–5).

The forces of globalization are also evident in other areas, in particular, in communication and information transfer. For example, between 1985 and 1995, the world information technology market expanded at an average rate of 12 per cent every year, as indicated by the increase in personal computers, workstations, data communication equipment, packaged software and services (World Bank, 1999: 58). At the same time, the reduction in the cost of communication and the convergence in the telecommunication industry have further promoted the continuous expansion in telecommunication, as evident in the growth of mobile telephones and internet use (World Bank, 1999: 56–70).

Like other countries, Canada has been subjected to the forces of globalization, but it is not clear how much Canada has taken full advantage of the opportunities offered in the global age. Historically, Canada has relied on the United Kingdom as its principal trading and investment partner, but US investment in Canada, which began to grow in the first two decades of the twentieth century, has expanded substantially in the period after the Second World War (Clement, 1977; Naylor, 1975). By 2000, 85 per cent of the total exports from Canada went to the United States, and 74 per cent of the imports to Canada came from the United States (Statistics Canada, 2001). These statistics clearly indicate the importance of the United States as a trading partner to Canada, but they also reflect Canada's relatively weak trading position with other countries and regions of the world. For example, after the United States, the next most important trading partner to Canada is the European Union, which received 5 per cent of Canada's total exports, and which accounted for 9 per cent of the total imports to Canada in 2000 (Statistics Canada, 2001). In contrast, Japan only accounted for 2 per cent of Canada's exports, and 3 per cent of Canada's imports in 2000. These statistics suggest that despite the trend of globalization, Canada has been relying almost exclusively on the United States as a trading partner, and not diversifying its trading relations into other regions of the world.[14]

Many historical and contemporary factors influence Canada's current trading position and future position in the global economy. One factor concerns Canada's existing human resources and its language and social capacity that can be converted into advantages in global exchange. In this context, the linguistic and social diversity immigrants bring to Canada can be seen as human capital to develop stronger relations with different regions of the world. Cultural and linguistic diversity is an asset in many areas. For example, when Canadian companies set up subsidiaries overseas, they often look for people who have the experience and language capacity to operate in a particular country. As well, Canadian companies trying to enter the local markets of foreign countries often find it necessary to rely on the cultural expertise of immigrants originated from those countries.[15] When Prime Minister Jean Chrétien led a trade delegation to China in 1994 under the banner Team Canada, the media reported the role played by expatriates from China and Hong Kong, whose cultural understanding and social contact have greatly facilitated the accomplishments of the delegation (*Financial Post*, 1994a). Cultural, social, and language skills can facilitate trade agreements and cultural exchanges, especially in countries and regions where linguistic and cultural differences can create obstacles in forging sustainable relationships.

There are also other areas where cultural diversity has increased the opportunity for Canada. For example, the large arrival of Chinese immigrants to Canada in the 1980s and 1990s has substantially expanded the ethnic consumer market, and as a result, promoted the internationalization of ethnic businesses in cities such as Vancouver and Toronto (Li, 1992; Li and Li, 1999; Wong, 1995, 1997). As well, the growth of the immigrant population from Asia has facilitated the transfer of international capital to Canada, which in turn, has transformed many small-scale family-operated immigrant businesses to corporate firms with transnational connections (Li, 1993).

In the age of globalization, Canada would have much to lose for not branching out into a more diverse but increasingly integrated world. Thus far, Canada has not treasured the cultural and linguistic richness of its immigrants, nor taken full advantage of it as a cultural asset for economic and cultural development.

Conclusion

The question of diversity is contentious in the immigration debate. It is widely held that the growth of immigration from non-traditional source countries since the late 1960s has increased the diversity of Canada, and along with it, has led to social strain and adjustment problems for urban Canada where there is a concentration of immigrants. Thus, diversity is mainly cast as a new problem related to changes in immigration, and the discourse focuses on the cost of diversity to Canada.

In reality, census data over time show that Canada's diversity has not changed much, if diversity is described as the component of Canada's population that is non-British and non-French. This framework, which characterizes Canada in terms of the British and the French as charter groups, and the Third Force of other Canadians, is essentially the one used by the Royal Commission of Bilingualism and Bilingualism in the 1960s, and has since been widely adopted as a convenient model to study Canada's diversity. The census data indicate that Canada's Third Force, which includes those not of British or French origin, has consistently been made up of roughly 26 per cent to 28 per cent of Canada's population between 1961 and 1991. Within this group, Europeans other than the British and the French have accounted for a substantial proportion. The growth of immigration from non-European source countries since the 1970s has only increased the non-European component within the Third Force, but has not altered the relative size of the Third Force itself. Thus, the discourse of increased diversity has to do with the growth of non-white population in Canada, and not the weakening of the numeric dominance of the charter groups.

The discourse on diversity has developed a codified language, a syntax, and a rationale to describe the problems of diversity without resorting explicitly to 'race'. In reality, the discourse has much to do with the racial question of many new immigrants from Asia, Africa, and other non-European countries. In the immigration discourse, diversity is synonymous with 'non-white' immigrants and the value and cultural differences they represent. Immigration is seen as bringing too many cultural and social changes to Canada and creating too many adjustment problems in social relations as well as putting strains in housing, schools, transportation, and other areas. Much of the concern regarding diversity is based on Canada's long-standing European tradition and cultural perspective, which interpret non-white differences as incompatible with Canada, and therefore undermine its cohesion.

The claim that immigrant-induced diversity is fragmenting Canada is groundless. In fact, evidence indicates that over time immigrants succumb to the forces of conformity and converge with native-born Canadians in many respects. As well, there is little evidence to suggest that the official policy of multiculturalism provides resources and institutional bases for immigrants to remain culturally and linguistically segregated. On the contrary, data on linguistic diversity in Canada show that such diversity has been weakening, and most linguistic minorities have difficulties maintaining a non-official mother tongue or home language much beyond the immigrant generation.

The analysis in this chapter suggests that the discourse of diversity is racially tinted. The result is that the problems of diversity are exaggerated while its global possibilities are not properly recognized. Thus far, Canada has been relying heavily on the United States as its principal trading partner, and has not taken full advantage of opportunities in the global market. It would appear that Canada has been maintaining a narrow vision of cultural protectionism that defines everything non-European as non-traditional and threatening to its cultural security and complacency. Alternatively, Canada may abandon its cultural parochialism and treat racial and linguistic diversity in Canadian society seriously as potential resources with which multilateral trade, international diplomacy, and other global exchanges can be further advanced. By recognizing the value of cultural differences and racial diversity, Canada would be in a better position in a world that is increasingly globalized in economy and culture.

Chapter 8

Immigrants and the City

Like native-born Canadians, immigrants gravitate towards urban areas partly as a result of Canada becoming more urbanized and partly because of the economic and social attractions of cities. However, immigrants, particularly the new arrivals, have a higher tendency than native-born Canadians to settle in metropolitan centres. This tendency, together with the density of immigrants in a few large cities, adds another dimension to the immigration debate. Essentially, the debate has to do with whether the concentrated presence of immigrants in metropolitan centres has provided a stimulus to the economic vitality and growth of cities or has aggravated urban problems and strained public services. Oftentimes, the debate is complicated by the fact that many recent immigrants are from source countries outside Europe and the United States, and the increased presence of immigrants of visible minority origin in Canadian cities adds a racial dimension to the immigration debate.

The debate is clearly based on facts and emotions. New immigrants do avoid less-populated areas of Canada and settle in major cities where economic opportunities are readily available and where they are likely to find emotional and social support from members of the same ethnic group. The continuous arrival of immigrants increases their population base in large cities and this, in turn, affects the urban social and physical landscape. Not all the urban changes can be attributed to the population increase of immigrants. The expansion of large cities triggered by both natural increases and internal and international migration also produces inevitable social changes, such as increases in housing development, infrastructural construction, and commercial expansion as well as in greater mobility of residents in neighbourhoods and in the workplace. Some long-time residents view such changes, and the scale of them, as destroying a romanticized conventional lifestyle and replacing it with one less familiar and therefore less desirable to them. Since part of the social change is the increased presence of immigrants, especially those of different races, they are blamed for social changes deemed undesirable. In this way, the immigration debate is often coloured by strong emotions and partial facts.

Immigration and the Growth of Cities

Urbanization has been a global trend closely associated with economic development, and it is likely to intensify rather than weaken despite globalization and its capacity to integrate nations and markets. The growth of cities in size and in economic concentration means urban areas now account for a substantial proportion of national economies. The World Bank estimates that as much as 85 per cent of the gross national product (GNP) of high-income countries is generated in urban areas (World Bank, 2000: 126).[1] Many reasons explain why cities are often the engines of economic growth and why they account for a large share of a country's production. Densely populated areas create economies of scale that enable goods and services to be produced efficiently; such areas provide convenient access to a large labour pool, a concentrated market of consumers, and a network of complimentary firms and business headquarters (Sassen, 2001; World Bank, 2000: 125). As investment capital and labour are drawn to metropolitan centres, they further expand the urban scales and create even more favourable conditions for future investment and labour mobility. This is why the intensity of economic development correlates positively with the degree of urbanization among nations of the world (World Bank, 2000: 126).

Like other high-income countries, Canada's cities provide the opportunities, consumer choices, diversities of lifestyle, and the economic and social vitality that become attractive to many people. The process of urbanization has been intensifying in Canada since the late nineteenth century. In 1901, about 37 per cent of Canada's population resided in urban areas, but by 1976, the urban population reached 76 per cent (Statistics Canada, 1983). The 1996 Census indicates that large centres are particularly attractive to Canadians; about 60 per cent of Canada's population resided in Census Metropolitan Areas (CMAs) in 1996,[2] and three cities alone—Toronto, Vancouver, and Montreal—accounted for one-third of Canada's total population.[3]

Statistics on the urban distribution of immigrants are clear: compared to native-born Canadians, immigrants are more inclined to be in large cities. The 1996 Census indicates that although nationally immigrants made up 17.4 per cent of the total population, 85 per cent of immigrants, as compared to 55 per cent of native-born Canadians, resided in CMAs. In Toronto and Vancouver, the size of the immigrant population relative to the local population is particularly noticeable. In 1996, 42 per cent of Toronto's population and 35 per cent of Vancouver's population were immigrants. In addition, many cities had roughly one-fifth to one-quarter of the population born outside of Canada; such cities were Montreal, Hamilton, St Catharines/Niagara, Kitchener, London, Windsor, Calgary, Edmonton, and Victoria.

Each year, the majority of new arrivals go to cities, particularly the three largest cities of Canada, and this trend is expected to continue. For example, between

1995 and 1999, over 40 per cent of new immigrants went to Toronto every year, another 15 to 20 per cent went to Vancouver, and about 10 to 12 per cent ended up in Montreal (see Table 8.1). Therefore, these three cities received over 70 per cent of new immigrants who came between 1995 and 1999. In all, 14 large and medium urban centres account for about 85 to 90 per cent of total annual immigrant arrivals in Canada.

The rationale behind immigrants' choice of urban centres is rather obvious. Immigrants are attracted to large cities because of the opportunities and services available, and because of the presence of large ethnic communities that provide newcomers with emotional and other support. As immigrant communities in metropolitan centres grow, a multiplier effect is produced in that a larger immigrant community also generates a higher rate of growth, since immigrants are likely to sponsor their family members to join them (see Akbar, 1995). A growing immigrant population also draws newcomers because the expanded market creates more opportunities for employment and business development. Moreover, a larger immigrant population produces extensive family and friendship networks on which new immigrants can rely for information, sponsorship, and other types of

Table 8.1   Immigration by Census Metropolitan Area, 1995–9 (%)

Census Metropolitan Area	1995	1996	1997	1998	1999
Toronto	44.8	42.9	45.5	43.5	43.9
Montreal	10.4	10.3	10.5	12.0	12.4
Vancouver	18.3	20.3	19.1	17.0	14.6
Ottawa-Hull	2.7	2.6	2.7	3.0	3.4
Edmonton	2.7	2.2	2.1	2.1	2.0
Calgary	3.3	3.1	3.2	3.4	3.6
Quebec City	0.8	0.6	0.7	0.8	0.7
Winnipeg	1.5	1.5	1.5	1.4	1.5
Hamilton	1.3	1.3	1.2	1.2	1.4
London	0.9	0.7	0.7	0.8	0.8
Halifax	1.5	1.3	1.2	1.0	0.7
Victoria	0.5	0.4	0.3	0.2	0.0
Regina	0.3	0.3	0.3	0.3	0.3
Saskatoon	0.4	0.3	0.4	0.4	0.4
Elsewhere in Canada	10.8	12.3	10.7	13.0	14.3
Total	100.0	100.0	100.0	100.0	100.0
[Number]	[212,869]	[226,071]	[216,014]	[174,159]	[189,816]

Source: Citizenship and Immigration Canada, *Facts and Figures, 1999*, Catalogue MP 43-333/2000E, p. 6 (Ottawa: Minister of Public Works and Government Services Canada, 2000); Citizenship and Immigration Canada, *Facts and Figures, 1997*, Catalogue MP 43-333/1998E, p. 4 (Ottawa: Minister of Public Works and Government Services Canada, 1998).

assistance. Over time, new immigrants' lives are influenced and shaped by the urban setting and social institutions, but in turn, immigrants also bring changes to Canadian cities.

The economic and political importance of metropolitan centres rests on their size and their growth potential. Thus, cities such as Toronto, Vancouver, and Montreal command substantial influence because they are the largest urban markets in Canada, and because their vitality is also prompted by their prospects of continuous growth. The impact of immigration in Canada is most apparent here. For example, between 1986 and 1996, many large cities in Canada experienced substantial population growth. Toronto's population grew from 3.4 million in 1986 to 4.2 million in 1996, an increase of 24 per cent; Montreal increased from 2.9 million to 3.3 million people, or 13 per cent; and Vancouver's population rose from 1.4 million to 1.8 million people, or 31 per cent (see Table 8.2). Other cities like Ottawa-Hull, Edmonton, and Calgary also expanded in population during the same period, although the absolute increase was smaller because of a smaller population base.

When the growth in urban population is apportioned to increases in the native-born population and increases in immigrants, it becomes clear that between 1986 and 1996, the growth in the number of immigrants accounts for about two-thirds of the population increase in Toronto, over half in Vancouver, about one-third in Montreal, and over a quarter in the Ottawa-Hull area (see Table 8.2). In both Edmonton and Calgary, the growth of the immigrant population accounts for about 22 per cent of the total population. In short, if there were no increase in the immigrant population from 1986 to 1996, the population growth in the three largest cities would have been substantially reduced, in the magnitude of over half a million people in Toronto, about 242,000 people in Vancouver, and about 127,000 people in Montreal. In this sense, the large Canadian cities benefit from immigration in sustaining a high rate of population growth, which in turn promotes their economic and social vitality.

The arrival of new immigrants not only augments the size of the total population, but also expands the labour force. The economics of growth are complex, but in essence they are driven by expansions in consumption and increases in investment. A larger population brings a bigger consumer market, which attracts additional capital investments to increase production. Thus, the injection of capital investment creates new employment and a larger work force and, in turn, more consumption. Census data show that the growth of the immigrant population has contributed substantially to the expansion of the labour force in large urban centres. For example, between 1986 and 1996, 87 per cent of the growth in the labour force of Toronto and 53 per cent of the growth in Vancouver can be attributed to the increase in the immigrant population.[4] These statistics further indicate the importance of immigration in sustaining a high rate of growth in Canada's largest cities.

Immigrant Enclaves

The rise in the immigrant population in major North American cities has triggered the growth and proliferation of what is known as 'immigrant enclaves'. The notion

Table 8.2 Immigrants in Selected Census Metropolitan Areas (CMAs), 1986 and 1996 Censuses

CMA	1986		1996		1986–96	
	Population	% Immigrant	Population	% Immigrant	Population Increase	% Population Increase Due to Growth in Number of Immigrants
Toronto	3,427,170	36.0	4,232,905	41.9	805,735	67.0
Montreal	2,921,360	15.7	3,287,645	17.8	366,285	34.7
Vancouver	1,380,730	28.4	1,813,935	34.9	433,205	55.8
Ottawa-Hull	819,265	13.4	1,000,940	16.2	181,675	28.5
Edmonton	785,465	18.2	854,225	18.5	68,760	22.3
Calgary	671,325	20.6	815,985	20.9	144,660	22.5

Source: Statistics Canada, 1996 Census of Canada, Table pr2cma.ivt, *Profile of Census Metropolitan Areas and Census Agglomerations*, 95F0182XDB-2,97-11-04, available on website <http://library.usask.ca/data/social/census96/profile/immigration.html>; Statistics Canada, 1986 Census of Canada, *Population: Selected Characteristics for Census Metropolitan Areas and Census Agglomerations*, Catalogue 94-128 (Ottawa: Minister of Supply and Services Canada, 1988).

of immigrant enclave has been developed mainly by American sociologists to describe the emergence of an ethnic sub-economy among some immigrant groups, in which common language, cultural similarity, and ethnic affinity provide a basis for organizing a sheltered economy (Portes and Jensen, 1989; Sanders and Nee, 1987; Wilson and Portes, 1980; Wilson and Martin, 1982; Zhou and Logan, 1989). In such an economy, ethnic businesses are believed to thrive on the ethno-specific immigrant community that creates both the consumer market and the labour pool for business development. As well, ethnic businesses do not just compete with each other, but they also develop a high degree of interdependence for supply and circulation of goods and services. The American studies have postulated that the immigrant enclave economy provides an alternative opportunity of mobility for immigrants, and that immigrants in the enclave enjoy returns to their capital investment similar to those in the open market (Portes and Jensen, 1989; Wilson and Portes, 1980; Zhou and Logan, 1989). The immigrant enclave also provides a context for the cultivation of social capital, which some minority immigrants can mobilize in order to overcome obstacles of adjustment and for social advancement.[5]

In Canada, cities such as Toronto and Vancouver have witnessed substantial proliferations of immigrant enterprises and business concentrations, primarily as a result of the increase in the immigrant population (Li, 1992, 1993; Marger and Hoffman, 1992; Teixeira, 1998). The expansion of ethnic businesses is not only evident in city cores or in neighbourhoods where some immigrant groups have historically congregated, but also in suburban areas and middle-class neigbourhoods that do not have a history of immigrant business development.

In Richmond, BC, for example, which is just south of Vancouver, the arrival since the 1980s of large numbers of Chinese immigrants mainly from Hong Kong has transformed residential and commercial patterns (Li, 1992). Historically, Richmond was an ethnically and linguistically homogeneous suburb of Vancouver. Throughout the 1980s and 1990s, it became a vibrant cosmopolitan centre largely as a result of internal and international migration, as well as corporate investments and immigrant business expansions. Between 1980 and 1988, immigrants from Asian countries accounted for 56 per cent of all immigration to Richmond, and immigrants from Hong Kong, Taiwan, and mainland China made up 23 per cent of the total (Li, 1992: 125). Along with the increase in the immigrant population came the expansion of commercial malls and ethnic businesses particularly geared to the consumer tastes of middle-class and affluent immigrants. Richmond attracted substantial capital investments from immigrant entrepreneurs and investors, as well as from corporate firms based in Asia (see Li, 1993). Throughout the 1980s, the ethnic businesses in Richmond changed, as immigrant family-operated firms gave way to corporate businesses, which expanded the capital investment and business scale in areas such as real estate development, and food and entertainment establishments (Li, 1992). By the 1990s, Richmond became known as a choice commercial and residential centre because of its cosmopolitan taste, immigrant culture, and middle-class flavour. To a large extent, the emergence of Richmond as a commercial and cultural centre was made possible by the increase in the immigrant population, which in turn attracted international and domestic capital investments. Similar findings were reported by Marger and Hoffman (1992), whose study shows that the size of the immigrant community and the capital and human resources immigrant entrepreneurs bring to Canada help to promote the expansion of immigrant enterprises in Toronto.

The immigrant enclave is sometimes misunderstood as a segregated sub-economy in which immigrants' economic life is isolated from mainstream society, and to which non-immigrant businesses have no access. This misunderstanding nurtures an image of immigrant enclaves as urban ghettoes that support an immigrant underclass, balkanize the economy, and fragment Canadian society. In reality, the immigrant enclave responds to the growth of the immigrant consumer market, attracting ethnic and non-immigrant businesses. The immigrant enclave often thrives on the middle-class affluence and consumer power of immigrants.

In a study of the Chinese enclave economy in Toronto, Li and Li (1999) used advertisements in Chinese newspapers to extrapolate the size of the Chinese immigrant consumer market, which was estimated to be in the range of $431 million to $3.5 billion a year in 1996. The study shows that both Chinese and non-Chinese businesses advertised in the Chinese enclave market. Chinese businesses accounted for 69 per cent of the advertisements in Chinese newspapers but only 55 per cent of the advertising revenue; in contrast, non-Chinese businesses accounted for 30 per cent of the advertisements and 45 per cent of advertising revenue. Furthermore, Chinese businesses were more inclined to market professional and other services, whereas non-Chinese firms focused on products and goods.

It would be naïve to assume that such an ethnic sub-economy and the larger economy are completely segregated, and that immigrants only participate in the ethnic sub-economy. In reality, there are many overlaps between the two economies, and it can be expected that immigrant consumers optimize their choice in participating in the non-ethnic economic sector as well as in the enclave market. Thus, competitive pricing, geographic proximity, cultural appeal, and linguistic convenience influence the consumer choice of enclave consumers. At the same time, it can be expected that both ethnic and non-ethnic entrepreneurs are cognizant of market and cultural factors as important in attracting immigrant consumers. Indeed, non-ethnic firms often try to penetrate the lucrative enclave market by adopting those cultural and linguistic features and practices that appeal to specific immigrant groups as a marketing strategy.[6]

No doubt, the growth of immigrant enclaves is mainly sustained by the increase in the immigrant population and its consumer power. Market surveys of consumption patterns conducted in Toronto and Vancouver reveal that certain segments of the immigrant market are particularly lucrative. For example, in Toronto, nearly half of the Chinese respondents surveyed in 1996 owned a home, three in four bought their cars with cash, and 43 per cent had travelled to Asia within the past two years; in Vancouver, 70 per cent of those surveyed in 1995 drove imported cars and 23 per cent had US bank accounts (*Toronto Star,* 1997; *Vancouver Sun,* 1995). The Canadian Advertising Foundation has estimated the purchasing power of visible minorities in Canada to be worth $300 billion a year, and has provided survey results to indicate that 46 per cent of visible minority respondents would be more likely to buy a product if the advertisement includes visible minority (*Globe and Mail,* 1995a). As one reporter wrote, 'With immigrants settling from all over the world, Canadian retailers and advertisers are finding that they need to engage in sophisticated marketing to win the fastest-growing consumer sector' (*Globe and Mail,* 1995a). Many Canadian corporations have responded to the growing immigrant consumer market by adopting innovating strategies in order to increase their share of the market. These strategies include sponsoring cultural events in immigrant communities, offering services in non-official languages, hiring consultants to design advertisements in non-official languages, using visible minority models to promote products, and contracting market surveys to identify consumer clusters of particular cultural tastes (*Financial Post,* 1994b; *Globe and Mail,* 1995a, 1997a; *Toronto Star,* 1996a). Major banks, too, have been aggressive in setting up specialized banking sections targeting the affluent Asian immigrant market, and providing special services to customers to facilitate their investments in Canada as well as their transnational banking activities *(Globe and Mail,* 1995b). These developments suggest that the consumer markets in urban centres have become more multicultural in products and in marketing strategy, as Canadian companies respond to global tastes.

Since the 1980s, domestic and international capital investments have tried to capture this growing market. Canada's Business Immigration Program has also encouraged international capital to accompany business immigrants to Canada, and in turn, has facilitated the growth of immigrant enterprises (see Borowski and Nash, 1994; Harrison, 1996; Li, 1997; Wong, 1993). By the mid-1990s, the proliferation of immigrant businesses was conspicuous in Vancouver and Toronto. For example, in 1996, as many as 50 Chinese-theme malls or shopping centres were noted in the Greater Toronto Area, many concentrated in the affluent suburbs of Richmond Hill, Markham, and Scarborough (*Toronto Star,* 1996b). Some of these malls were new developments while others were conversions of ailing ones. In describing the success of these new Asian malls, one reporter cited Market Village on Steeles Avenue at the northern edge of Toronto as 'the hub of Hong Kong transplanted to Toronto, and a microcosm of the largest, wealthiest and potentially most influential immigration population this country has ever seen' (*Toronto Star,* 1996b). In Vancouver, the combination of offshore capital and immigrant entrepreneurship led to the development of several Asian-theme malls in Richmond, as well as major real estate projects in Vancouver downtown (Li, 1998: 134–5). There is no doubt that the scale of international migration to Toronto and Vancouver and the corresponding economic and social changes have assisted these cities to flourish as cosmopolitan centres, and have resulted in what Hiebert (2000: 28) calls 'the internationalization of the population of Canada's primary cities'.

If the growth of the immigrant population and the proliferation of immigrant businesses can be seen as further internationalizing the cosmopolitan centres of Canada, it is equally accurate to describe immigrant businesses as being transformed by the competitive market and urban culture of Canada. A case in point is the changes in the ethnic media, which historically were produced locally within the ethnic community, usually with limited resources and geared towards local readers. The rise in the immigrant population and the growth of middle-class immigrants have expanded the readership market, and globalization has enabled international capital and production technology to be injected into previously local media operations. By the 1990s, many ethnic media in large cosmopolitan centres were subsidiaries of multinational corporations, and their global network, production technology, and concentrated capitalization allowed them to improve their products and compete directly with established Canadian media. For example, there were three major Chinese daily newspapers in Toronto in 1997, with a reported daily circulation of 108,673 (Li and Li, 1999: 58).[7] Such success in capturing a sizable immigrant readership market is because of their thorough coverage of international, national, and local news, and their advertising market. The immigrant enclave economy is different but not separate from the mainstream economy. On the contrary, it is highly sophisticated and advanced, offering a unique way to integrate immigrants into Canadian society.

Schools and Neighbourhoods

While immigration contributes to the growth and vitality of major urban centres, it also creates strains and hardships in certain sectors. One such area is the schools, which have to deal with the challenge of teaching a relatively large proportion of immigrant children, whose mother tongue is often not one of the official languages. Given the tendency of immigrants to settle in large cities, the pressure for schools appears to be most acute in Toronto and Vancouver. Hiebert (1999) has noted that many schools in Greater Vancouver have half of their students born outside of Canada, and in certain districts, such as East Vancouver, Richmond, and Surrey, immigrant children approach 100 per cent of the student population in some local schools.

In 1986, immigrant children accounted for 16 per cent of the school-age population (ages 6 to 18) in Toronto, and 14 per cent in Vancouver (see Table 8.3). By 1996, just 10 years later, immigrant children made up about 23 per cent of the school-age population in Toronto and 20 per cent in Vancouver. The impact of immigration on schools is more apparent when one examines the increase in the school-age population that can be attributed to immigration. In Toronto, the growth in the immigrant population has accounted for 54 per cent of the increase in the school-age population between 1986 and 1996, whereas in Vancouver and Montreal, the figures are 39 per cent and 26 per cent respectively. These percentages translate into an absolute increase of 65,758 for Toronto, and 28,403 for Vancouver, and 9,492 for Montreal. These statistics suggest that part of the pressure on the school system comes from the sheer increase in the school-age population, which accompanies the growth in the native-born population as well as the immigrant population. But the magnitude of increase in the immigrant population, its linguistic diversity, and its tendency to concentrate in some neighbourhood schools pose additional challenges for the school system.

Table 8.3 Changes in School-Age (6–18) Population and Percentage Immigrants, 1986 and 1996 Censuses

CMA	1986		1996			1986–96	
	School-Age Population	% Immigrant	School-Age Population	% Immigrant		Increase in School-Age Population	% Increase Due to Growth in Number of Immigrants
Toronto	588,350	16.0	709,452	22.5		121,102	54.3
Montreal	492,300	8.0	529,524	9.2		37,224	25.5
Vancouver	219,750	14.2	292,392	20.4		72,642	39.1
Ottawa-Hull	140,500	6.6	174,024	9.2		33,524	19.8
Edmonton	148,650	9.8	164,700	7.6		16,050	-12.7
Calgary	116,200	12.0	151,380	9.8		35,180	2.5

Source: Compiled from 1986 and 1996 Censuses of Canada, Public Use Microdata File on Individuals. The numbers have been weighted to population size.

In the long run, immigrant children would learn the official languages and integrate into Canadian schools, but in the short term, they often require the school system to have to commit additional resources in the area of remedial language training. Oftentimes, the deployment of additional resources in language training is seen as a cost or a burden triggered by immigration. In reality, teaching English or French as a second language has also become a vibrant industry creating employment for many Canadian teachers. The 1998 Survey of Providers of Training in English or French as a Second Language, conducted by Statistics Canada with the support of several federal departments, shows that 290,000 participants enrolled in official-languages classes in 331 private schools and 150 public institutions in 1998. The industry employed 11,000 people and generated revenues of $300 million (Statistics Canada, 1999). One-third of the schools reported their intention to add new markets to their current targets. Foreign students accounted for 39 per cent of the enrollment in these classes, and the industry has grown 22 per cent between 1994 and 1998 (Statistics Canada, 1999). These statistics suggest that what is typically perceived as 'undesirable' costs incurred as a result of having immigrants and immigrant children without the language skills can also have the 'desirable' effect of sustaining an industry of language service that generates substantial revenues and employment.

There has been a strong reaction to the large influx of immigrant children in some schools from parents of native-born Canadians, mainly based on concerns that educational resources would go to the language upgrading of immigrants thus reducing resources available for general educational improvement, as well as concerns that such reductions, combined with the language difficulty of some immigrant students in the classroom, would lower the quality of education for their own children. It is not clear whether some parents are concerned about the perceived decline in educational quality or about the changing racial composition of schools. At least some of the reactions to immigrants and immigrant children appear to have been based on racial jealousy and concerns unrelated to education. In an article that explains why some white Canadians moved to Tsawwassen from Richmond, BC, a reporter quoted a respondent who complained that the high honour roles in Richmond schools mainly went to immigrant children, thus 'making it difficult for their own, less bookish children to get into the increasingly choosy University of British Columbia' (*Globe and Mail*, 1995c). But there were also complaints about immigrant students not related to educational equality, such as about the garish lifestyle and conspicuous consumption of immigrant students of Asian origin.[8] These changes—in the composition of the student body and the emergence of racial tensions—also exert pressures on school boards to upgrade the curriculum, improve testing, and broaden hiring in order to combat racism in education and to accurately reflect the multicultural characteristics of the population (*Globe and Mail*, 1993).

The adjustments in schools are part of the social changes that have taken place in many city neighbourhoods. The fact that immigrants account for 46 per cent of Toronto's population and 37 per cent of Vancouver's means that many neighbourhoods are being transformed, albeit to different degrees, by the arrival of immigrants. In Vancouver, for example, the foreign-born population made up half or more of the residents in about 15 per cent of the census enumeration areas in 1996 (Ley, 1999).

Although there is no evidence to indicate that immigrants in large cities are forming an underclass or congregating in ghettoes, certain residential patterns of immigrants can be discerned (Ley, 1999; Ley and Smith, 1997). In Vancouver, tracts with high concentrations of immigrants are located in the city proper, but suburban areas such as Richmond and Burnaby also have high levels of immigrants (Ley and Smith, 1997). Immigration statistics between the period 1991 and 1996 also showed that new immigrants settled heavily in the suburban areas of Richmond, Burnaby, and Surrey, as well as in the city proper (Hiebert, 1999). In Toronto, however, immigrants are not necessarily found in the inner city cores; tracts of high-immigrant concentration are located along the subway and in the northwestern suburb of Scarborough (Ley and Smith, 1997).

Urban Canada is not segregated in the sense that racial and ethnic groups live in separate neighbourboods and in isolation from each other. In fact, Fong and Gulia (2000) showed that in the five years between 1986 and 1991, neighbourhoods in Toronto, Vancouver, and Montreal became more diverse racially and ethnically. Fong and Gulia (2000: 172–3) suggested that the phenomenon of 'white flight' found in the United States is 'not a feature of neighbourhood change in Canada . . . (and) the general trend is for more members of each racial and ethnic group to share neighbourhoods with other groups'. However, the trend to more diversified neighbourhoods results from visible minorities seeking out neighbourhoods with Europeans, despite the fact that Europeans are still sensitive to the presence of minorities (Fong and Gulia, 2000).

Urban residential patterns have been influenced by social class as well as by ethnicity, and there are substantial variations among ethnic groups and among cities in terms of the concentration of ethnic groups in neighbourhoods (Darroch and Marston, 1971; Driedger, 1999; Hiebert, 1999). However, Fong (1999) found that socioeconomic status well explains the experience of spatial assimilation for European groups, but less well in the case of Asians and blacks. Fong explained that Asians and blacks tend to live in neighbourhoods with higher proportions of their own groups because Asians benefit from the social capital of their ethnic group and experience low returns on the socioeconomic resources in increasing spatial contact with whites, and because blacks may be steered away from white neighbourhoods because of discrimination (Fong, 1997a, 1997b). It appears that the tendency of some immigrants to reside in neighbourhoods with a high concentration of members of the same ethnic group is influenced by many factors, including the support networks available from such neighbourhoods, the socioeconomic status of immigrants, the social reception of traditional residential neighbourhoods, as well as other structural factors.

Studies on high-poverty neighbourhoods indicate that immigrants, especially visible minorities, are more likely than native-born Canadians to be located in such areas (Kazemipur and Halli, 1997, 2000a, 2001).[9] These findings do not imply that immigrants are overwhelmingly concentrated in poor areas of cities. In fact, Ley and Smith (1997) have shown that the distribution of urban poverty can be largely explained by socioeconomic factors, and to a much lesser extent by ethnocultural variations. Similarly, Fong (1997c) found that neighbourhood qualities among racial and ethnic groups are affected not only by group characteristics, but also by the city's structural contexts, in terms of ethnic group size, labour market status, housing market status, and other structural factors. Nevertheless, the finding that the poverty rate tends to be about 10 per cent higher among immigrants than non-immigrants in Toronto and Vancouver and about 16 per cent higher in Montreal suggests that immigrants, especially more recent ones, are more adversely affected by the increase in poor neighbourhoods in Canada because of a variety of factors, including possible discrimination, discounting of foreign credentials and poor timing of immigration in relation to the economic cycle of Canada (Kazemipur and Halli, 1997, 2000b, 2001).

Affluent Areas and Prosperous Immigrants

With the growth of the immigrant population in cities throughout the 1980s and the arrival of some affluent immigrants from Asia and other parts of the world, there has been a tendency for prosperous immigrants to move into exclusive neighbourhoods that are traditionally dominated by upper-middle-class white Canadians. Along with the changes in the social landscape of some established neighbourhoods is the proliferation of immigrant businesses and Asian-theme malls into parts of cities that hitherto have been relatively unaffected by racial diversity and global culture. These developments have caused tensions, as some long-time residents interpret the coming of foreign-looking immigrant neighbours and the expansion of immigrant businesses advertised in a foreign language as encroachments to what they perceive as traditional European neighbourhoods.

Much of the anxiety towards the expansion of the immigrant population into traditional middle-class neighbourhoods is directed towards immigrants of visible minority origin, especially those from Asia. There is no doubt that immigrants from Asia have constituted over half of the total immigration between 1970 and 2000 (see Table 2.3 and Chapter 2). But there are indications that it is a combination of their race and affluence, as well as their conspicuous presence in traditionally white neighbourhoods that trigger social animosity from some long-time residents (see Li, 1998). In contrast to the racial antagonism in some American cities, the social tension of immigration in large urban centres of Canada appears to be relatively mild by comparison.

Towards the end of the 1980s and early 1990s, there were heated debates in Vancouver concerning changes in the urban landscape of predominantly white upper-middle-class neighbourhoods. Mansion-style homes were being built in record numbers in response to demands that were created by increased Asian immigration. In the course of the debate, the terms *monster houses* and *unneighbourly houses* were used in the media and public discourse to refer to what some people considered to be ostentatious houses that overshadowed surrounding homes. Over time, however, 'monster houses' acquired a subtle but clearly understood meaning to refer to big houses that were deemed architecturally unpleasant and environmentally destructive, and that were believed to be built by greedy developers to suit the poor taste of wealthy Asian immigrants from Hong Kong (Li, 1994b: 23). The case of 'monster houses' in Vancouver illustrates how some affluent immigrants of a different race who venture into established white neighbourhoods are stigmatized as foreigners with little regard for the aesthetic values and traditional lifestyle of Canada.

The controversy of 'monster houses' began around the mid-1980s when housing prices in Vancouver started to rise precipitously and builders began constructing larger new homes in prestigious neighbourhoods to maximize the land value. The mid-1980s also witnessed increased Asian immigration, especially from Hong Kong; many came as business immigrants and affluent investors with substantial investment capital. Some of these immigrants bought mansion-style homes in the affluent neighbourhoods of Vancouver West, such as Shaughnessy, Kerrisdale, and Oakridge, and this led to hostility towards Asian immigrants, especially towards the Chinese, and the opulence of their large homes. The construction of these mansion-style houses on the west side of Vancouver prompted many protests by residents to officials and councillors throughout the late 1980s and early 1990s. Many heated public meetings were held; in response to public pressure, the City Council of Vancouver between 1986 and 1989 made substantial changes in the zoning by-laws aimed at restricting the height and size of houses relative to the lot (Stanbury and Todd, 1990). As they increased their presence on the West Coast, Asian immigrants, particularly Chinese immigrants, also became the new target of racial antagonism and were continuously blamed for destroying traditional Vancouver neighbourhoods and for transforming Vancouver into another Hong Kong. The media reported anti-Chinese signs in affluent neighbourhoods and unfriendly slogans on T-shirts (*Vancouver Sun*, 1989). Two Angus Reid surveys conducted in 1989 showed that about 60 per cent of the respondents in British Columbia agreed with the statement that 'immigrants are driving housing prices up', whereas nationally, only about 30 per cent agreed with the statement (Angus Reid Group, 1989). However, in the same year, a report published by the Laurier Institute indicates that the major factors contributing to the housing demand in Vancouver had to do with many demographic factors, including natural increase, net migration, and changing household structures (Baxter, 1989).

By the end of the 1980s, there was a general perception that the overheated real estate market in Vancouver was largely caused by wealthy Hong Kong immigrants and offshore Asian investors buying into the housing market, and that the problem of 'monster houses' was exacerbated by the wealth of immigrants and their cultural tastes that supported the demand for the bulky, 'unneighbourly' houses. As several commentators pointed out, the hostility towards the Chinese had to do with the simple fact that they were able to move into established white middle-class neighbourhoods and buy big houses without hardship, for prices beyond the reach of average white Canadians (*Vancouver Sun*, 1989; *Western Living*, 1988: 37).

The perception of Asian immigrants driving up real estate prices and causing radical changes to traditional neighbourhoods was reinforced in many newspaper reports that further popularized this common belief. For example, in a front-page newspaper article entitled 'Hong Kong Connection: How Asian Money Fuels Housing Market', a reporter said Asian investors were driving up housing prices and Hong Kong buyers were concentrating in west side neighbourhoods; the reporter further lamented how bilingual English and Chinese signs were changing the streets of Kerrisdale, a neighbourhood she described as 'once a WASP bastion' (*Vancouver Sun*, 1989).

In letters of complaint about 'monster houses' to City Hall, many residents blatantly blamed Chinese and Asian immigrants for a wide range of issues, sometimes unrelated to houses, including their social behaviour and foreign cultural tastes (Li, 1994b: 27). Complaints about 'monster houses' sometimes had to do with average Canadians not being able to afford them, and sometimes they were generalized into 'Vancouver's problem' believed to be caused by non-European immigrants (Li, 1994b: 27). The opposition to 'monster houses' was sometimes directed towards the design of new homes and sometimes towards the foreign-looking owners and their alleged differences in lifestyle and taste. Over time, 'monster houses' came to symbolize unwelcome outsiders and foreign values deemed contrary to the nostalgic Canadian lifestyle.

Some white Canadians, through their protest actions and neighbourhood associations against the building of 'ugly large homes', almost equated their actions to a crusade to save Vancouver from being over-urbanized. In the process, Asian immigrants became scapegoats for many of Vancouver's problems. The protest movement also helped to racialize immigrants, in the sense that their habits, preferences, and spending styles took on a racial meaning that demarcated the difference between white Canadians and Asian immigrants.

By the mid-1990s, the issue of 'monster houses' began to calm down—Vancouver passed numerous by-laws to control the building of new houses, and housing construction slowed as real estate prices fell. However, there were also indications that racial tensions in Vancouver remained high in the mid-1990s as some white Canadians moved out of central Vancouver to settle in neighbourhoods that were more racially homogeneous (*Globe and Mail*, 1995c). The case of 'monster houses' indicates the existence of social and racial barriers for non-white immigrants when they venture into affluent white neighbourhoods and alter the physical and racial landscape of urban Canada.

Toronto also experienced racial tension as Asian immigrants began to settle in the northwestern suburban areas of the city. In 1984 the Chinese Canadian community in Scarborough, Ontario, was the target of a public debate. Earlier, many Chinese residents and businesses had moved to Scarborough and other suburbs when rising Toronto land prices made suburban living more attractive. By 1984, the apparent increase in the Chinese population caused considerable public concern. In particular, many local residents were unhappy about the development of

Dragon Mall in the Agincourt area in Scarborough, which housed Chinese restaurants, grocery stores, and shops, and attracted many Chinese patrons on weekends. A meeting to discuss the alleged traffic and parking problems caused by the Chinese drew 500 people, and after it one participant frankly admitted that there was an anti-Chinese sentiment (*Toronto Star,* 1984). The incident and the underlying racial tension prompted the mayor to appoint a task force on Multicultural and Race Relations in Scarborough. Four years later, Alderman Doug Mahood conceded that many of the traffic problems were the results of 'poor planning by city staff' but 'a lot of the wrath was taken out on the Chinese' (*Toronto Star,* 1988).

An element of public concern seems to be related to the fact that the so-called Asian malls such as Dragon Centre were able to prosper in ethnic businesses that catered to the growing Chinese middle-class consumer market, while surrounding traditional retail businesses were struggling because of the growth of large-scale suburban shopping malls. As a shopkeeper in the Agincourt area described it in 1988, 'many of the original merchants have left because their business dropped off—the Anglo community just doesn't shop here as before' (*Toronto Star,* 1988). Hostility arose because of the prosperity of the Chinese businesses; the Chinese were seen as foreigners encroaching in large numbers on the affluent suburbs unaccustomed to racial diversity.

In 1995, another controversy surfaced concerning the growing number of Asian immigrants and the expansion of Chinese businesses in Markham, a suburb north of Toronto. In June of 1995, Carole Bell, the deputy mayor of Markham and regional councillor of York Region, warned in a regional council retreat that the growing concentration of ethnic groups was causing conflict, and prompted some residents to move out of Markham. She said that citizens demanded councillors to pass by-laws prohibiting what she called 'signage in a language we can't read', and that as an example, many new developments in Unionville were exclusively marketed to the Chinese community (*The Liberal,* 1995: 3). Bell's statement suggested that the growing concentration of Chinese and Asian immigrants in Markham and the development of malls with foreign language signs were driving long-time residents to leave (*Toronto Star,* 1995a). Despite strong protests from the Chinese Canadian community and the written condemnation of her statement by 12 mayors from across Greater Toronto, Bell refused to apologize and reiterated her position as reflecting the true perception in the community (*Toronto Star,* 1995a, 1995b). A Markham resident was reported to have said that she was tired of driving through town and seeing signs only in Chinese, and that she was glad Bell didn't apologize (*Toronto Star,* 1995b). Eventually, the municipality council of Markham appointed an advisory committee to address the public concerns—7 of the 14 members were from the Chinese Canadian community. In addition, the councillors adopted a statement that said, 'We welcome all races, nationalities and cultures to live and work together and we value everyone's contribution' (*Toronto Star,* 1995c).

These incidents in Toronto and Vancouver illustrate the social tension as immigrants settle in urban Canada and as traditional neighbourhoods adjust to the increasing presence of immigrants, especially those of visible minority origin. Undoubtedly, the increased volume of immigration to Canada's cities has created some practical problems of adjustment, in residential patterns and neighbourhood development. But some of the adjustment problems appear to be based on race and on the unwillingness of long-time Canadians to accept immigrants' racial diversity beyond the European tradition.

Conclusion

Urbanization is a global trend that is related to economic development and industrial growth, and urban areas in high-income countries now account for the majority share of gross national product of these countries. Immigrants tend to congregate in urban centres of Canada in part because of the growth and vitality of cities and in part because the existing immigrant communities and ethnic neighbourhoods of large cities provide certain convenience and support to immigrants. The greater tendency of immigrants to reside in large cities of Canada than the native-born population makes immigration an important engine of growth in urban population and labour market. As well, it is a source of tension as immigrants adapt to Canadian cities and as neighbourhoods adjust to a larger presence of immigrants from different racial and ethnic background.

Toronto, Vancouver, and Montreal, the three largest cities of Canada, now receive over 70 per cent of new immigrants to Canada every year. In 1996, 42 per cent of Toronto's population and 35 per cent of Vancouver's population were immigrants. Furthermore, between 1986 and 1996, the growth of the immigrant population accounts for two-thirds of the population growth in Toronto, over half in Vancouver, and one-third in Montreal. Thus, immigration has helped the large cities of Canada to sustain a high growth rate in population as well as in the labour market and consumer market.

The surge of the immigration population in Canadian cities has also prompted the expansion of immigrant enclaves. Research on the enclave economy indicates that such an economy is vibrant and complex and often offers immigrants opportunities of employment and business development. The immigrant enclave economy tends to thrive on the basis of a protected ethnic consumer market, an enlarged immigrant labour pool, as well as an injection of immigrant capital. Cities such as Toronto and Vancouver have witnessed the proliferation of immigrant businesses not just in urban core areas, but also in suburbs and middle-class neighbourhoods. The immigrant economy has revitalized some urban areas, but has also created social tension when some long-time residents see the expansion of ethnic businesses and immigrant enclaves as encroaching on traditional neighbourhoods.

The scale of international migration to cities like Toronto and Vancouver has helped these cities flourish as cosmopolitan centres; in turn, immigration businesses have been transformed by the competitive market and urban culture of Canada. Research also shows that the immigrant enclave economy does not operate in isolation from the larger economy. In fact, the growth of the immigrant consumer market has attracted corporate businesses of Canada to adopt market strategies to reflect the ethnic preferences and cultural tastes of the increasingly multicultural consumer market.

The growth of the immigrant population in cities has also created additional demands on various public services. The school system in particular has felt the pressure of the growth of the school-age immigrant population, and has to accommodate many immigrant children who do not speak either official language. The problem is further aggravated by the fact that some neighbourhood schools have an exceptionally large number of immigrant students because of high immigrant concentrations in these areas. These short-term adjustment problems have prompted strong reactions from some of the native-born population, on the grounds that the quality of their children's education is being compromised. But it also appears that some reactions are directed towards the racial origin of immigrants and their conspicuous consumptions and affluent lifestyles.

There is little evidence to suggest that urban Canada is becoming more racially segregated as a result of the expansion in the immigration population. Nevertheless, there are identifiable areas in Toronto, Vancouver, and other cities where immigrants are more highly concentrated. Research on poor neighbourhoods also indicates that immigrants, especially visible minorities, are more likely than native-born Canadians to reside in these areas. This does not mean immigrants are concentrated in poor urban areas, but it does suggest that the life chances of immigrants are affected by many factors, including economic and urban conditions.

Urban Canada has also witnessed the growth of prosperous immigrants, especially of racial minority origin. Many such immigrants begin to move into exclusive neighbourhoods traditionally dominated by white, upper-middle-class Canadians. Some long-time residents interpret the changing urban landscape and racial composition of their neighbourhood as encroachments to the traditional heritage and culture of Canada, and have lobbied to slow down the rate and direction of urban development.

There is substantial evidence to indicate that immigration is a source of growth of many Canadian cities. Canadian cities have to make social changes as non-white immigrants from Asia and other parts of the world globalize its urban social and physical landscapes. The process of integrating immigrants in cities involves short-term hardships and tensions, some of which are economic and others which are racial. Canadian cities have not seen an explosion of racial tension and conflict evident in other countries. Canada appears to be sensitive to an integration process that requires immigrants to adapt to Canadian society and Canadian urban centres to accommodate an increasingly multicultural population. Over a longer timeframe, the racial and social diversity of immigrants can be seen as helping Canada to internationalize its cities and to expand their cultural complexity and economic scale towards becoming global cities.

Chapter 9

Immigration and Canadian Society

In the preceding chapters, the immigration debate has been presented from several Canadian vantage points. Specifically, the merits of immigration have been assessed historically, demographically, economically, and socially. The immigration discourse is complex as it is shaped not only by objective facts and scientific findings, but also by subjective perceptions and normative values Canadians hold about Canada's past and its future. Such perceptions and values often influence the interpretation of facts and findings. As the discourse evolves, certain discernible features can be identified. For example, the immigration debate is primarily framed from the standpoint of Canada's self-interest, on which the merits of immigration and the contributions of immigrants are articulated in terms of benefits to Canada, and not in the context of global relations. The validity of such assumptions is widely adopted as self-evident in the immigration discourse; in turn, the presumed rationale shapes the language, the subtext, the tenor, and the substance of the debate.

In this last chapter, the immigration discourse is examined in the context of three environments within which certain conceptual biases and false assumptions have affected the immigration debate and influenced the sentiments and conclusions about the merits of immigration. These environments pertain to policy development, public discourse, and academic research. The normative constraints in each of these environments have at times contributed to certain myths and misunderstandings about immigrants and about their performance in Canada, and at times they have introduced a hidden racial dimension in the immigration debate. For example, in immigration policy development, it is often believed that such development can engineer the desirable consequences of immigration, but in reality, performance outcomes of immigrants are influenced by many structural and institutional factors of Canadian society. The public discourse of immigration is often highly regarded as a democratic articulation of Canadians' views towards immigration and their preferred choice of newcomer. In reality, the immigration discourse is often tinted with the racial question and with Canada's traditional bias towards non-whites. Academic research pertaining to race has also contributed to racial profiling of immigrants in attributing social value of immigrants on the basis of their racial origin, and has unwittingly promoted the social significance of race in scientific investigations.

This chapter ends with a recapitulation of the major themes of the book, summarizing the arguments presented in earlier chapters and concluding from them. The role of immigration for the future of Canada is also discussed, especially in light of continuous social changes in the age of globalization.

The Immigration Question Revisited

Despite the many issues and controversies that revolve around immigration, the fundamental question that captures much of the public debate and academic research has to do with assessing the merit of immigration on the basis of its benefits to Canada. The question underscores a widely accepted assumption about immigrants, which holds that the worth of immigrants is contingent upon the ability of newcomers to benefit the existing population in Canada. In other words, despite the contribution of immigration to nation building in the past, Canada does not see future immigration as essential unless newcomers can benefit the resident population. This utilitarian mentality towards immigration has largely guided the immigration debate and the research agenda about immigration. It is often reinforced on the grounds that Canada has every right to safeguard its national boundary and to determine who should or should not be new Canadians, and that unlike the past, Canada's knowledge-based economy does not need sheer manual labour from new immigrants. Such thinking contributes to the widely held belief that the worth of immigrants is measured by human capital, investment capital, and other quantifiable values to Canada. As a result, the immigration debate in Canada seldom considers immigration in the context of global inequality or economic globalization. The noted exception is the concern over brain drain from Canada, which is really a concern over the loss of human capital from Canada to the United States, where higher wages and lower taxes have attracted the periodic migration of skilled workers across the border.

Attempts to answer the apparently simple question about the worth of immigrants turn out to be rather complicated. Some of the complexities have to do with methodological and conceptual difficulties in gauging the net benefits of immigration. Other complexities are related to ideological biases towards immigrants, particularly those of colour, which distort the types of questions being raised in the immigration debate as well as the nature of the answers. The preoccupation over gauging the cost and benefit of immigration also means that economic considerations take precedence over other considerations, in part because economic behaviours and outcomes are relatively easy to quantify, and in part because economic performance can be directly translated into a monetary value to reflect a cost or a benefit. In contrast, the social worth of immigration, in terms of immigrants' capacity to enrich Canada's culture, values, social diversity, and international connections tend to be ignored. In fact, under the popular presumption that interprets immigrants' superficial differences as immutable differences of people, real and imagined differences of recent immigrants are viewed as 'costs' to Canada and not as potential sources of enrichment.

In the final analysis, the immigration debate is also about how Canada should guide its gates and should protect its national boundary. It is a debate about defining the type of people that should be accepted as new Canadians, and the type that should be kept out of Canada. Canada's commitment to democracy and equality, as enshrined in the *Charter of Rights and Freedoms*, would seem to make it obvious that superfluous factors related to one's race, origin, language, and heritage cannot be used as grounds to determine 'desirable' and 'undesirable' immigrants. By and large, Canada's statutory laws and regulations respect the principles of a liberal democratic society and maintain *de jure* equality for all. In practice, the social definition of desirable immigrants, the normative preference of immigrants of European origin, and the traditional bias towards non-whites in Canadian society influence the cultural boundary of Canada and the perceptions of Canadians towards newcomers. In this sense, the immigration debate is as much about defining the legal criteria for admitting newcomers as mapping the cultural and normative boundaries of Canada.

Immigration presents an obvious dilemma for Canada as a nation. On the one hand, advanced industrial countries such as the United States, the United Kingdom, Australia, and Germany are competing with Canada for those with human capital and financial capital to enrich their country and economy. It is a classic case of brain drain—the transfer of human resources and capital from the less developed to the highly developed parts of the world. On the other hand, the expansion of the capitalist market and economic globalization, along with other social and political changes, has resulted in the displacement of people, and the marginalization of people's livelihood. Such people are crossing national borders as underground immigrants, refugee claimants, guest workers, and illegal migrants. The challenge for a country like Canada is how to maintain a flexible and open border so that the flow of capital and human resources can be facilitated, and at the same time, protect its national interest and worth by keeping out those who are marginalized and displaced. Ultimately, it is a challenge for the developed world to re-examine not just immigration, but also the fundamental forces that trigger the movements of people across national boundaries.

The Limits of Policy Development

The development of immigration policy is an important tool that the state can engineer to shape the outcome of immigration. It is obvious that immigration policy determines the immigrant stock in that it serves as a gatekeeper in specifying the number and the type of immigrants that should be accepted. Thus, immigration policy can be seen as one powerful factor that influences the volume of immigration as well as the quality of immigrants (see Borjas, 1999; Isbister, 1996; Reitz, 1998).

While the understanding of immigration policy development is certainly sound, the method by which the efficacy of immigration policy is assessed relies on outcome indicators as manifested in the performance of immigrants. For example, the earnings of immigrants are typically treated as a feature of immigrants or as a consequence that derives from their human capital quality; in turn, immigrants' human capital content and other attributes are considered outcomes of policy choice. Therefore, if new immigrants' earnings fall behind those of native-born Canadians more than what previous cohorts of immigrants earned when they first arrived, it is tempting to attribute this disparity to immigration policy as the cause for failing to screen out those with less competitive human capital. In reality, the earnings of immigrants are determined by many factors, including the human capital of individuals, the way the human capital is valued or devalued in the economy, the opportunities available to new arrivals, and many other individual and societal features. At best, it is the level of human capital that immigrants bring with them to Canada that can be considered a characteristic of immigrants, but even in this instance, immigration policy can only be effective in influencing that portion of the immigration stream that is subject to selection decisions. The manner by which the human capital of immigrants is valued or devalued is a feature of Canadian society and not an attribute of the holders of such capital. Simply put, if the Canadian labour market rewards people differentially on the basis of race and gender in addition to human capital, then racism and sexism should be considered features of Canadian society, and not that of women or racial minorities, who in this case, are being victimized by societal features of inequality.

It can be seen that inferring from the behavioural outcomes of immigrants to the policy of immigrant selection as a cause can be misleading. Immigration policy can only influence the admission of immigrants to Canada, but it is the interaction of immigrants' attributes and societal features that really determine the subsequent behavioural outcomes of immigrants. Reitz (1998) has tried to specify some of these societal features in what he calls the 'warmth of the welcome', which includes, besides the immigration policy itself, institutional characteristics as manifested in educational opportunities, welfare accessibility, and labour market features. Reitz's analysis shows that variations in these institutional features in Canada, the United States, and Australia explain a large portion of the difference in relative earnings of new immigrants in each respective society.

It is no accident that Canada's immigration policy does not restrict the admission of immigrants purely on the basis of selectivity, that is, on the basis of selection criteria as specified in immigration regulations. The very fact that Canada's immigration law is designed to serve many purposes, including family reunification and humanitarianism, is another strong rebuttal to those who insist on measuring the efficacy of immigration policy on the basis of immigrants' economic performance and other behavioural outcomes. But there is an obvious gap between what the statute and regulations specify and what the social expectations of immigrants entail. Immigrants, irrespective of how they are selected or admitted, are expected to match the economic performance of the native-born population, in order to prove their worth to Canada.

Policy makers' desire to fine-tune the selection component of the immigration policy is understandable, since immigration policy, as compared to other societal features, represents one of the factors that can be modified with relative ease, and provides a chance for producing some desirable outcomes on future immigrants. However, it has become increasingly clear that changes in the immigration policy alone are insufficient to induce the optimal immigrant profiles or immigrants' behavioural outcomes, not only because the selection policy just applies to a portion of immigrants being admitted, but also because once in Canada, many more societal features take over to influence immigrants and their performance. An effective policy of immigration and integration inevitably involves policy changes in such other areas as strengthening multiculturalism education, removing institutional barriers that deny equal opportunities to newcomers, and combatting racism and sexism that further disadvantage those already in an insecure entrance status.

In immigration policy debates, there is tendency to focus on the economic-class immigrants, who are selected on the basis of substantial human and investment capital and are expected to contribute economically to Canada. In contrast, there is only nominal service being paid to the family-class immigrants and refugees, who are considered unsolicited and therefore with limited economic value, but are admitted as a result of the law making provisions to admit them. Much of the critique of the immigration policy in the 1990s coming from conservative quarters had to do with the notion that Canada was admitting too many unsolicited immigrants, and therefore losing control of the immigration program for not having large enough economic-class immigrants. This critique is often backed by the argument that Canada is entering into an information-based new economy, which only needs highly trained and skilled immigrants, and not the type that is represented in the family-class or refugee-class immigrants.

The utilitarian perspective creates a *de facto* two-tier system in the immigration program pertaining to the *selection* of economic immigrants and the *admission* of unsolicited immigrants, as demarcated by the implicit economic value being attached to each tier. The differential value being placed on the two-tier system is consistently reinforced by income data that show that economic-class immigrants earn more than those admitted under the family class or refugee class. While higher income often reflects higher human capital, the corollary is also obvious. The lower the earnings of immigrants, the lower their imputed values, and the less they are seen to contribute to Canada. In this way, the worth of immigrants is put in pure economic terms and captured in a narrowly defined measurement, and nothing else. In this perspective, there is little consideration for the fact that immigrants often immigrate as a family unit, and that beside the capacity to earn, an immigrant family also contributes to the building of society in ways that often escape economic measurements, in such areas as entrepreneurship, family values, work ethics, and social capital, in addition to raising and socializing children for Canada's future generation.

Even in economic terms, there is often a lack of ingenuity in immigration debates in not being able to recognize many latent values of immigration beyond what simple economic data show. For example, the argument to confine the admission of unsolicited immigrants within Canada's capacity to settle new immigrants is often made on the grounds that such self-selected immigrants frequently lack language and other skills needed to survive in Canada, and that expanding the government-sponsored immigrant settlement programs is a costly but necessary precondition for admitting more unsolicited immigrants. In short, Canada's capacity to settle immigrants is defined by the spending on settlement programs, and family-class immigrants and refugees are considered a financial burden to Canada because of their perceived cost of settlement.[1]

Even a casual examination of the budgetary expenditures and 'non-respendable' revenues of the Department of Citizenship and Immigration suggests that the actual cost of settling new immigrants is relatively small, especially when the various fees paid by immigrants are taken into account. Furthermore, settlement programs also serve several latent functions. For example, for the fiscal years 1999–2000 and 2000–1, the department spent about $366.5 million on various newcomers' programs in the forms of grants and contributions, which constituted about 43 per cent of the actual expenditure of the department in 1999–2000 and 41 per cent in 2000–1 (see Table 9.1). The cost of these settlement programs, relative to the department's total spending, has been declining slightly over the four-year period, from 46 per cent in 1997–8 to 41 per cent in 2000–1.

The federal government recovers a substantial amount of money from immigrants in the form of immigration visa fees, landing fees, and other charges to offset the cost of the services provided to them.[2] For example, for the fiscal year 2000–1, immigrants applying to come to Canada paid processing fees in the amount of $297.3 million, in addition to paying right of landing fees in the amount of $166.9 million. In all, immigrants coming to Canada paid a total fee in the amount of $464.2 million in 2000–1, $403.5 million in 1999–2000, $347.1 million in 1998–9, and $329.9 million in 1997–8 (see Table 9.2). The revenue contributed by new immigrants was higher than the amount spent in each respective year by the federal government on various programs for integrating immigrants and resettling refugees. Undoubtedly, the fees paid by immigrants are meant to recover the cost for processing them, and it is not clear whether the charges are sufficient to cover all the processing costs as well as settlement costs. At the very least, the net cost for processing and settling new immigrants is likely to be much lower than what the total grants and contributions for integrating newcomers and resettling refugees show on the surface. Furthermore, in addition to providing various services, the spending of the Department of Citizenship and Immigration also helps to create employment for many Canadians. The department hired almost 4,000 full-time equivalents in each of the four fiscal years between 1997–8 and 2000–1, not counting the indirect employment that its grants and contributions helped to create in the provinces where the transfer payment and contributions were made.

The federal spending on integrating newcomers and resettling refugees also

Table 9.1   Actual Expenditure for Integrating Newcomers and Resettling Refugees, and Number of Employees of Citizenship and Immigration Canada, 1997–8 to 2000–1

Actual Expenditure for Integrating Newcomers and Resettling Refugees	*1997–8*	*1998–9*	*1999–2000*	*2000–1*
Grants (million $):				
Grant for the Canada–Quebec Accord	90.0	101.4	102.9	104.1
Grants to provinces	46.3	0.1	51.4	52.8
Contributions (million $):				
Immigration Settlement and Adaptation Program	25.1	28.5	32.2	39.8
Host Program	2.4	2.7	2.4	2.7
Language Instruction for Newcomers to Canada	102.2	119.0	95.6	93.6
Resettlement Assistance Program	37.2	42.3	80.9	67.8
International Organization for Migration	1.4	1.5	1.1	1.1
Total Grants and Contributions (million $):	304.6	295.5	366.5	366.4
As % of department's total expenditure	45.5	41.9	42.8	40.5
Number of department's full-time equivalent employees	3,879	3,815	3,910	3,891

Source: Citizenship and Immigration Canada, Performance Report, 1998, 1999, 2000, and 2001, available at <http://www.cic.gc.ca/english/pub/>.

serves some latent functions. For example, among the total settlement spending of the federal government is an annual grant to Quebec to run its own separate settlement program under the *Canada–Quebec Accord of 1991*. The Accord guarantees a minimal compensation of $90 million for 1995–6 and after, given to Quebec by the federal government for operating parallel settlement programs, subject to an annual upward adjustment depending on increases in immigrants to Quebec or increases in federal expenditures.[3] For the fiscal year 2000–1, the compensation to Quebec was $104.1 million, or 28 per cent of the total federal grants and contributions spent on integrating newcomers and resettling refugees. For the calendar years of 1998 and 1999, Quebec received about 15 per cent of the total annual number of new immigrants to Canada, and for 2000, about 14 per cent (Citizenship and Immigration Canada, 2001c).

There are sound political grounds in justifying Quebec's disproportionate share in compensation relative to its intake of annual immigrants. As the *Canada–Quebec Accord* states, one objective is 'the preservation of Quebec's demographic

Table 9.2   Non-Respendable Revenues of Citizenship and Immigration Canada 1997–8 to 2000–1

Non-Respendable Revenues	1997–8 (million $)	1998–9 (million $)	1999–2000 (million $)	2000–1 (million $)
Immigration cost recovery fees	210.2	229.4	258.7	297.3
Right of landing fees	119.7	117.7	144.8	166.9
Citizenship cost recovery fees	20.6	18.9	21.0	23.4
Right of citizenship fees	12.9	14.3	13.7	14.7
Interest on immigration loans program	0.3	0.6	0.8	0.9
Obligations of transportaiton companies	4.8	4.2	4.6	2.8
Total revenues	368.5	385.1	443.6	506.0
Total revenues as % of total actual expenditure	55.0	54.7	51.8	56.0

Source: Citizenship and Immigration Canada, Performance Report, 1998, 1999, 2000, and 2001, available at <http://www.cic.gc.ca/english/pub/>.

importance within Canada and the integration of immigrants to that province in a manner that respects the distinct identity of Quebec' (Employment and Immigration Canada, 1991b: 2). Thus, the disproportionately higher compensation to Quebec can be justified on the grounds that Quebec desires to develop its immigrant services not only to help immigrants to settle in Quebec, but also in a manner that preserves Quebec's distinct identity. To fulfill this political desire requires additional resources or costs. But it is precisely objections to such additional political costs incurred in the federal government spending that triggered objections from provinces, notably British Columbia and Ontario.

A reporter summarized the discontent of British Columbia in 1997 as follows:

> The province, with 13 per cent of the country's population, is absorbing 22 per cent of immigrants—about 45,000 newcomers this year. . . . To make things worse, BC has been getting a paltry share—11 per cent of federal funds for settlement services and adult language training. This is in contrast to Quebec, which takes 12 per cent of immigrants and gets a clear 35 per cent off the top of all settlement funds. The other province that feels particularly shortchanged is Ontario, taking 54 per cent of immigrants while getting only 36 per cent of the money (*Vancouver Sun*, 1997).

The disproportionate distribution of immigrant settlement funds among provinces became a contentious issue between the federal government and various heavy immigrant-receiving provinces. In order to settle with the disgruntled provinces, the federal government could only raise the spending on immigrant settlement services, since the existing spending could not be equalized without jeopardizing the Accord with Quebec. In 1997, the federal government reached an agreement with British Columbia, Ontario, and Alberta to raise the federal immigrant settlement spending, under which an additional $20 million a year would be given to BC, $35 million to Ontario, and about $5 million to Alberta (*Globe and Mail*, 1997b, 1997c). In return, BC would abandon a controversial residency requirement for welfare and drop a $47-million lawsuit against the federal government over the issue (*Globe and Mail*, 1997c). These developments clearly illustrate that there are politics intertwined with the immigration debate, and that at least some of the costs related to immigrant settlement should be seen as political costs aimed at preserving and improving the intergovernmental relations of Canada. However, in immigration debates, the immigrant settlement cost is typically singled out as a financial burden to Canada, with little regard to immigrants' financial contributions to offset the cost, or to the latent functions that government spending also serves. The above analysis illustrates a need to broaden the immigration policy debate beyond the simplistic notions of cost and benefit. It also indicates that immigration policy development is only one of the many factors that influences immigration outcomes, and that many societal features also affect the integration and performance of immigrants.

Biases in Public Discourse on Immigration

Public discourse on immigration is often coloured by the race question, especially in view of the changing composition of immigration since the late 1960s that involves the decline of immigrants from Europe and the United States to Canada and the corresponding rise of non-white immigrants from what comes to be known as 'non-traditional' source countries.[4] The assessment of immigration by the Canadian public is not necessarily based on scientific findings, but often premised on subjective experiences and partial interpretations. In the end, it is difficult to segregate the immigration debate from the race question, since the 'colour' of immigrants becomes a key component of the discourse even though it is articulated subtly and indirectly. Thus, the value of immigrants may be discounted or distorted in the immigration debate simply on the basis of the changing racial composition of immigrants.

There is substantial evidence from opinion surveys to indicate that some segments of the Canadian public are unhappy about the growing number of non-white immigrants coming to Canada, and consequently are reluctant to support a more liberal immigration policy to enlarge the intake of immigrants. The reluctance is premised on the view that non-white immigrants represent unbridgeable differences that would undermine the social landscape, the normative order, and the European tradition of Canada. From this vantage point, the reservation towards immigration is to a large degree a reservation towards people of colour. Mercer (1995: 171) made a similar point when he wrote, 'Canadians have chiefly interpreted themselves and the immigration experience from a Eurocentric perspective . . . ; in racial terms, Canadians have seen themselves as white.'

The racial message of the immigration discourse is often formalized and indeed legitimized in opinion polls seeking to find out what Canadians think about immigration as well as in media reports analyzing these results. Government departments frequently use public opinions to solicit citizens' views regarding social issues and to measure their support of government policies.[5] In discussions and consultations about immigration, the government is particularly interested to find out from Canadians the level of immigration and the type of immigrants that are acceptable to them. The media and polling companies also support public opinion surveys about immigration because the topic is sensational, controversial, and newsworthy. It is in seeking Canadians' views on 'diversity' in opinion polls that the racial subtext of the immigration discourse becomes most apparent (Li, 2001b).

Certain standard questions have been routinely used in such polls as a means to gauge what is often referred to as the 'tolerance' level of Canadians towards 'diversity'. For example, in a national immigration survey conducted in January 2000 by Ekos Research Associates for the federal government, the following question was asked: 'Forgetting about the overall number of immigrants coming to Canada, of those who come would you say there are too many, too few or the right amount who are members of visible minorities?' (Ekos Research Associates, 2000: 6). The same question had been asked in earlier polls. A news report on the survey was widely printed in several major newspapers (see, for example, *Globe and Mail*, 2000a; *Vancouver Sun*, 2000). Reporter Nahlah Ayed revealed that 27 per cent of the respondents in the 2000 survey indicated that there were 'too many' visible minority immigrants, compared to 25 per cent who said so in 1999, and 22 per cent in 1998. The *Vancouver Sun* used the headline 'Survey Finds Less Tolerance for Immigrants' to highlight the story (*Vancouver Sun*, 2000). It becomes clear that the view of visible minority immigrants being too numerous, which was given by a quarter of the survey respondents, is elevated to the level of Canadians' tolerance of diversity, and the minute change of percentage of this segment over time (from 25 per cent in 1999 to 27 per cent in 2000) is given the scientific stature in revealing 'Canadians becoming less tolerant'.

There is a clear racial message that can be ascertained in the way the survey question is framed and interpreted, even though the words *race* or *non-white* are not used. First, the wording of the question indicates that pollsters and interest groups funding the survey can legitimately ask the general public to consider 'race' as a factor in immigration, and to assess the social worth of 'non-whites' in terms of whether there are too many or too few of them, provided a term like *race* or *colour* is avoided. The term *visible minorities* replaces a racially charged term such as *coloured people*, but the pollsters framing the question as well as respondents answering it are clear about what the term *visible minorities* means. Another phrase that has been used in polls to substitute for *coloured people* is *people who are different from most Canadians*. Pollsters sometimes use this codified phrase to ask respondents to indicate whether they think such people should be kept out of Canada (see *Globe and Mail*, 1992). The attractiveness of a term like *visible minorities* is that its softer appearance and its use in the *Employment Act* (S.C.

1986, c. 31) make it a convenient label that can be innocently adopted to discuss the social worthiness of 'race' and 'non-whites' without running the risk of being branded 'racist'. Most Canadians would probably find it objectionable if asked to express an opinion about whether there are too many or too few 'non-whites' in a situation in which they participate, such as a school, a corporation, or a social occasion, in part because this is too racially blatant, and in part because the principle of racial equality is clearly defined in the *Charter* and the Canadian tradition.[6] Yet, when the question about visible minorities is asked in a public poll, it appears to be much more acceptable, and indeed neutral, as a tool to find out how far Canadians are prepared to accept non-whites or coloured races. In short, opinion polls sanctify the racial phenomenon by giving Canadians a public forum to evaluate the 'coloured' segment of the population as 'too many' or 'too few' purely on the basis of 'race', as though such an evaluation is natural and proper in itself.[7] The way the 'colour' question is camouflaged in opinion polls reifies the notion of 'race' by legitimizing the right of Canadians to pass judgment on newcomers based on their superficial features. Furthermore, Canadians' opinions on immigrants' race are not seen as a social problem that has to be addressed; rather, they are presented as a democratic choice of citizens regarding how many 'diverse' elements in Canadian society they are prepared to 'tolerate'.

There is further evidence to suggest that pollsters and interest groups actively pursue the question about opinions regarding immigrants' 'race' in opinion surveys, and then present such opinions as citizens' intolerance of 'diversity' or their 'cultural insecurity' that should be taken into account in policy formulation. For example, in an immigration consulting meeting organized by Citizenship and Immigration Canada in Montebello, Quebec, on 6–7 March 1994, results of a public opinion survey conducted by Ekos Research Associates were presented, and it was reported that 'growing intolerance appears to have a racial dimension (since) 87 per cent of respondents who believe that too many immigrants are drawn from visible minorities also believe that immigration levels are too high . . . , (and that) Canadians are concerned about a "slipping away of our values" and a loss of Canadian identity' (Public Policy Forum, 1994).[8] Shortly after, in an article in the *Globe and Mail* on 28 March 1994, it referred to the finding in the Ekos survey that showed 'most Canadians believe there are too many immigrants, especially from visible minorities', and used it to explain how '"cultural insecurity" amid change fuels resentment among a majority of Canadians towards Asian, African and Arab migrants' (*Globe and Mail*, 1994b). It is clear from the prevailing interpretation that respondents' opinions on 'race' are not considered 'racist' in the public immigration discourse, but rather, they are regarded as Canadians' genuine expression of 'growing intolerance' or 'cultural insecurity' based on a legitimate concern that too many 'non-whites' would render Canadian values 'slipping away'. Furthermore, the message is clear that Canadians' reservations over too many immigrants is misunderstood when in fact they are only concerned about too many 'non-white' immigrants and not immigrants *per se*.[9] In this way, the racial message in the immigration discourse is covered up as non-racist, and indeed elevated to the level of noble concerns by citizens who only want to protect Canada's ideological tradition and the national unity.

The fact that the racial message in the immigration discourse is typically regarded as legitimate concerns of citizens also implies that polling results have a substantial influence on the outcomes of the immigration debate. Lucienne Robillard, then minister of citizenship and immigration made this point clear when she announced in 1996 the government's intention not to increase the immigration level because 'the Canadian population is divided, according to the last poll we had' (*Globe and Mail*, 1996b). Often, Canadians' reservations over admitting more immigrants and their opinions regarding too many 'non-white' immigrants are treated by the media as an indication of a public 'backlash', and not a problem of Canadian society that has to be addressed (*Globe and Mail*, 1996b).[10] The term *backlash* implies a public disapproval of a policy direction that produces a widely perceived undesirable social change.

The public immigration discourse in Canada is in a difficult epistemological position. On the one hand, the discourse has legitimized the importance of public opinions in assessing the value of immigration; on the other hand, it has racialized the immigration question in allowing the colour of immigrants to be used as an acceptable basis for assigning a value to immigrants. The public discourse on immigration illustrates that subjective perceptions and normative values about race can distort the tone and the tenor of the immigration debate, and that such distortion can also affect the way objective facts and scientific findings are gathered and presented.

Racialization of Immigrants in Academic Research

The construction of the racial subtext in the immigration discourse has been facilitated by a long academic tradition that studies how respondents in opinion surveys place different values on people of different 'race' or origin. In this tradition, prejudiced attitudes of individuals are treated as though they are free-floating ideas without a material base (see Bonilla-Silva, 1996; Wellman, 1977), and the scientific inquiry is further reduced to the empirical question of explaining why some individuals are prejudiced and others not. Furthermore, the legitimacy of researchers approaching respondents to ask them to rank-order people on racial grounds is never questioned, and respondents have accepted such research as proper and natural.

Academics have encouraged respondents to articulate racial prejudice freely in their research and then proceeded to coin various concepts to describe prejudiced attitudes as though they reflect natural preferences of people. In so doing, several widely accepted concepts popularized by researchers have contributed to distorting racial prejudice by making them appear as natural and legitimate, and therefore less offensive. For example, the notion of social distance is widely adopted in attitudinal surveys to capture the degree to which respondents are prepared to accept members of a different 'race' in various types of social relations, for example, as a close kin, fellow club members, neighbours, co-workers, or citizens

(Bogardus, 1925, 1968; Owen, Eisner, and McFaul, 1981). This notion and similar constructs have been used widely, including in several major attitudinal surveys in Canada (Berry and Kalin, 1995; Berry, Kalin, and Taylor, 1977; Kalin and Berry, 1996).

A question on 'social distance' was used in the 2000 survey conducted by Ekos Research Associates and commissioned by Citizenship and Immigration Canada. In the survey, respondents were asked to indicate how they feel about someone from a given country moving into their neighbourhood. The results, presented as a measurement of social distance, show that respondents were more positive towards those from the United Kingdom and France than those from China, Jamaica, or Somalia; furthermore, the results were compared to similar findings in a 1992 survey (Ekos Research Associates, 2000). A 1991 national survey conducted by Angus Reid Group and commissioned by Multiculturalism and Citizenship Canada also included a similar question that involved presenting respondents with a list of selected ethnocultural groups and asking them to indicate how comfortable they are with members of each group, ranging from 'not at all comfortable with' to 'very comfortable' (Angus Reid Group, 1991: 49–51).[11] The results, described as 'comfort levels', show that those of European origin had a higher 'comfort' rating than those of non-white origin—Chinese, Black, Moslem, Arab, Indo-Pakistani, and Sikh (Angus Reid Group, 1991: 51). Thus, in calling what researchers find as 'social distance' and 'comfort levels', researchers have unwittingly encouraged respondents to rank order social groups on the basis of origin and skin colour, with little regard that such an exercise contributes to racializing immigrants and minority groups by accepting the legitimacy of placing social value on race or colour.

This type of research is sometimes justified on the grounds that the normative hierarchy of racial groups unraveled in attitudinal surveys actually reflects their status hierarchy in society, and that documenting racist attitudes is one necessary step towards eliminating them.[12] This type of research accepts the premise that 'race' is a valid scientific construct, and supports its continuous usage as a meaningful concept by systematically asking respondents to place value judgment on people based on 'colour'. In his critique of research that reifies 'race'—that is, research that gives an objective appearance to 'race' when in fact it is not there— Miles (1982: 34–8) argues that such research gives primacy to 'race' as though it is an active agent in and of itself, when in fact 'race' is a consequence of social construction. At the very least, social scientists have been insensitive in systematically encouraging the articulation of 'racial' differences by conditioning respondents to choose preferences based on 'race', 'origin', or 'skin colour', and then by attributing a pseudoscientific label such as 'comfort level' or 'social distance' to beautify and to legitimize such choices. Over time, as these questions on 'racial' preferences are repeatedly asked by academics in studies, the legitimacy of asking such questions is engraved in the minds of people in that their frequent recurrence in survey questionnaires becomes, *ipso facto,* a justification of their social merit and scientific validity. When these academic tools are increasingly popularized in opin-

ion polls and in the immigration discourse, the public articulation of 'racial' preferences itself and the means by which such preferences are articulated also become
entrenched and institutionalized.

The immigration discourse in Canada has a strong racial dimension, in part
because of the changing racial composition of immigrants to Canada, but also in
part because academic research has contributed to racializing immigrants and
minority groups by encouraging the public to articulate their racial preferences and
then legitimizing such preferences as harmless and democratic choices.

Summary and Conclusion

This book begins with the discussion that immigration is a global phenomenon
that involves movements of people across national boundaries. Many historical
factors have contributed to such large movements in the past, but in the contemporary context, globalization has contributed to the blurring of national boundaries and has encouraged a high degree of human mobility along with the
relatively free flow of information, technology, products, and capital. Undoubtedly,
the expansion of the capitalist market and economic globalization have provided
many new opportunities that facilitate the mobility of people, especially those who
possess human capital and financial capital. But the direction of international
migration tends to be from less developed to highly developed regions of the
world. In this process, advanced industrial countries such as Canada benefit from
the transfer of human capital from different parts of world. Globalization enables
wealthy nations to have greater access to the global skilled labour market, and
their immigration policies are generally framed so that they can take advantage of
global human resources and capital for their economic development.

The context of globalization and immigration explains why a country like
Canada mainly frames its immigration debate in terms of its self-interest. From this
vantage point, immigration is only worthwhile if it can be shown that immigrants
benefit Canada. There is no dispute that immigrant societies such as Canada have
been populated and built by immigrants and their descendants. However, preva-
lent thinking in the immigration discourse considers immigration to be essential to
the building of Canada during periods of land settlement and agricultural growth;
since Canada is now in an information-based age, the future of economic growth is
believed to rest on expansions in technical skills and innovations, and not manual
labour, and thus, the merits of immigration to Canada's future are therefore not
clear. Such thinking has influenced the immigration discourse, and has conditioned the direction of the debate in terms of the cost and benefit of immigration to
Canada.

Attempts to answer the question regarding the cost and benefit of immigration
has been marred by many difficulties, including the imprecision of the concept
'immigrant', which has been used in different ways—as a legal term, a social construct, and an academic concept. The legal definition of immigrants mainly pertains to the legal immigrant status that is granted to those who have landed in
Canada as immigrants and have not become Canadian citizens. However, in the

official discourse, a distinction is often made between the economic immigrants, or those selected on human capital and other labour market criteria, and 'unsolicited' or 'self-selected' immigrants made up of the family class or refugee class. This distinction also implies that solicited immigrants have more to offer to Canada, and that self-selected immigrants are less productive and indeed can be costly to Canada. Immigrant as a social concept is not precise, but it is used to refer to non-white newcomers, typically from Asia, Africa, and other regions outside of Europe and the United States. In this usage, the notion of immigrant conveys the problems of immigration and the potential injurious effect immigration and diversity have created for Canada. Academics, too, tend to use the concept immigrant differently, mainly to refer to people who have moved, who are known as first-generation immigrants. But the application of the concept is not consistent, as it sometimes includes, and other times, excludes children of immigrant, illegal immigrants, and transitory migrants. The difference in the application of the concept immigrant results in uneven expectations being placed on immigrants, as well as variations of interpretations based in part on a different understanding of what immigration entails. In addition to the conceptual ambiguity, there are also cultural biases that influence the expectations of immigrants in Canadian society. Immigrants are seen as outsiders who are expected to adapt to Canadian lifestyle, in terms of its norms, values, and traditions, and who should conform over time to the economic performance and other behavourial standards of native-born Canadians.

Assessments of the merits of immigration have also been influenced by the changing racial composition of immigrants, as non-white immigrants began to immigrate to Canada in large numbers after the changes in immigration regulation in 1967. These changes have added an emerging racial dimension to the immigration debate, and they have distorted the objectivity of the immigration discourse in allowing the colour or origin of immigrants to be an object of evaluation.

Immigration affects Canada's population, and produces other changes for society. Historically, immigration contributed to population increase, especially during periods of high economic growth. However, until recently, natural increase has had a greater effect on population growth than immigration. In the second half of the twentieth century, immigration accounted for about one-quarter of the net population increase every decade. Currently, the decennial population increase in Canada would have been trimmed more than half without immigration. However, the continuous decline in fertility in Canada and the corresponding aging of the population suggest that sometime in the first quarter of the twenty-first century, Canada's natural increases will produce a net loss in population because of more deaths than births; the only source of population growth would have to come from international migration. Eventually, even a constant arrival of 225,000 new immigrants a year will be insufficient to counteract the decline in population. Assuming such a medium growth scenario, Canada's population will peak around the year 2041 and then decline slowly but steadily thereafter. These projections suggest that Canada's world position is likely to erode in comparison to the United States, which has been expanding in population size and in the scale of the advanced economy.

There is also no evidence to indicate that Canada's 'absorptive capacity' of new immigrants has been saturated, especially when such capacity is defined as a ratio of newcomers to the native-born population over time. In short, the demographic analysis suggests that the existing demographic evidence cannot justify a policy to reduce future immigration, and that Canada has much to gain in maintaining an expansionist policy in immigration in light of its future demographic trends.

Much research on immigration has been conducted in Canada, and in the main, the research has attempted to place a value on immigration by gauging the net benefits of immigration to Canada. Thus far, the models developed are mainly limited to assessing economic benefits based on calculations using measurable quantities such as earnings, unemployment insurance benefits, taxes, and welfare payments (see, for example, DeVoretz, 1995; Economic Council of Canada, 1991). The research has indicated that there is no evidence of immigration creating an economic burden or an underclass in Canada, and the weight of the evidence also suggests that immigrants on average have contributed to Canada economically, and that their performance compares favourably to native-born Canadians.

Academics follow two strategies in assessing the economic contributions of immigrants. The first strategy treats immigration as a means of aggrandizing the population size of Canada and expanding per capita productivity. The second strategy compares the economic performance of immigrants to that of the native born, and to the extent that the former is performing similarly to the latter, immigrants are deemed to be contributing in the same way as native-born Canadians. Research using the first strategy has produced mixed findings that show a small positive or negative effect on per capita productivity or income as a result of expanding the intake of immigrants. On the basis of such inconclusive findings regarding aggregate economic benefits of immigration, it would be difficult to justify increasing or reducing the level of immigration.

Research that compares the economic performance of immigrants and native-born Canadians has clearly shown that immigrants on average perform as well as the native-born, and in some instances, outperform them. The findings are fairly consistent in showing that immigrants, compared to the native-born, rely less on employment insurance and welfare transfer payment, and over the course of their lives, immigrants' contribution in taxes exceeds the costs of social benefits and social assistance they receive through transfer payment. To the extent that immigrants pay more in taxes than they take out in transfer payments, and to the extent that they use social benefits about the same as or less than native-born Canadians, they can be said to create a net economic benefit for Canadian society.

Studies comparing the earnings of immigrants also show that immigrants on average earn as much as native-born Canadians, even though more recent entry cohorts earn less. There have been concerns about the apparent erosion in the economic performance of more recent immigrants to Canada: they earn less on arrival than earlier immigrants as compared to the earnings of the native-born; more recent cohorts seem to have difficulties catching up with the average earnings of native-born Canadians. At the same time, research on urban poverty shows that immigrants, especially more recent arrivals, have a higher chance to reside in poor areas of cities than native-born Canadians. It is not entirely clear why recent immigrants tend to perform less well than their predecessors in relative earnings. It is probably a combination of factors pertaining to immigrants' characteristics such as their level of human capital and language capacity as well as societal features such as economic conditions, market valuation of foreign credentials, and opportunity structure that explains the changing relative performance of new immigrants. However, it is also not certain whether the relative earnings of recent immigrants will decline further or rebound over time.

It would be incorrect to conclude from the earnings of recent arrivals that immigrants are not performing as well as native-born Canadians. On the contrary, immigrants on average, tend to earn as much or more than native-born Canadians. However, when differences between immigrants and native-born Canadians in education, experiences, and other work-related factors and individual characteristics are taken into account, immigrants, especially women and racial minorities, suffer an income penalty. The substantial research on immigrants' earnings suggests that many factors contribute to net income disparities, including the devaluation of foreign credentials, gender pay inequity, racial discrimination, job opportunities, and economic conditions. In short, earnings and earnings disparities reflect both features of Canadian society as well as characteristics of immigrants. It is simplistic and incorrect to infer from net earnings disparities that immigrants have less to offer to Canada than native-born Canadians. On the contrary, net earnings disparities often imply that social inequality rather than individual inadequacy is affecting the earnings opportunities and life chances of social groups and individuals.

While research has identified economic hardship facing some immigrants, it has also documented the affluence and growing economic power of other immigrants. Research on immigrant enclaves and ethnic markets has shown that the immigrant consumer market is fast growing, and that Canadian corporations and businesses are battling for the immigrant market with innovative marketing strategies. There is no doubt that immigration has promoted the population growth and economic prosperity of large urban centres. In Vancouver and Toronto, for example, the increase in immigration between 1986 and 1996 has contributed to more than one-half and more than two-thirds of the population increase respectively. Since over 60 per cent of the annual immigrant arrivals tend to go to these two cities, a substantial reduction in the immigration level will adversely affect the future growth of these cities.

Academic research has been effective in addressing a rather limited aspect of the immigration question, mainly pertaining to quantifiable attributes of immigrant life that are essentially economic in nature. However, immigrants also bring cultural and social benefits to Canada—entrepreneurship, family values, cultural diversity, and social capital—all of which are difficult to quantify and assess. Even in narrowly defined terms, academic research on the economic performance suggests that immigrants do not constitute a dependent population in Canada draining public money. On the contrary, they perform at par or outperform native-born Canadians and contribute to the growth of the economy and the cities. Given such evidence, it would be fair to say that Canada has prospered as a nation from immigration in the past, notwithstanding the fact that it also has to deal with short-term adjustment problems associated with settling and integrating newcomers. In view of the demographic trends of Canada, it would make sense for Canada to strengthen its immigration program and to expand its immigration intake to ensure the future growth and prosperity of the nation.

Immigration involves a national policy that affects the long-term development of a nation. Like other demographic forces, the full effect of immigration becomes much more apparent over decades. The delayed long-term effect makes it even more important that immigration policy should have a forward-looking perspective in being able to identity world trends and global development in order to design an immigration program that takes into account future changes.

One of the changes has been globalization. If globalization is loosely defined as a trend towards a more integrated world of nations in which there is a softening of national boundaries and increased mobility of goods, services, people, and ideas, then we should expect a future world in which more people will be moving across nations, either temporarily or permanently. The World Bank estimates that at the beginning of the twenty-first century, about 2.5 per cent of the world population, or roughly 130 million people, live outside their countries of birth, and this number is rising at a rate of about 2 per cent a year (World Bank, 2000: 38). There is no doubt that globalization has facilitated the movements of people across national boundaries, especially for those in possession of human capital and investment capital that are sought after by advanced developed countries. At the same time, there are an increasing number of displaced persons in the world; 23 million refugees had crossed national borders by 1995, in addition to another 20 million persons displaced within their own countries (World Bank, 2000: 37). These trends suggest that the future world has to deal with two related problems of globalization: the increased migration of highly trained and well-resourced persons across nation-states and the surge of asylum seekers from less developed countries seeking entry to the developed parts of the world.

The challenge for highly developed countries like Canada has been to design a system to select the best-qualified immigrants and to keep out the pauperized mass of asylum seekers. Thus far, highly developed nations have been successful in defining legitimate refugees as those suffering mainly from political persecution, and have used this narrow notion of refugees to exclude the majority of asylum seekers on the grounds that they are 'economic migrants' and not *bona fide* 'refugees'. The question is whether the highly developed countries can continue to profit from free trade and human mobility of globalization without dealing with the issue of global inequality and poverty that is triggering the displacement of people. It is not just those in dire straits who are searching for economic security elsewhere; others with rising expectations of improved material conditions also seek a better life in the advanced industrialized world. The response from highly developed countries has been to erect taller fences and to intensify border controls to keep out those they define as 'undesirables', at the same time reducing the border barriers for trade and for those with skills and capital. It is a paradoxical approach to the contradictions of globalization, but the contradictions will likely intensify unless the highly developed countries begin to seriously address the root problem of world poverty and inequity.

In the course of managing the contradictory forces of immigration, highly developed countries find it necessary to adopt differential policies and discourses towards different migratory flows, such as towards skilled immigrants and bogus asylum seekers, or towards legal and illegal immigrants. These paired concepts clearly underscore the need for receiving countries to promote the merits of skilled immigrants, as well as to publicize the dangers of hordes of unwelcome foreigners, deemed financially burdensome and morally harmful. Oftentimes, the danger of unwelcome foreigners is exaggerated. But the ideological construction of such dangerous foreigners helps to racialize and at times, to demonize them, in order to justify extreme measures designed to counteract a social menace that is seen as threatening the security and integrity of democratic societies. In other words, the ideological construction becomes strategic and necessary to win the moral grounds for adopting harsh measures against undesirable elements. The recent 'children overboard' scandal in Australia illustrates well how the government has manipulated photographs and evidence during the 2001 election to falsely accuse asylum seekers of throwing children to sea in order to force the Australian government to accept them. It also shows how the government has used the fabrication to construct the social image of asylum seekers as demons to justify extreme measures against them, including confining them to long-term internment in remote locations.[13] The incident also suggests how the immigration debate can be easily distorted and politicized. In Canada, the arrival on the West Coast of several rusty boats carrying migrants and refugee claimants from China triggered strong public condemnations and harsh government responses. The government incarcerated most of the migrants and claimants and processed them with unusual speed. In all, a total of 599 Chinese migrants had arrived by boat in 1999; of the 576 who claimed refugee status, only 16 were granted it by July of 2000. The Canadian government spent a total of $36 million in processing and incarcerating the Chinese migrants (*Globe and Mail,* 2000b). A minister referred to the migrants as 'lawbreakers' who abused Canada's generosity, and as a result had stirred up an anti-immigration backlash (*National Post,* 1999). A national opinion poll conducted in August of 1999 shows that about half of the respondents wanted to immediately deport the migrants to China, and the other half were in favour of allowing them to apply as refugees or to stay while their applications were reviewed (*Globe and Mail,* 1999). These incidents illustrate how highly developed countries have responded to 'undesirable' migrants and refugee claimants, and have adopted moral discourses and harsh policy measures to block their entry.

Canada has maintained a *de facto* dual policy regarding immigration: the selection of immigrants and admission of their family members, and the management of asylum seekers. Much of the attention towards immigration policy development is directed towards selecting immigrants of high human capital quality and keeping out the asylum seekers. Canada has only moderate success in both areas. The question of asylum seekers is related to the problem of global inequality, and Canada's policy is at best a defensive measure. There is some evidence to indicate that despite Canada's emphasis on selecting immigrants with human capital endowment or investment capital, it is only attracting the middle-tier quality immigrants while the best-qualified immigrants often choose to go to the United States (Reitz, 1998).

Canada's policy of immigration selection is a reactive policy in that it assumes an unlimited supply of potential immigrants wanting to come to Canada, and focuses tailoring immigration to the country's short-term economic needs as defined by the demand of skilled immigrants. If the trend to globalization continues, it is likely that the international market of potential immigrants with human capital or investment capital that highly developed countries want will decline in stock, and recipient countries will be competing intensely for the limited supply of 'desirable' immigrants. Canada is not positioning itself for such a competition. It has often been cited that the United States will always attract the best-qualified and most entrepreneurial immigrants because of the higher remuneration rate, lower taxes, and better growth potentials. But Canada has much to offer in such areas as the publicly funded health care system, the social safety net program, accessible postsecondary education, a liberal citizenship policy, and an official policy of multiculturalism. However, Canada is not actively promoting itself to prospective immigrants about many of its attractive features, probably for fear that it will also attract 'undesirables'.

In the long run, Canada may be better able to attract the kind of immigrants it wants by ensuring that new immigrants have a fair chance in Canada, irrespective of racial origin. In particular, it is in the area of multiculturalism that Canada has much to improve in order to increase its attractiveness to highly marketable immigrants who are shopping around the world for a country that can best reward their talents economically and socially. The immigration discourse in Canada is lined with a racial bias towards non-white immigrants, and official multiculturalism is ineffective in combatting racial discrimination and in leveling inequality. In the past, some countries were able to protect their economic advantage by maintaining a closed-door policy to those they deemed culturally and racially incompatible with the resident population. In an increasingly globalized world in which cultural and racial diversity is an asset to facilitate the flow of capital, goods, services, and ideas, even countries that were previously unreceptive to immigration are beginning to recognize the merits of immigration.[14]

Canada has benefited from immigrants in the past by maintaining a relatively open system, in terms of accepting immigrants and granting citizenship to them. Many European countries are now beginning to recognize the limits of an isolationist position, and embark on a more open immigration system. It is inconceivable that Canada would want to retrench its position on immigration at a time when others are beginning to recognize what Canada has been doing. A country like Canada has a choice of policy to change its future course. It can adopt an isolationist position in order to safeguard its cultural and racial homogeneity, and it can reduce the admission of immigrants with the optimism that the country can continue to grow in an information age even without population growth. Alternatively, it can embrace the opportunity of becoming a truly multicultural and multiracial nation, and with its enriched cultural and economic endowment, can become actively engaged in a globalized world. The short-term cost of making a mistake is probably negligible, but in the long run, Canada may have to pay a heavy price for its lack of foresight in not being able to recognize how immigration can continue to contribute to the building of an economically and culturally diverse Canada that is adaptable to the twenty-first century and beyond.

Appendix

Table A.1 Immigrants Admitted Annually to Canada, 1867–2000, and Unemployment Rate, 1946–2000

Year	Immigrants Admitted	Unemployment Rate	Canada's Population	Immigrants as % of Canada's Population
1867	10,666		3,463,000	0.3
1868	12,765		3,511,000	0.4
1869	18,630		3,565,000	0.5
1870	24,706		3,625,000	0.7
1871	27,773		3,689,000	0.8
1872	36,578		3,754,000	1.0
1873	50,050		3,826,000	1.3
1874	39,373		3,895,000	1.0
1875	27,382		3,954,000	0.7
1876	25,633		4,009,000	0.6
1877	27,082		4,064,000	0.7
1878	29,807		4,120,000	0.7
1879	40,492		4,185,000	1.0
1880	38,505		4,255,000	0.9
1881	47,991		4,325,000	1.1
1882	112,458		4,375,000	2.6
1883	133,624		4,430,000	3.0
1884	103,824		4,487,000	2.3
1885	76,169		4,537,000	1.7
1886	69,152		4,580,000	1.5

Table A.I *(continued)*

Year	Immigrants Admitted	Unemployment Rate	Canada's Population	Immigrants as % of Canada's Population
1887	84,526		4,626,000	1.8
1888	88,766		4,678,000	1.9
1889	91,600		4,729,000	1.9
1890	75,067		4,779,000	1.6
1891	82,165		4,833,000	1.7
1892	30,996		4,883,000	0.6
1893	29,633		4,931,000	0.6
1894	20,829		4,979,000	0.4
1895	18,790		5,026,000	0.4
1896	16,835		5,074,000	0.3
1897	21,716		5,122,000	0.4
1898	31,900		5,175,000	0.6
1899	44,543		5,235,000	0.9
1900	41,681		5,301,000	0.8
1901	55,747		5,371,000	1.0
1902	89,102		5,494,000	1.6
1903	138,660		5,651,000	2.5
1904	131,252		5,827,000	2.3
1905	141,465		6,002,000	2.4
1906	211,653		6,097,000	3.5
1907	272,409		6,411,000	4.2
1908	143,326		6,625,000	2.2
1909	173,694		6,800,000	2.6
1910	286,839		6,988,000	4.1
1911	331,288		7,207,000	4.6
1912	375,756		7,389,000	5.1
1913	400,870		7,632,000	5.3
1914	150,484		7,879,000	1.9
1915	33,665		7,981,000	0.4
1916	55,914		8,001,000	0.7
1917	72,910		8,060,000	0.9
1918	41,845		8,148,000	0.5
1919	107,698		8,311,000	1.3
1920	138,824		8,556,000	1.6
1921	91,728		8,788,000	1.0
1922	64,224		8,919,000	0.7
1923	133,729		9,010,000	1.5
1924	124,164		9,143,000	1.4
1925	84,907		9,294,000	0.9

Table A.1   (continued)

Year	Immigrants Admitted	Unemployment Rate	Canada's Population	Immigrants as % of Canada's Population
1926	135,982		9,451,000	1.4
1927	158,886		9,637,000	1.6
1928	166,783		9,835,000	1.7
1929	164,993		10,029,000	1.6
1930	104,806		10,208,000	1.0
1931	27,530		10,377,000	0.3
1932	20,591		10,510,000	0.2
1933	14,382		10,633,000	0.1
1934	12,476		10,741,000	0.1
1935	11,277		10,845,000	0.1
1936	11,643		10,950,000	0.1
1937	15,101		11,045,000	0.1
1938	17,244		11,152,000	0.2
1939	16,994		11,267,000	0.2
1940	11,324		11,381,000	0.1
1941	9,329		11,507,000	0.1
1942	7,576		11,654,000	0.1
1943	8,504		11,795,000	0.1
1944	12,801		11,946,000	0.1
1945	22,722		12,072,000	0.2
1946	71,719	3.4	12,292,000	0.6
1947	64,127	2.2	12,551,000	0.5
1948	125,414	2.3	12,823,000	1.0
1949	95,217	2.8	13,447,000	0.7
1950	73,912	3.6	13,712,000	0.5
1951	194,391	2.4	14,009,000	1.4
1952	164,498	2.9	14,459,000	1.1
1953	168,868	3.0	14,845,000	1.1
1954	154,227	4.6	15,287,000	1.0
1955	109,946	4.4	15,698,000	0.7
1956	164,857	3.4	16,081,000	1.0
1957	282,164	4.6	16,610,000	1.7
1958	124,851	7.0	17,080,000	0.7
1959	106,928	6.0	17,483,000	0.6
1960	104,111	7.0	17,870,000	0.6
1961	71,698	7.1	18,238,000	0.4
1962	74,856	5.9	18,583,000	0.4
1963	93,151	5.5	18,931,000	0.5
1964	112,606	4.7	19,290,000	0.6

Table A.1   (continued)

Year	Immigrants Admitted	Unemployment Rate	Canada's Population	Immigrants as % of Canada's Population
1965	146,758	3.9	19,644,000	0.7
1966	194,743	3.6	20,015,000	1.0
1967	222,876	4.1	20,378,000	1.1
1968	183,974	4.8	20,701,000	0.9
1969	164,531	4.7	21,001,000	0.8
1970	147,713	5.9	21,297,000	0.7
1971	121,900	6.4	21,962,082	0.6
1972	122,006	6.3	22,219,560	0.5
1973	184,200	5.6	22,493,842	0.8
1974	218,465	5.4	22,808,446	1.0
1975	187,881	7.1	23,142,275	0.8
1976	149,429	7.0	23,449,793	0.6
1977	114,914	8.0	23,726,345	0.5
1978	86,313	8.3	23,963,967	0.4
1979	112,093	7.5	24,202,205	0.5
1980	143,135	7.5	24,516,278	0.6
1981	128,639	7.6	24,820,382	0.5
1982	121,176	11.0	25,117,424	0.5
1983	89,188	11.9	25,366,965	0.4
1984	88,271	11.3	25,607,555	0.3
1985	84,334	10.7	25,842,590	0.3
1986	99,325	9.6	26,100,587	0.4
1987	151,999	8.8	26,449,888	0.6
1988	161,494	7.8	26,798,303	0.6
1989	191,493	7.5	27,286,239	0.7
1990	216,396	8.1	27,700,856	0.8
1991	232,744	10.3	28,030,864	0.8
1992	254,817	11.2	28,376,550	0.9
1993	256,741	11.4	28,703,142	0.9
1994	224,364	10.4	29,035,981	0.8
1995	212,859	9.4	29,353,854	0.7
1996	226,039	9.6	29,671,892	0.8
1997	216,014	9.1	29,987,214	0.7
1998	174,159	8.3	30,248,210	0.6
1999	189,816	7.6	30,499,219	0.6
2000	227,371	6.8	30,769,669	0.7

Source: Data for immigrants admitted,1867 to 1999, are from Citizenship and Immigration Canada, *Facts and Figures 1999*, Catalogue MP43-333/2000E, p. 2 (Ottawa: Minister of Public Works and Government Services Canada, 2000); and for 2000, from *CANSIM*,

Label: D27 (updated 25 Sept. 2001), Title: Immig. by Country of Last Residence (original source: SDDS 3601 Employment and Immigration Canada); Data for unemployment, 1946 to 1975, are from Statistics Canada, *Historical Statistics of Canada*, 2nd edn, Catalogue CS11-516E, pp. D223-247 (Ottawa: Minister of Supply and Services Canada, 1983); and for 1976 to 2000, *CANSIM*, Label: D984954 (updated 30 Jan. 2001), Title: CDA LF Characteristics Annual Averages/Unemployment Rate (original source SDDS 3701 STC (71-220, 71-529)); Data for Canada's Population, 1867 to 1945, are from Statistics Canada, *Historical Statistics of Canada*, 2nd edn, Catalogue CS11-516E, pp. A1-14 (Ottawa: Minister of Supply and Services Canada, 1983); and for 1946 to 1970, *CANSIM*, Label: D31248 (updated 25 June 1996), Title: Population of Canada, by Province (original source: SDDS 1901 STC (13-521 & 13-201)); and for 1971 to 2000, *CANSIM*, Label: C892268 (updated 6 Nov. 2001), Title: Population by Age by Sex Canada (original source: SDDS 3604 Demography Division).

Table A.2 Immigrants Admitted Annually to Canada by Country/Region of Last Permanent Residence, 1955–2000

Year	Britain	Other Europe	Total Europe	Africa	Asia	Australasia	USA	Central America	West Indies	South America	Other Countries	Total
1955	30,420	60,351	90,771	475	3,662	1,700	10,395	109	793	1,654	387	109,946
1956	52,619	92,935	145,554	1,079	3,537	1,924	9,777	106	1,058	1,551	271	164,857
1957	114,347	143,064	257,411	2,970	3,371	3,345	11,008	172	1,162	2,376	349	282,164
1958	26,003	76,049	102,052	1,355	4,450	2,344	10,846	159	1,192	2,168	285	124,851
1959	19,037	65,263	84,300	843	5,608	1,512	11,338	160	1,196	1,750	221	106,928
1960	20,384	62,322	82,706	833	4,218	1,657	11,247	202	1,168	1,823	257	104,111
1961	12,285	39,652	51,937	1,088	2,887	1,432	11,516	147	1,126	1,301	255	71,689
1962	16,055	37,595	53,650	2,171	2,733	1,384	11,643	183	1,586	1,103	133	74,586
1963	25,193	43,703	68,896	2,431	3,912	1,692	11,736	168	2,397	1,779	140	93,151
1964	29,959	52,434	82,393	3,874	6,526	2,305	12,565	186	2,199	2,257	301	112,606
1965	40,718	67,098	107,816	3,196	11,684	2,711	15,143	205	3,095	2,471	437	146,758
1966	65,065	82,853	147,918	3,661	14,238	4,059	17,514	224	3,935	2,604	590	194,743
1967	64,601	94,890	159,491	4,608	21,247	6,179	19,038	422	8,403	3,090	398	222,876
1968	39,434	80,878	120,312	5,204	22,076	4,818	20,422	374	7,623	2,693	452	183,974
1969	33,212	54,764	87,976	3,297	23,706	4,414	22,785	593	13,093	4,767	900	161,531
1970	27,620	47,708	75,328	2,863	21,451	4,388	24,424	711	12,456	4,943	1,149	147,713
1971	16,281	35,552	51,833	2,841	22,369	2,906	24,366	636	10,843	5,058	1,048	121,900
1972	19,133	32,160	51,293	8,308	23,325	2,148	22,618	865	8,234	4,309	906	122,006
1973	28,102	43,781	71,883	8,307	43,193	2,671	25,242	1,141	19,281	11,057	1,425	184,200
1974	39,748	48,946	88,694	10,450	50,566	2,594	26,541	1,391	23,670	12,528	2,031	218,465
1975	36,076	36,822	72,898	9,867	47,382	2,174	20,155	1,510	17,800	13,270	2,825	187,881
1976	21,714	27,146	48,860	7,752	43,236	1,845	16,933	1,356	14,406	10,628	1,094	146,110
1977	18,536	22,180	40,716	6,372	31,380	1,547	12,918	1,330	11,789	7,840	1,022	114,914

Table A.2 (continued)

Year	Britain	Other Europe	Total Europe	Africa	Asia	Australasia	USA	Central America	West Indies	South America	Other Countries	Total
1978	12,251	17,811	30,062	4,261	24,029	1,237	9,949	950	8,222	6,782	821	86,313
1979	13,406	19,452	32,858	3,958	50,540	1,395	9,617	732	6,262	5,898	836	112,096
1980	18,924	22,244	41,168	4,330	71,602	1,555	9,926	800	7,254	5,433	1,049	143,117
1981	21,964	24,335	46,299	4,887	48,831	1,318	10,559	1,030	8,566	6,136	992	128,618
1982	17,075	29,081	46,156	4,513	41,686	938	9,360	1,651	8,674	6,871	1,298	121,147
1983	6,036	18,276	24,312	3,659	36,906	478	7,381	3,654	7,216	4,816	735	89,157
1984	5,395	15,506	20,901	3,552	41,920	535	6,922	4,078	5,630	4,085	616	88,239
1985	4,719	14,140	18,859	3,545	38,597	506	6,669	5,016	6,132	4,356	622	84,302
1986	5,522	17,187	22,709	4,770	41,600	503	7,275	6,078	8,874	6,686	724	99,219
1987	9,537	28,026	37,563	8,501	67,337	753	7,967	6,873	11,227	10,801	1,076	152,098
1988	10,444	30,245	40,689	9,380	81,136	745	6,537	5,671	9,439	7,255	1,077	161,929
1989	9,759	42,346	52,105	12,199	93,261	894	6,931	5,870	10,909	8,685	1,147	192,001
1990	9,003	42,942	51,945	13,442	111,744	988	6,084	7,781	11,689	8,898	1,659	214,230
1991	8,283	39,788	48,071	16,090	120,019	953	6,599	13,407	12,925	10,584	2,184	230,832
1992	7,731	37,140	44,871	19,636	139,272	1,191	7,537	12,526	14,952	10,389	2,468	252,842
1993	7,665	38,927	46,592	16,917	147,268	1,319	8,010	7,736	16,563	9,579	1,763	255,747
1994	6,320	32,301	38,621	13,699	141,513	1,108	6,230	3,503	9,976	7,915	1,194	223,759
1995	6,367	34,768	41,135	14,567	128,922	1,050	5,152	2,828	10,027	7,519	830	212,030
1996	5,837	34,180	40,017	14,879	144,406	1,228	5,846	3,414	9,334	6,113	837	226,074
1997	4,846	33,819	38,665	14,525	138,326	1,404	5,036	3,506	8,235	5,690	658	216,045
1998	4,036	34,468	38,504	12,675	101,393	1,055	4,775	2,696	6,354	4,966	773	173,191
1999	4,626	34,319	38,945	15,678	112,978	839	5,522	2,913	6,747	5,582	761	189,965
2000	4,845	38,127	42,972	19,829	140,108	938	5,824	3,068	7,148	6,779	705	227,371

Table A.2 *(continued)*

Note: The data for Europe include 'Britain' and 'Other Europe'.

Source: Data are based on *CANSIM*, Label: D27-28, D36-D41, D125596-D125598 (updated 25 Sept. 2001), Title: Immigration by Country of Last Residence (original source: SDDS 3601 Employment and Immigration Canada), except for Africa, Central America, and South America, 1955–81, which are included in 'other countries' for those years in the *CANSIM* data set. Estimates for immigrants from Africa, Central America, and South America, 1955–81, are based on the following sources: Department of Citizenship and Immigration, *Annual Report, 1955–56*, Table 6, pp. 32–3 (Ottawa: Queen's Printer and Controller of Stationery, 1956); Department of Citizenship and Immigration, *Annual Report, 1956–57*, Table 6, pp. 36–7 (Ottawa: Queen's Printer and Controller of Stationery, 1957); Department of Citizenship and Immigration, *Immigration Statistics 1957*, Table 6, pp. 16–17 (Ottawa: Queen's Printer and Controller of Stationery, 1958); Department of Citizenship and Immigration, *Immigration Statistics 1958*, Table 6, pp. 16–17 (Ottawa: Queen's Printer and Controller of Stationery, 1959); Department of Citizenship and Immigration, *Immigration Statistics 1959*, Table 6, pp. 16–17 (Ottawa: Queen's Printer and Controller of Stationery, 1960); Department of Citizenship and Immigration, *Immigration Statistics 1960*, Table 6, pp. 16–17 (Ottawa: Queen's Printer and Controller of Stationery, 1961); Department of Citizenship and Immigration, *Immigration Statistics 1961*, Table 6, pp. 16–17 (Ottawa: Queen's Printer and Controller of Stationery, 1962); Department of Citizenship and Immigration, *Immigration Statistics 1962*, Table 6, pp. 16–17 (Ottawa: Queen's Printer and Controller of Stationery, 1963); Department of Citizenship and Immigration, *Immigration Statistics 1963*, Table 6, pp. 16–17 (Ottawa: Queen's Printer and Controller of Stationery, 1964); Department of Citizenship and Immigration, *Immigration Statistics 1964*, Catalogue ci. 61–964, Table 6, pp. 16–17 (Ottawa: Queen's Printer and Controller of Stationery, 1965); Department of Citizenship and Immigration, *Immigration Statistics 1965*, Catalogue ci. 61–963, Table 6, pp. 16–17 (Ottawa: Queen's Printer and Controller of Stationery, 1966); Department of Manpower and Immigration, *Immigration Statistics 1966*, Catalogue MP22-1/1966, Table 7, pp. 14–15 (Ottawa: Queen's Printer and Controller of Stationery, 1967); Department of Manpower and Immigration, *Immigration Statistics 1967*, Catalogue MP22-1/1967, Table 9, pp. 12–13 (Ottawa: Queen's Printer and Controller of Stationery, 1968); Department of Manpower and Immigration, *Immigration Statistics 1968*, Catalogue MP22-1/1968, Table 3, p. 5 (Ottawa: The Queen's Printer, 1969); Department of Manpower and Immigration, *Immigration Statistics 1969*, Catalogue MP22-1/1969, Table 3, p. 5 (Ottawa: Queen's Printer for Canada, 1970); Manpower and Immigration, *Immigration Statistics 1970*, Catalogue M22-1/1970, Table 3, p. 5 (Ottawa: Information Canada, 1971); Manpower and Immigration, *Immigration Statistics 1971*, Catalogue M22-1/1971, Table 3, p. 5 (Ottawa: Information Canada, 1972); Manpower and Immigration, *Immigration Statistics 1972*, Catalogue MP22-1/1972, Table 3, p. 5 (Ottawa: Information Canada, 1974); Manpower and Immigration, *Immigration Statistics 1973*, Catalogue MP22-1/1973, Table 3, pp. 5–7 (Ottawa: Information Canada, 1975); Manpower and Immigration, *Immigration Statistics 1974*, Catalogue MP22-1/1974, Table 3, pp. 5–7 (Ottawa: Information Canada, 1975); Manpower and Immigration, *Immigration Statistics 1975*, Catalogue MP22-1/1975, Table 3, pp. 5–7 (Ottawa: Minister of Supply and Services Canada, 1976); Manpower and Immigration, *Immigration Statistics 1976*, Catalogue MP22-1/1977, Table 3, pp. 5–7 (Ottawa: Minister of Supply and Services Canada, 1977); Employment and Immigration Canada, *Immigration Statistics 1977*, Catalogue MP22-1/1977, Table 3, pp. 5–7 (Ottawa: Minister of Supply and Services Canada, 1978); Employment and Immigration Canada, *Immigration Statistics 1978*, Catalogue MP22-1/1978, Table 3, pp. 5–7 (Ottawa: Minister of Supply and Services Canada, 1980); Employment and Immigration Canada, *Immigration Statistics 1979*, Catalogue MP22-1/1979, Table 3, pp. 5–7 (Ottawa: Minister of Supply and Services Canada, 1981); Employment and Immigration Canada, *Immigration Statistics 1980*, Catalogue MP22-1/1980, Table 3, pp. 10–15 (Ottawa: Minister of Supply and Services Canada, 1982). For 1955–81, figures for 'other countries' in the table are calculated by subtracting Africa, Central America, and South America from the original 'other countries' category of the CANSIM data.

Table A.3   Total Fertility Rate, Canada, 1921–96

Year	Total Fertility Rate
1921	3.5
1926	3.4
1931	3.2
1936	3.0
1941	2.8
1946	3.4
1951	3.5
1956	3.9
1961	3.8
1966	2.8
1971	2.2
1976	1.8
1981	1.7
1986	1.7
1991	1.8
1996	1.6

Source: Data for 1921 to 1986 are from Bali Ram, *Current Demographic Analysis: New Trends in the Family, Demographic Facts and Features.* Catalogue 91-535E, Appendix Table 3.1, p. 82 (Ottawa: Minister of Supply and Services Canada, 1990); for 1991 from Z. Wu, *Fertility and Family Surveys in Countries of the ECE Region: Standard Country Report, Canada*, Appendix Table 2, p. 52. New York and Geneva: United Nations 1999; for 1996 from M.V. George et al., *Population Projections for Canada, Provinces and Territories 2000-2026*, Statistics Canada, Catalogue No. 91-520-XPB, p. 4 (Ottawa: Minister of Industry, 2001).

Notes

Chapter 1 Questions of Immigration

1. Many OECD (Organization for Economic Cooperation and Development) countries continue to depend on immigrant and foreign labour as one important source to supplement their labour needs; see, for example, Tables 1.1 and 1.2. Historically, countries such as the United States and Canada relied heavily upon immigration for labour supply and population growth. From the late nineteenth century to the period prior to the First World War, the United States was undergoing rapid industrialization and urban growth, and immigration rose substantially during this period, peaking in 1907 when 1.3 million immigrants arrived in the United States and added over 3 per cent to the US labour force (Smith and Edmonston, 1997). In Canada, immigration also rose sharply during the same period, which coincided with rapid industrial development in Eastern Canada and agricultural settlement of the West; immigration peaked in the few years prior to the First World War, reaching 375,000 in 1912 and over 400,000 in 1913 (see Table A.1; Kelly and Trebilcock, 1998). Immigrants continue to make up a substantial part of the population in the United States and Canada (see Table 1.1).

2. One of the early scholars who developed a typology of migration is Petersen (1958). In contrast to free migration, Peterson makes a further distinction between forced migration that provides no choice to those who have to move and impelled migration that offers some discretion to the migrants regarding whether to move.

3. The World Trade Organization (WTO) is a good example of such a framework that deals with rules of trade between nations. Founded in 1995 by the 128 signatories of the General Agreement on Tariffs and Trade (GATT), WTO is dedicated to the principle of freer trade, and as of December 2001 has a membership of 143 countries including China (see World Trade Organization, 2001).

4. Informalization refers to the growth of the informal economy that encompasses 'the production and sale of goods and services that are licit but produced and/or sold outside the

regulatory apparatus covering zoning, taxes, health and safety, minimum wage laws, and other types of standards' (Sassen, 2001: 294). The informal economy differs from the underground economy that entails illegal activities.

5. The term *immigrants* in the official statistics of Australia includes those born in another country who have been granted the right to live permanently in Australia, as well as foreign-born long-term residents (12 months or more). See, for example, Australian Bureau of Statistics, *Australian Social Trends 1997, Population Composition: Birthplace of Overseas Australians*, available at < http://www.abs.gov.au/ausstats > .

6. There are different theories regarding the origin of the Indians in North America and varying estimates about the length of their history. A popular theory suggests that the ancestors of North American Indians crossed the Bering area and moved down the Mackenzie Corridor. Archeological finds in the Yukon unearthed evidence of artifacts as far back as between 27,000 and 23,000 BC, even though remains of hunting sites date back to the period after 10,000 BC, that is, after the height of the Glacier Age with the final opening of the Mackenzie Corridor (see Price, 1979).

Chapter 2 Immigration and Canada

1. Satzewich (1991: 35) argues that international migration is selective because, contrary to the noble ideals of freedom of mobility, it is 'structured in part by the supply and demand for labour associated with the process of accumulation, and in part by the state'.

2. What constitutes the modern state and how much autonomy the state has are the subjects of considerable debate. Pal (1993) categorizes three main approaches to these debates: neo-Marxism, neo-structuralism, and public choice. These approaches differ in how the state's autonomy is conceptualized and in how social relations limit and promote such autonomy.

3. See ss. 92 and 95 of the *British North America Act* (1867), reprinted in Egerton, 1911.

4. The net gain of immigration over emigration was 63,000 for 1911 to 1921, and 42,000 for 1921 to 1931 (Statistics Canada, 1983: D498-511).

5. Statistics for 1955 and after are from Table A.2 in the appendix; see the end of the table for a listing of original sources.

6. Major changes in Canada's Immigration Regulations were made in 1952, 1962, 1967, 1977, 1978, and 1985. For details of these changes, see Revised Statutes of Canada 1952, c. 325; Order-in-Council P.C. 1962-86; Order-in-Council P.C. 1967-1616; Statutes of Canada 1976-7, c. 52; Order-in-Council P.C. 1978-486; Order-in-Council P.C. 1985-3246. A new immigration bill, Bill C-11 entitled *Immigration and Refugee Protection Act*, was passed by the House of Commons on 13 June 2001, and received royal assent on 1 Nov. 2001 (S.C. 2001, c. 27). On 14 June 2002, the government published the new immigration regulations; see *Canada Gazette*, 2002, Part II, vol. 136, no. 9, pp. 1-449.

7. For a comparison of immigration to the United States and Canada, see Green (1995), Reitz (1998), and Thompson and Weinfeld (1995).

8. The tier structure was first introduced in 1989 (P.C. 1989-2440) to enable provinces with a poor record in attracting business immigrants to benefit from a lower level of minimum investment.

9. The change from 3 per cent to 10 per cent enabled Alberta to be qualified under Tier I; provinces and territories already qualified for Tier I were Newfoundland, Nova Scotia,

Prince Edward Island, New Brunswick, Manitoba, Saskatchewan, and Yukon and North-west Territories.

10. The 1993 Immigration Regulations also stipulated that offences such as failure to comply with terms and conditions governing approvals, submitting false information in relation to an application for approval, and making misleading representations about an approved business or fund are subject to prosecution.

11. Newspapers have reported several dubious business ventures in which investor immigrants seem to have been misled by promoters eager to profit from shady investments for personal gains. Many investor immigrants are reported to have lost substantial capital and some are taking legal actions against promoters. See, for example, *Star Phoenix*, 17 Dec. 1992, p. D1, 21 Dec. 1992, p. A9, and 30 Dec. 1992, p. A4.

12. Financial and other data pertaining to entrepreneurial and investor immigrants are based on information provided on application forms of entrepreneurial and investor immigrants being issued immigration visas abroad between 1987 and 1990. The data are based on special tabulations from data originated from the Immigration and Refugee Affairs Division, Department of External Affairs, Canada.

13. Data are compiled from Immigration Statistics, Department of Manpower and Immigration Canada, 1966–76; Immigration Statistics, Department of Employment and Immigration, 1977–91; Immigration Statistics, Department of Citizenship and Immigration, 1992–96.

Chapter 3 The Social Construction of Immigrants

1. See Consolidated Update of the Immigration and Refugee Protection Regulations, including all amendments effective as of 30 Sept. 1999 [on-line], Citizenship and Immigration Canada, under Manuals and Operations Memoranda < http://www.cic.gc.ca > . See also the *Immigration and Refugee Protection Act* (S.C. 2001, c. 27), and the new Immigration and Refugee Protection Regulations announced on 14 June 2002 (*Canada Gazette*, Part II, vol. 136, no. 9, pp. 1–449).

2. These categories of admission are defined in Immigration Regulations and are widely adopted in official policy analysis. For example, a document entitled 'Regulatory Impact Analysis Statement' reported in the *Canada Gazette* immediately following 28 Jan. 1993 amendment to the Immigration Regulations describes immigrants and their selection as follows: 'Immigrant applicants are generally divided into three "classes": family, refugee, and independents. The independent class includes assisted relatives, skilled workers and business applicants. . . . Assisted relatives and skilled workers are assessed against a series of selection criteria. The criteria are: education, Specific Vocational Preparation (SVP), experience, occupational demand, arranged employment or designated occupation, demographic factor, age, knowledge of English and French languages and personal suitability' (*Canada Gazette*, Part II, vol. 127, no. 3, 28 Jan. 1993, p. 632). See Table 3.1 for the updated selection criteria for economic immigrants.

3. See Table 5.1 in Chapter 5 regarding the number of immigrants admitted annually under different admission categories between 1980 and 2000.

4. According to the *Language Instruction for Newcomers to Canada: Handbook for Service Provider Organizations (LINC)*, 'to be eligible under LINC a person must be either a permanent resident or a newcomer who has been allowed to remain in Canada, to whom CIC

intends to grant permanent resident status and who has not acquired Canadian citizenship'. Citizenship and Immigration Canada, March 2000 < http://www.cic.gc.ca > .

Chapter 4 Immigration and Canada's Population

1. From 1985 to 1990, the planned level of annual immigration (mid-point) as announced by the government rose from about 100,000 to 250,000 a year, but the actual level of annual immigration exceeded the planned level. From 1990 to 1995, the planned level (mid-point) was around 250,000 yearly, but the actual level fell short of it (Citizenship and Immigration Canada, 2001d: 7).

2. Demographers consider a fertility rate of 2.1, or an average number of 2.1 births per woman over her lifetime, as the required level of births that is needed to allow a population to replace itself naturally. By 1997, the total fertility rate for most industrial countries had fallen below 2.1; only the US had a fertility rate of 2.06 that was close to the replacement level (George et al., 2001: 13).

3. In the 1994 study, Statistics Canada provided various estimates of population projections well into the twenty-first century, based on various assumptions of population growth. Under the scenario of high population growth, fertility is expected to reach 1.9 per women by 2016; life expectancy at birth of 81 years for men and 86 years for women in 2016; and annual immigration to reach 330,000 by 2005. Under the scenario of medium population growth, fertility is expected to stay at 1.7 children per women; annual immigration will remain at 250,000; and life expectancy at birth of 78.5 years for men and 84 years for women by 2016. For the scenario of low population growth, fertility will continue to decline to 1.5 births per women; life expectancy is presumed to be 77 years for men and 83 years for women; and immigration will continue to decline to 150,000 by 2005 (George et al., 1994: 65).

4. In the 2001 study, Statistics Canada made the following assumptions. The low-growth scenario assumes a declining fertility that falls to 1.3 births per woman by 2005–6, a declining annual immigration that reaches 180,000 by the same year, and life expectancy of 78.5 for males and 83 for females. The assumptions for medium-growth scenario are: total fertility of 1.48 by 2001, a constant immigration of 225,000 by 2001–2, and life expectancy of 80 years for males and 84 years for females by 2026. The high-growth scenario assumes a rise in fertility beginning in 2002, reaching 1.8 children per woman by 2026, an annual immigration that reaches 270,000 by 2005–6, and life expectancy of 81.5 years for males and 85 years for females by 2026 (George et al., 2001: 59).

5. The term *sustainable development* first appeared as a planning objective in a 1980 document published by the International Union for the Conservation of Nature entitled 'The World Conservation Strategy'. In 1983, the United Nations established the World Commission on Environment and Development, also known as the Brundtland Commission, to devise long-term strategies for the world community to achieve sustainable development by taking into account the interrelations among people, resources, environment, and development (World Committee on Environment and Development, 1987). According to the Commission, sustainable development is development that meets the needs of the present generation without compromising the needs of future generations to meet their needs. As such, it is an integrated concept based on social, economic, and environmental concerns,

and premised on the principles of intergeneration, international, and intranational equity. Canada endorsed the principle of sustainable development, and the government of Canada amended the *Auditor General Act* in 1995 to establish a Commissioner of the Environment and Sustainable Development within the Office of the Auditor General (Statutes of Canada, 1995, c. 43).

Chapter 5 Economic Benefit of Immigration

1. In 1991, the economic class in fact constitutes 37.6 per cent of the total 230,781 immigrants admitted that year (see Table 5.1).

2. Section 7 of the former *Immigration Act* requires the minister in charge of immigration to report to Parliament every year with an immigration plan regarding the total number of immigrants, convention refugees, and others to be admitted to Canada (Revised Statutes of Canada, 1985, c. I-2, s. 7; Statutes of Canada, 1992, c. 49, s. 3). As an example, the immigration plan for 2001 indicates that Canada plans to admit 200,000 to 225,000 immigrants during that year, with the economic class making up 58 per cent, the family class, 27 per cent, and the refugee class, 13 per cent (Citizenship and Immigration Canada, 2001d). The *Immigration and Refugee Protection Act* of 2001 requires the minister responsible for immigration to report to Parliament once a year the number of foreign nationals who became and expected to become permanent residents in the following year, the number of temporary resident permits issued, and the number of persons granted permanent resident status under the minister's discretion; in addition, the report has to include a gender-based analysis of the impact of the Act and the linguistic profile of foreign nationals who become permanent residents (S.C. 2001, s. 94).

3. Earnings are typically seen as 'returns' to education, since education represents a form of investment in human capital that brings a yield or return when one joins the labour market (see Becker, 1993).

4. Chiswick (1977, 1978) employed immigrants' years of residence in the host society to measure 'assimilation effect', but the technique was criticized by Borjas (1985) on the grounds that such a measurement when applied to cross-sectional data confounds the real assimilation effect with the cohort effort. The study by Bloom, Grenier, and Gunderson (1995) used pooled data from the 1971, 1981, and 1986 Canadian censuses, and measured assimilation effect and cohort effect separately in their model.

5. The American economic literature on immigration also shows rather inconclusive results regarding the impact of immigration on labour, fiscal burden, and productivity; see, for example, Borjas (1994) and Isbister (1996).

6. In the 1991 report published by the Economic Council of Canada, the authors argue that 'while the hosts do not pay for immigrants' education, neither do they receive any benefit from it', and that 'when an immigrant comes, he or she retains title to his or her own human capital and to all the earnings it brings' (Economic Council of Canada, 1991: 34). Accordingly, the authors consider the argument of 'brain drain' from the sending countries and 'brain gain' to the receiving country not sustainable. Despite the apparent logic, the claim of the host members not benefiting personally from immigrants' education is premised on a notion that society does not have collective interests but only individual interests. Extrapolating from this rationale, Canadians without children and Canada as a

country would have nothing to gain in supporting a public educational system, since the individuals being educated would benefit from their education personally by taking up jobs after they complete schooling and keeping their earnings to themselves, and individual tax-payers who have no children would have nothing personally to gain.

Chapter 6 Human Capital of Immigrants

1. Human capital is similar to physical or financial capital in that it increases output, but unlike physical or financial capital, education is embodied in human capital and cannot be separated from the person possessing it (see Becker, 1993: 15–26).

2. This perspective has been widely adopted in both the United States and Canada to study immigrants. For example, Borjas (1994: 1671) reviewed the US studies on the economics of immigration, and pointed out that 'these studies view the labor market performance of immigrants in the host country as a measure of the immigrant contribution to the econ-omy's skill endowment and productivity'. The Economic Council of Canada (1991) adopted a similar theoretical perspective in its study of immigration to Canada. For a critique of the study by the Economic Council of Canada, see Li (1992) and also Chapter 4.

3. The status attainment model bears a striking similarity to the structural functional argu-ment of stratification in sociology and the human capital theory in neoclassical economics (Horan, 1978; Wright, 1979). The basic model describes individuals' careers in terms of both ascribed and achieved statuses (Blau and Duncan, 1967; Duncan, Featherman, and Duncan, 1972). Educational attainment, seen as an important link between social origin and occupational attainment, is in turn dependent upon family background and individual value orientation (Sewell and Hauser, 1972, 1975; Sewell, Haller, and Ohlendorf, 1970).

4. Under the New Regulations, a skilled worker applicant may be granted a maximum of 5 points for family relationship in Canada, under the selection category of 'adaptability', sim-ilar to the maximum points allocated for assisted relatives under the old system (see Table 3.1). It is true that the immigration system recognizes family unification as the basis for family-class immigration, but family ties are seen as an extension of one's family and not so much social capital in this context.

5. This analysis is primarily based on results reported in Li (2000).

6. The dependent variable is 'annual earnings from employment and self-employment', which is the sum of gross wages and salaries and net self-employment income before paying indi-vidual income taxes. Wages and salaries are always positive, but net self-employment income can have a negative value. Earnings from employment and self-employment are used here to indicate outcomes of labour market participation, and some individuals had earnings from both sources. The independent variables measuring individual variations in human capital and work-related features include: years of schooling, experience estimated by subtracting from age the years of schooling and the six years before schooling began, experience squared, knowledge of the official languages, the number of weeks worked in 1995 (1 to 52), the nature of work in terms of whether the weeks worked were full-time or part-time, occupation (14 categories), and the industry of work (14 categories). In addition, a variable 'years since landing in Canada' is used as a proxy of Canadian experience for immigrants. The variable is measured as the number of years since an immigrant has immi-grated to Canada, and native-born Canadians are coded as 0. The 'years of schooling' is

constructed from several variables. For individuals with postsecondary education, the variable 'years of schooling' is the sum of years of university or non-university education, whichever is higher, and 12 years of elementary and secondary grades. For those with secondary school graduation certificate, it is coded as 12. For those with less than secondary school graduation certificate, the highest grade coded is 11 even though higher completed grades may have been reported. Individuals with only 'grade 5–8' education are coded as having an average of 6.5 years of schooling, and those with 'less than grade 5', an average of 2 years of schooling. In addition, two other variables measuring the characteristics of the local market are used in the analysis; they pertain to the unemployment rate and the percentage of immigrant population in the CMA as calculated from the 1996 census microdata file.

7. The following sections are primarily based on an analysis originally reported in Li (2001a).

8. Using data on nativity and age of immigration, a typology of four kinds of degree holders is constructed. Since age of immigration is reported as a range in the census, inferences on the type of degree immigrants held can only be based on such crude information. First, 'native-born Canadian degree holders' are defined as those born in Canada and holding at least one university degree. Second, 'immigrant Canadian degree holders' are those who immigrated to Canada as a child, before age 13, and who reported having at least one degree in the census. Since these immigrants came as children, the degree is assumed to have been obtained in Canada after immigration. Third, immigrants who immigrated to Canada between the ages of 13 and 24 with at least one degree at the time of the census are classified as 'immigrant mixed-education degree holders', since depending on the exact age of immigration, these immigrants may have obtained some components of their education or degree outside Canada. Finally, immigrants who immigrated at the age of 25 or older and held at least one degree are considered 'immigrant foreign-degree holders', since given their age of immigration, their first degree probably was obtained outside of Canada. There is no doubt that these estimates would have measurement errors, but at least they provide an empirical basis for estimating market outcomes of Canadian degree, foreign degree, and mixed-education degree.

9. Variables being controlled include: CMA (Census Metropolitan Area) level at which the individual resided (4 categories ranging from 'not CMA' to 'large CMAs over 1 million people'), the nature of work in terms of whether the weeks worked were full-time or part-time, the major field of study (8 categories), occupation (14 categories), industry of work (14 categories), knowledge of the official languages (4 categories), the number of degrees held (2 categories in terms of 'bachelor degree' or 'advanced degree'), work experience estimated by subtracting from age the years of schooling and the six years before schooling began, work experience squared, and the number of weeks worked in 1995 (1 to 52). In addition, a variable 'years since landing in Canada' is used as a proxy of Canadian experience for immigrants, and native-born Canadians are coded as zero.

Chapter 7 Immigration and Diversity

1. For an analysis of social changes in Canadian society in the latter half of the twentieth century and forces that contribute to changes, see Li (1996), and for a discussion of Canada's changing values, see Nevitte (1996).

2. In response to rising political discontent in Quebec, the federal government appointed a 10-

person Royal Commission to examine bilingualism and biculturalism in Canada in the summer of 1963. The Order-in-Council striking the Commission stated that the Commissioners were 'to inquire into and report upon the existing state of bilingualism and biculturalism in Canada and to recommend what steps should be taken to develop the Canadian Confederation on the basis of an equal partnership between the two founding races, taking into account the contribution made by other ethnic groups to the cultural enrichment of Canada and the measures that should be taken to safeguard that contribution' (P.C. 1963–1106, cited in Canada, Report of the Royal Commission on Bilingualism and Biculturalism, 1967). The Royal Commission wrote a five-volume report—the first volume was published in 1967 and the last one in 1970. Throughout the reports of the Royal Commission, the framework used was a trichotomy composed of the British, the French, and other Canadians, which paid little attention to the First Nations as people with distinct aboriginal rights and entitlements. See Canada, Report of the Royal Commission on Bilingualism and Biculturalism (1965, 1969).

3. Calculations on ethnic origins of the Canadian population are complicated by changes in the questions used in various censuses. Since 1981, respondents to Canadian censuses were allowed to choose 'multiple origins' as an answer to the ethnic origin question. As a result, 1,838,615 individuals, or 7.6 per cent of the total population in 1981, chose 'multiple origins' as an answer to the 'ethnic origin' question. In the 1991 Census, 7,794,250 individuals, or 28.9 per cent of the total population, chose 'multiple origins'. Furthermore, 88.5 per cent of those who chose multiple origins in 1991 made a selection that involved either British or French and other combinations (see Statistics Canada, 1984, 1993).

4. In the 1996 Census, 10.2 million persons, or 36 per cent of the total population, reported more than one ethnic origin, and about 5.9 million persons, or 20 per cent of Canada's population, indicated having 'Canadian origins' (see Statistics Canada, 1998b: 11).

5. Boyd and Norris (2001) demonstrated that among those born in Canada, most of the increase in the reporting of Canadian origin came from those who declared British origin in 1986; however, such increase from 1991 to 1996 also came from the French population.

6. This section is mainly based on materials originally published in Li (2001b).

7. In June and July of 1994, the Democracy Education Network organized 58 study circles in six Canadian cities as a part of the federal government's consultation on the immigration policy. Its summary report states that one of the four concerns expressed by participants has to do with 'integration and settlement' and 'the dilemmas of diversity' (Democracy Education Network, 1994: 2).

8. A case in point can be found in Toronto's experience in the late 1970s when the city witnessed several incidents of non-whites being pushed off subway platforms and hit by incoming trains. These events were so racially charged that the provincial government appointed the Ontario Task Force on Human Relations to investigate. In its report, the Task Force wrote: 'With what appeared to some as unseemly haste, large numbers of black, brown and yellow skinned people suddenly appeared on the streets, the buses, and in public places. Some English-speaking residents who had not perceived the extent to which Toronto had become a multicultural entity, now discovered that they lived in a multi-racial community, and indeed, were now members of a minority themselves. Needless to say, they had difficulty adjusting to the cultural shock. . . . These factors, and many less discernable

[*sic*] have created an atmosphere in which overt violence is perceived to be less unacceptable by the hoodlum element which perpetrates the crimes against the visible minority' (Pitman, 1977: 38). At that time, the number of visible minorities in Canada was relatively small, since they only made up 6.3 per cent of Canada's population in 1986 and 11.2 per cent in 1996 (Statistics Canada, 1998b). The Toronto case illustrates how the notion of excessively large numbers of non-white immigrants in the immigration debate is often normatively constructed.

9. For further evidence of the immigration discourse and the messages delivered, see Citizenship and Immigration Canada, 1994a, 1994b, 1994c; Employment and Immigration Canada, 1989b, 1990.

10. For example, a policy research subcommittee formed by the Canadian government, called Policy Research Sub-Committee on Social Cohesion, defined social cohesion as 'the ongoing process of developing a community of shared values, shared challenges and equal opportunity within Canada, based on a sense of trust, hope and reciprocity among all Canadians' (quoted in Jenson, 2000: 8).

11. Clearly, in this context 'average Canadians' means European Canadians since they are the majority in Canada, and 'concerns of special interest groups' imply conflicting interests that undermine the collective interest of the majority.

12. The Reform Party campaigned during the 1993 election to eliminate the federal multiculturalism programs as a means to reduce the deficit (*Globe and Mail,* 14 Dec. 1993, pp. A1, A2). After the election, the Reform Party continued its attack on multiculturalism on the grounds that it is divisive and unnecessarily costly. For example, Art Hanger, a member of the Reform Party and a member of the Parliament representing Calgary Northeast, said in the House of Commons in 1994, 'It appears to me to be somewhat contradictory to state that immigrants under the present system are being integrated into Canadian society. My understanding of what integration means is that an immigrant embraces the Canadian way of life and Canadian culture, while having the freedom to preserve his own culture, but if he chooses to do so he should have to do so at his own expense, on his own time without government assistance. Multiculturalism as it is now practised, emphasizes differences and tends to separate the different ethnic communities, while being funded by the federal government' (Canada, House of Commons Debates, 27 Jan. 1994, p. 455).

13. By 1997, the world foreign direct investment stock has reached US$3.5 trillion, about 30 per cent was accounted for by developing countries (World Bank, 2000: 37–8).

14. In 1995, 78 per cent of Canada's total exports went to the United States and 75 per cent of its imports came from the United States; by 2000, the figures were 85 per cent and 74 per cent, respectively (Statistics Canada, 2001). Thus, Canada's trading relationship with the United States appears to have strengthened during this period.

15 See, for example, *Globe and Mail,* 1996a.

Chapter 8 Immigrants and the City

1. According to the World Bank, urban areas generate 55 per cent of the GNP in low-income countries, and 73 per cent in middle-income countries (World Bank, 2000: 126). Thus, the economic importance of cities relative to the national economy increases as the income level of a country rises.

2. Statistics Canada defines a Census Metropolitan Area (CMA) as an urban core having a population of at least 100,000 (Statistics Canada, 1996).

3. Unless otherwise stated, statistics from the 1996 Census in this chapter were calculated by the author from the Public Use Microdata File on Individuals.

4. Compiled from the 1986 and 1996 Censuses, Public Use Microdata File on Individuals.

5. The role of social capital in the lives of immigrant settlement in Canada is largely underresearched. The American literature has suggested the importance of social capital in providing resources and opportunities for immigrants; see, for example, Jasso and Rosenzweig (1995) and Zhou and Bankston (1996), in addition to the literature on the immigrant enclave cited earlier.

6. Li and Li (1999) found that non-Chinese firms often employed intermediaries such as advertising firms and special sales agents with the necessary language skills to market their products and services. As of 1994, *The Financial Post* (1994c) estimated that there were 40 marketing firms geared to Chinese Canadian customers in Toronto. These findings further illustrate that linguistic and cultural diversity can be an economic asset for businesses trying to capture specialized domestic markets or to compete in the global economy.

7. The three newspapers are *Ming Pao, Sing Tao,* and *World Journal*. The *World Journal* operates as a subsidiary of Taiwan's *United Daily News* and started distributing the Chinese language newspaper in Toronto in 1976. *Sing Tao,* a subsidiary of *Sing Tao* of Hong Kong, began publishing in Toronto in 1978. *Ming Pao,* also a subsidiary of a Hong Kong newspaper, entered the Toronto market in 1993 (see Li and Li, 1999).

8. Parents complained about the luxury cars that some immigrant teenagers were driving to school. As one respondent told a reporter, 'The Asian kids have better cars than the teachers do' (*Globe and Mail*, 1995c).

9. High-poverty neighbourhoods are those areas with 40 per cent or more of their residents having an income that falls within the threshold of an officially defined low-income level, known as the low-income cutoff (see, for example, Kazemipur and Halli, 2000a).

Chapter 9 Immigration and Canadian Society

1. There are routine public concerns being expressed over the cost of settling new immigrants. For example, an editorial in the *Globe and Mail* made the following point: 'In the 1997–98 fiscal year, Ottawa paid $95.6 million for adult language instruction and another $63.3 million in related programs. . . . Ontario alone spent $97.6 million in 1997 to teach English and French to children who spoke neither language. These are significant settlement costs' (*Globe and Mail*, 1998a). In an article entitled 'Stop Spending on Immigrants' that appeared in the *Globe and Mail,* a commentator was more direct in his attack on the spending on settling immigrants and on their drain of tax money: 'The 1.5 million immigrants who have come to this country in the past seven years have had a detrimental impact on the impoverished of this society. They have siphoned off billions of tax dollars to address their needs. . . . Instead, over the past decade, we have spent billions of dollars on immigrants through English-as-a-second-language classes, welfare, resettlement programs, subsidized housing and refugee claims' (*Globe and Mail*, 1998b).

2. At the time of writing, each arriving immigrant who is 19 years of age and over, including refugees, pays $975 for 'the right of landing', in addition to paying an application fee earlier,

which in the case of a principal applicant and the spouse is $500, and a business immigrant, $1,000 (Citizenship and Immigration Canada, 1999b).

3. The formula for calculating the annual compensation by the federal government to Quebec is set out in Annex 'B' of the *Canada–Quebec Accord* (Employment and Immigration Canada, 1991b).

4. This section and the next are mainly based on materials in Li (2001b).

5. Government-funded opinion polls are routinely conducted, but the results are not always released publicly. For example, in an internal report written for Citizenship and Immigration Canada, the author states that the report is based on surveys collected by Ekos in November 1996, Environics in December 1996, and Angus Reid in February 1997, which include 'questions asked specifically on behalf of CIC (Citizenship and Immigration)' (Palmer, 1997: 1). In a news story reported by *Toronto Star* on 19 Aug. 1996, the paper said it had to use the *Access to Information Act* to obtain results of a public opinion poll on immigration commissioned by the federal government (*Toronto Star,* 1996c).

6. Section 15 of the Canadian *Charter of Rights and Freedoms* states: 'Every individual is equal before and under the law and has the right to the equal protection and equal benefit of the law without discrimination and, in particular, without discrimination based on race, national or ethnic origin, colour, religion, sex, age or mental or physical disability' (S.C. 1982, c. 11).

7. It is sometimes pointed out that Canada has a right to choose its immigrants, and Canadians have a say in exercising this right. Advocates of immigration restriction also suggest that Canadians do experience problems caused by immigrants coming from a different background; an often-cited problem has to do with public schools being overwhelmed by immigrant children not speaking the official languages, resulting in non-immigrant parents worrying about declining educational quality (see *Globe and Mail,* 1994c). My argument is not about whether Canada has a right to choose its immigrants or not, or whether there are problems of adjustment for immigrants and Canadian society. The simple fact remains that the *Charter* guarantees the equality of rights and non-discrimination for all, and the choice of preferred immigrants cannot be based on 'race' or 'colour' in violation of the *Charter,* in the same way that immigrant selection cannot be based on 'gender'. In asking respondents to indicate their 'racial preference' of immigrants and in giving a 'racial preference' as the answer, Canadians are in fact using 'race' or 'colour' as a criterion in choosing their preferred immigrants.

8. Michael Valpy, a well-known columnist, was sympathetic to the dominant interpretation of 'cultural insecurity' in the immigration discourse. He wrote: 'Ekos found that opposition to high immigration levels does not rest primarily on economic insecurity—the traditional blue-collar fears of immigrants-are-taking-our-jobs. Rather it rests most of all on cultural insecurity. The cultural fear is a product of resurging anxieties—particularly anglophone anxieties—about eroding Canadian identity. It is about the lack of sufficient Canadian homogeneous tribalness to form national consensuses on public policy direction' (*Globe and Mail,* 1994a: A2). Some readers expressed different views, but these opposition voices were ineffective to influence the dominant perspective in the immigration discourse. For example, a reader wrote: 'I expected Canadians to regard freedom, honesty, hard work, personal accountability and tolerance as their most cherished values. I am not aware of any immigrant group not subscribing to these ideals. However, I am definitely aware of the mil-

lions who cheat on taxes, engage in UT and welfare fraud, expect 42 weeks' government handout after 10 weeks' employment, indulge in cross-border shopping with false customs declarations . . . and [are] intolerant to and unwilling to respect the culture of aboriginals (the 'true' Canadians), and these millions are mostly members of Mr. Valpy's "old Canada"' (*Globe and Mail*, 1994d: A26). Such opposition voices are largely ignored in the immigration discourse.

9. The corollary of this argument is that some Canadians are concerned over too many 'non-white' immigrants and that they would probably not have said that there are too many immigrants if these immigrants were 'white'.

10. Alan Li, President of the Chinese-Canadian National Council, argued for the need to regard negative public opinions on immigration as a social problem in itself: 'Unless the government takes a more proactive stance on immigration, public perceptions will not change. These are misconceptions that the government hasn't taken steps to correct' (*Globe and Mail*, 1996b: A6).

11. The wording of the question is as follows: 'I would like you to think of recent immigrants to Canada. These are persons who were born and raised outside of Canada. How comfortable would you feel being around individuals from the following groups of immigrants: (British, French, Ukrainians, etc.)?' (Angus Reid Group, 1991).

12. Some may argue that the academic tradition of studying individual racist attitudes using tools such as the 'social distance' scale is necessary in order to understand and to combat racism. In reality, findings of such research are seldom used to combat racism; rather, they are often represented by pseudoscientific labels such as 'social distance' or 'discomfort levels' to camouflage the racist nature, and indeed to justify 'racial' concerns. These survey tools are also so overused that they have conditioned respondents in accepting the legitimacy of passing judgment on others based on 'race' or 'colour'. The point is not to condemn survey tools in studying racism or racist behaviours. However, academics have to take a more objective stance by calling racist behaviours 'racist' and not some other fancy terms. As well, they have to conduct research with a clear view that racist behaviours are constitutionally and morally unacceptable, and with an objective to expose and to disallow racist practices. A good example of such a critical approach is the work of Henry (1989), and Henry and Ginzberg (1985), and Henry et al. (2000).

13. During the 2001 national election, the Australian government manipulated photographs to show how asylum seekers on rusty boats sailing to Australia threw children overboard to force the Australian Navy to rescue them, when in fact children and adults were at sea as a result of a sinking vessel. The manipulation helped the government to construct an ideological war against asylum seekers in order to win public support for adopting harsh measures against them by depicting them as heartless and sub-human. It further helped the governing party to swing voters to win enough votes to form a coalition government. As the truth of the incident began to unfold in 2002, however, there was a substantial backlash against the government (see, for example, *Sydney Morning Herald*, 2002; *Australian* 2002a, 2002b, 2002c).

14. Even a country like Japan, which historically has been unreceptive to immigrants, is showing signs that it has much to lose in the future if it continues its past practice. As one reporter wrote, 'Japan may not want to accept immigration, but stark demographics could leave it with little choice' (*Globe and Mail*, 2001b: A12).

References

Abbott, Michael G., and Charles M. Beach. 1993. 'Immigrant Earnings Differentials and Birth-Year Effects for Men in Canada: Post-War-1972', *Canadian Journal of Economics* 26(3): 505–24.

Abu-Laban, Yasmeen. 1998. 'Welcome/STAY OUT: The Contradiction of Canadian Integration and Immigration Policies at the Millennium', *Canadian Ethnic Studies* 30(3): 190–211.

Abu-Laban, Yasmeen, and Daiva Stasiulis. 1992. 'Ethnic Pluralism under Siege: Popular and Partisan Opposition to Multiculturalism', *Canadian Public Policy* 18(4): 365–86.

Akbar, Sajjad. 1995. 'Family Reunification Multipliers for Canada, 1971–86' in Don J. DeVoretz, ed., *Diminishing Returns: The Economics of Canada's Recent Immigration Policy*. Toronto and Vancouver: C.D. Howe Institute and Laurier Institute, pp. 65–82.

Akbari, Ather H. 1995. 'The Impact of Immigrants on Canada's Treasury, Circa 1990' in Don J. DeVoretz, ed., *Diminishing Returns: The Economics of Canada's Recent Immigration Policy*. Toronto and Vancouver: C.D. Howe Institute and Laurier Institute, pp. 113–27.

———. 1989. 'The Benefits of Immigrants to Canada: Evidence on Tax and Public Services', *Canadian Public Policy* 15(4): 424–35.

Akbari, Ather H., and Don J. DeVoretz. 1992. 'The Substitutability of Foreign-Born Labour in Canadian-Production: Circa 1980', *Canadian Journal of Economics* 25(3): 604–14.

Alberta Task Force on the Recognition of Foreign Qualifications. 1992. *Bridging the Gap: A Report of the Task Force on the Recognition of Foreign Qualifications*. Edmonton: Government of Alberta.

Aliaga, David. 1994. 'Italian Immigrants in Calgary: Dimensions of Cultural Identity', *Canadian Ethnic Studies* 26(2): 141–8.

Angus Reid Group. 1991. *Multiculturalism and Canadians: Attitude Study 1991*, submitted to Multiculturalism and Citizenship Canada.

———. 1989. *Immigration to Canada: Aspects of Public Opinion*. Winnipeg: Angus Reid Group

Australian, The. 2002a. 'Revealed: The Full Picture', 18 Feb., p. 1.

———. 2002b. 'PM's Man Blames Defence', 19 Feb., p. 1.

———. 2002c. 'Advisers Gave PM "Flawed" Account', 20 Feb., p. 4.

Avery, Donald. 1990. 'Canadian Immigration Policy and the "Foreign" Navvy, 1896–1914' in Michael S. Cross and Gregory S. Kealey, eds, *The Consolidation of Capitalism, 1896–1929*.

Toronto: McClelland & Stewart, pp. 47–73.

Baker, Michael, and Dwayne Benjamin. 1995a. 'The Receipt of Transfer Payments by Immigrants to Canada', *The Journal of Human Resources* 30(4): 651–76.

———. 1995b. 'Labor Market Outcomes and the Participation of Immigrant Women in Canadian Transfer Programs' in Don J. DeVoretz, ed., *Diminishing Returns: The Economics of Canada's Recent Immigration Policy*. Toronto and Vancouver: C.D. Howe Institute and Laurier Institute, pp. 208–42.

Basavarajappa, K.G., and R.B.P. Verma. 1985. 'Asian Immigrants in Canada: Some Findings from 1981 Census', *International Migration* 23(1): 97–121.

Basran, G.S. 1993. 'Indo-Canadian Families Historical Constraints and Contemporary Contradictions', *Journal of Comparative Family Studies* 24(3): 339–52.

Basran, Gurcharn S., Charan Gill, and Brian D. MacLean. 1995. *Farmworkers and Their Children*. Vancouver: Collective Press.

Basran, Gurcharn S., and Li Zong. 1998. 'Devaluation of Foreign Credentials as Perceived by Non-White Professional Immigrants', *Canadian Ethnic Studies* 30(3): 6–23.

Baxter, David. 1989. *Population and Housing in Metropolitan Vancouver: Changing Patterns of Demographics and Demand*. Vancouver: Laurier Institute.

Beach, Charles M., and Christopher Worswick. 1993. 'Is There a Double Negative Effect on the Earnings of Immigrant Women?', *Canadian Public Policy* 19(1): 36–53.

Beaujot, R., K.G. Basavarajappa, and R.B.P. Verma. 1988. *Income of Immigrants in Canada*. Catalogue 91-527E. Ottawa: Minister of Supply and Services Canada.

Beaujot, Roderic, and J. Peter Rappak. 1990. 'The Evolution of Immigrant Cohorts' in Shiva S. Halli, Frank Trovato, and Leo Driedger, eds, *Ethnic Demography: Canadian Immigrant, Racial and Cultural Variations*. Ottawa: Carleton University Press, pp. 111–40.

Becker, Gary S. 1993. *Human Capital: A Theoretical and Empirical Analysis with Special Reference to Education*. Chicago: University of Chicago Press.

Berry, John W., and Rudolf Kalin. 1995. 'Multicultural and Ethnic Attitudes in Canada: An Overview of the 1991 National Survey', *Canadian Journal of Behavioural Science* 27(3): 301–20.

Berry, John W., Rudolf Kalin, and Donald M. Taylor. 1977. *Multiculturalism and Ethnic Attitudes in Canada*. Ottawa: Minister of Supply and Services Canada.

Billingsley, B., and L. Muszynski. 1985. *No Discrimination Here*. Toronto: Social Planning Council of Metropolitan Toronto and the Urban Alliance on Race Relations.

Blau, Peter M., and Otis D. Duncan. 1967. *The American Occupational Structure*. New York: John Wiley & Sons.

Bloom, David E., Gills Grenier, and Morley Gunderson. 1995. 'The Changing Labour Market Position of Canadian Immigrants', *Canadian Journal of Economics* 46(28): 987–1005.

Bloom, David E., and Morley Gunderson. 1991. 'An Analysis of Earnings of Canadian Immigrants' in John M. Abowd and Richard B. Freeman, eds, *Immigration, Trade and the Labour Market*. Chicago: University of Chicago Press, pp. 321–67.

Bogardus, Emory S. 1925. 'Measuring Social Distances', *Journal of Applied Sociology* 9: 299–308.

———. 1968. 'Comparing Racial Distance in Ethiopia, South Africa, and the United States', *Sociology and Social Research* 52(Jan.): 149–56.

Bonilla-Silva, Eduardo. 1996. 'Rethinking Racism: Towards a Structural Interpretation', *American Sociological Review* 62(June): 465–80.

Borjas, George J. 1999. *Heaven's Door: Immigration Policy and the American Economy*. New Jersey: Princeton University Press.

———. 1994. 'The Economics of Immigration', *Journal of Economic Literature* 32(Dec.): 1667–717.

——. 1985. 'Assimilation, Changes in Cohort Quality, and the Earnings of Immigrants', *Journal of Labor Economics* 3(4): 463–89.

Borowski, Allan, and Alan Nash. 1994. 'Business Migration' in H. Adelman, A. Borowski, M. Burstein, and L. Foster, eds, *Immigration and Refugee Policy: Australia and Canada Compared*. Vol. 1. Toronto: University of Toronto Press, pp. 227–52.

Bourdieu, Pierre. 1986. 'The Forms of Capital' in John G. Richardson, ed., *Handbook of Theory and Research for the Sociology of Education*. Westport, CT: Greenwood Press, pp. 241–58.

Bourbeau, Robert. 1989. *Canada—A Linguistic Profile*. 1986 Census of Canada, Catalogue 98-131. Ottawa: Minister of Supply and Services Canada.

Boyd, Monica. 1992. 'Gender, Visible Minority and Immigrant Earnings Inequality: Reassessing an Employment Equity Premise' in Vic Satzewich, ed., *In Deconstructing a Nation: Immigration, Multiculturalism and Racism in '90s Canada*. Halifax: Fernwood, pp. 279–321.

——. 1985. 'Immigration and Occupational Attainment in Canada' in Monica Boyd et al., *In Ascription and Achievement: Studies in Mobility and Status Attainment in Canada*. Ottawa: Carleton University Press, pp. 393–445.

——. 1984. 'At a Disadvantage: The Occupational Attainments of Foreign-Born Women in Canada', *International Migration Review* 18(4): 1091–119.

Boyd, Monica, and Doug Norris. 2001. 'Who Are the "Canadians"?: Changing Census Responses, 1986–1996', *Canadian Ethnic Studies* 33(1): 1–24.

Breton, Raymond. 1999. 'Intergroup Competition in the Symbolic Construction of Canadian Society' in Peter S. Li, ed., *Race and Ethnic Relations in Canada*. Toronto: Oxford University Press, pp. 291–310.

——. 1988. 'The Evolution of the Canadian Multicultural Society: The Significance of Government Intervention' in A.J. Fry and Ch. Forceville, eds, *Canadian Mosaic Essay on Multiculturalism*. Amsterdam: Free University Press, pp. 25–44.

——. 1984. 'The Production and Allocation of Symbolic Resources: An Analysis of the Linguistic and Ethnocultural Fields in Canada', *Canadian Review of Sociology and Anthropology* 21(2): 123–44.

Brotz, Howard. 1980. 'Multiculturalism in Canada: A Muddle', *Canadian Public Policy* 6(1): 41–6.

Canada, Debates of the Senate. 1964. Senatorial Address of Hon. Paul Yuzyk, *Debates of the Senate Canada*. 3 Mar., pp. 50–8.

Canada, House of Commons. 1994. *House of Common Debates*. 27 Jan., p. 455.

——. 1983. *Proceedings of Special Committee on Participation of Visible Minorities in Canadian Society, Nos. 1–27*. Ottawa: Minister of Supply and Services Canada.

——. 1971. *House of Commons Debates*. 8 Oct., pp. 8545–8.

——. 1947. *Debates of the House of Commons*. 1 May, pp. 2644–9.

Canada, Royal Commission on Bilingualism and Biculturalism. 1969. *The Cultural Contribution of Other Ethnic Groups*. Vol. 4 of *Report of the Royal Commission on Bilingualism and Biculturalism*. Ottawa: Queen's Printer.

——. 1967. *Official Languages*. Vol. 1 of *Report of the Royal Commission on Bilingualism and Biculturalism*. Ottawa: Queen's Printer and Controller of Stationery.

——. 1965. *A Preliminary Report of the Royal Commission on Bilingualism and Biculturalism*. Ottawa: Queen's Printer and Controller of Stationery.

Canada, Royal Commission on Equality in Employment. 1984. *Report of the Commission on Equality in Employment*. Ottawa: Minister of Supply and Services Canada.

Canada Gazette. 2002. Part II, vol. 136, no. 9, pp. 1–449, Immigration and Refugee Protection Regulations, 14 June.

——. 1993. Part II, vol. 127, no. 3, pp. 605–61, Immigration Regulations, 1978, amendment, 28 Jan.

Chiswick, Barry R. 1978. 'The Effect of Americanization on the Earnings of Foreign-Born Men', *Journal of Political Economy* 86(5): 897–921.

———. 1977. 'Sons of Immigrants: Are They at an Earnings Disadvantage?', *American Economic Review* 67(1): 376–80.

Citizenship and Immigration Canada. 2001a. *Overview of Bill-C11 Immigration and Refugee Protection Act.* Released June 2001. < http://www.cic.gc.ca > .

———. 2001b. *Business Immigration Program Statistics 2000.* Released 20 Aug. 2001. < http://www.cic.gc.ca > .

———. 2001c. *Facts and Figures 2000.* Catalogue MP 43-333/2001E. Ottawa: Minister of Public Works and Government Services Canada.

———. 2001d. *Planning Now for Canada's Future: Introducing a Multi-Year Planning Process and the Immigration Plan for 2001 and 2002.* Ottawa: Minister of Public Works and Government Services Canada.

———. 2000. *Facts and Figures 1999.* Catalogue MP 43-333/2000E. Ottawa: Minister of Public Works and Government Services Canada.

———. 1999a. *Canada . . . The Place to Be: Annual Immigration Plan for the Year 2000.* Ottawa: Minister of Public Works and Government Services Canada.

———. 1999b. *Fee Schedule for Citizenship and Immigration Services.* Ottawa: Minister of Public Works and Government Services Canada.

———. 1998. IMDB Profile Series: The Economic Performance of Immigrants, Immigration Category Perspective. Ottawa: Citizenship and Immigration Canada.

———. 1996. *A Broader Vision: Immigration Plan, 1996 Annual Report to Parliament.* Catalogue Cil-1996. Ottawa: Minister of Supply and Services Canada.

———. 1994a. *What Are the Key Elements of a Strategy for Integrating Newcomers into Canadian Society?,* The Report of Working Group #5, 1994 Immigration Consultations.

———. 1994b. *Into the 21st Century: A Strategy for Immigration and Citizenship.* Catalogue MP-307-10-94F. Ottawa: Minister of Supply and Services Canada.

———. 1994c. *Canada and Immigration: A Discussion Paper.* Ottawa: Minister of Supply and Services Canada.

———. 1994d. *Immigration Consultations Report.* Catalogue MP43-334/1994E. Ottawa: Minister of Supply and Services Canada.

Clark, Harry R., and Lee Smith. 1996. 'Labor Immigration and Capital Flows: Long-Term Australian, Canadian and United States Experience', *International Migration Review* 30(4): 925–49.

Clement, Wallace. 1977. *Continental Corporate Power: Economic Linkages Between Canada and the United States.* Toronto: McClelland & Stewart.

Coleman, James S. 1988. 'Social Capital in the Creation of Human Capital', *American Journal of Sociology* 94: S95–S120.

Coulson, R.G., and D.J. DeVoretz. 1993. 'Human Capital Content of Canadian Immigrants, 1967–1987', *Canadian Public Policy* 19(3): 357–66.

Daily, Gretchen C., and Paul R. Ehrlich. 1992. 'Population, Sustainability, and Earth's Carrying Capacity', *BioScience* 42(10): 761–71.

Darroch, A. Gordon, and Wilfred G. Marston. 1971. 'The Social Class Basis of Ethnic Residential Segregation: The Canadian Case', *American Journal of Sociology* 77(3): 491–510.

Davies, Gordon W. 1977. 'Macroeconomic Effects of Immigration: Evidence from CANDIDE, TRACE, and RDX2', *Canadian Public Policy* 3(3): 299–306.

Democracy Education Network. 1994. *Talking about Immigration: The Study Circles of the Future of Immigration Policy.*

Denton, Frank, Christine Feaver, and Byron Spencer. 1999. 'Immigration and Population Aging', *Canadian Business Economics* 7(1): 39–57.

deSilva, Arnold. 1997. 'Earnings of Immigrant Classes in the Early 1980s in Canada: A Reexamination', *Canadian Public Policy* 23(2): 179–202.

———. 1992. *Earnings of Immigrants: A Comparative Analysis*. Ottawa: Economic Council of Canada.

DeVoretz, Don J., ed. 1999. *Canada's Brain Drain, Gain or Exchange? Policy Options*, research on Immigration and Integration in the Metropolis Commentary Series #99-01. Vancouver: Vancouver Centre of Excellence (RIIM).

———. 1995 *Diminishing Returns: The Economics of Canada's Recent Immigration Policy*. Toronto and Vancouver: C.D. Howe Institute and Laurier Institute.

DeVoretz, Don, and Samuel A. Laryea. 1998. *Canadian Human Capital Transfers: The USA and Beyond*, research on Immigration and Integration in the Metropolis Working Paper Series #98-18. Vancouver: Vancouver Centre of Excellence (RIIM).

deVries, John. 1990. 'Language and Ethnicity: Canadian Aspects' in Peter S. Li, ed., *Race and Ethnic Relations in Canada*. Toronto: Oxford University Press, pp. 231–50.

deVries, John, and Frank G. Vallee. 1980. *Language Use in Canada*. Ottawa: Minister of Supply and Services Canada.

Doern, G. Bruce, and Richard W. Phidd. 1983. *Canadian Public Policy: Ideas, Structure, Process*. Toronto: Methuen.

Driedger, Leo. 1999. 'Immigrant/Ethnic Racial Segregation: Canadian Big Three and Prairie Metropolitan Comparison', *Canadian Journal of Sociology* 24(4): 485–509.

Driedger, Leo, ed. 1978. *The Canadian Ethnic Mosaic: A Quest for Identity*. Toronto: McClelland and Stewart.

Duncan, Otis Dudley, David L. Featherman, and Beverly Duncan. 1972. *Socioeconomic Background and Achievement*. New York: Seminar Press.

Easterbrook, W.T., and Hugh G.J. Aitken. 1988. *Canadian Economic History*. Toronto: University of Toronto Press.

Economic Council of Canada. 1991. *Economic and Social Impacts of Immigration*. Ottawa: Minister of Supply and Services Canada.

Egerton, Hugh Edward. 1911. *Federations and Unions within the British Empire*. Oxford: Clarendon Press.

Ehrlich, Paul R., and Anne H. Ehrlich. 1990. *The Population Explosion*. New York: Simon & Schuster.

———. 1991. *Healing the Planet*. New York: Addison-Wesley.

Ekos Research Associates. 2000. *National Immigration Survey*, presentation to the Hon. Elinor Caplan, Minister of Citizenship and Immigration Canada.

———. 1992. *The Public Opinion Impact of the New Immigration Legislation*, report submitted to Employment and Immigration Canada.

Employment and Immigration Canada. 1993a. *Evaluation of the Immigration Investor Program: National and Provincial Macroeconomic Impacts*. Ottawa: Minister of Supply and Services Canada.

———. 1993b. *Immigration Consultations 1993: The Management of Immigration*. Document IM-240-1-93. Ottawa: Public Affairs Employment and Immigration Canada.

———. 1992a. *Evaluation of the Immigrant Investor Program: Interviews with Investors, Businesses and Other Stakeholders*. Ottawa: Minister of Supply and Services Canada.

———. 1992b. *Managing Immigration: A Framework for the 1990s*. Document IM 199/7/92. Ottawa: Public Affairs Branch, Employment and Immigration.

———. 1991a. *Immigration Statistics 1991*. MP22-1/1991. Ottawa: Minister of Supply and Services Canada.

———. 1991b. *Canada–Quebec Accord Relating to Immigration and Temporary Admission of Aliens*. Ottawa: Minister of Supply and Services Canada.

——. 1990. *Annual Report to Parliament: Immigration Plan for 1991–1995*. Document IM-094/10/90. Ottawa: Public Affairs and The Immigration Policy Group, Employment and Immigration.

——. 1989a. *Immigration Statistics*. MP22-1/1989. Ottawa: Minister of Supply and Services Canada.

——. 1989b. *Immigration to Canada: Issues for Discussion*. Document IM 061/11/89. Ottawa: Public Affairs and the Immigration Policy Branch.

——. 1985. *Immigration Statistics 1989*. MP22-1/1989. Ottawa: Minister of Supply and Services Canada.

——. 1984. *Immigration Statistics 1985*. MP22-1/1985. Ottawa: Minister of Supply and Services Canada.

——. 1983. *Immigration Statistics 1983*. MP22-1/1983. Ottawa: Minister of Supply and Services Canada.

Epstein, Alek, and Nina Kheimets. 2000. 'Immigrant Intelligentsia and Its Second Generation: Cultural Segregation as a Road to Social Integration?', *Journal of International Migration and Integration* 1(4): 461–76.

Financial Post, The. 1994a. 'The Unsung Heroes of Chretien's China Trip', 18 Nov., p. C7.

——. 1994b. 'Hong Kong Expatriate Shows Canadians How to Market into China', 18 Nov., p. C11.

——. 1994c. 'Focus on the Chinese in Canada', special edition, 18 Nov., pp. C1–24.

Fleras, Augie, and Jean Leonard Elliott. 1992. *Multiculturalism in Canada: The Challenge of Diversity*. Scarborough, ON: Nelson Canada.

Fong, Eric. 1999. 'The Spatial Assimilation Model Re-examined: An Assessment by Canadian Data', *International Migration Review* 33(3): 594–620.

——. 1997a. 'A Systemic Approach to Racial Residential Patterns', *Social Science Research* 26: 465–86.

——. 1997b. 'Residential Proximity with the Charter Groups in Canada', *Canadian Studies in Population* 24(2): 103–24.

——. 1997c. 'The Effects of Group Characteristics and City Context on Neighborhood Qualities among Racial and Ethnic Groups', *Canadian Studies in Population* 24(1): 45–66.

Fong, Eric, and Milena Gulia. 2000. 'Neighborhood Change within the Canadian Ethnic Mosaic', *Population Research and Policy Review* 19: 155–77.

Foschi, Martha, and Shari Buchan. 1990. 'Ethnicity, Gender, and the Perceptions of Task Competence', *Canadian Journal of Sociology* 15(1): 1–18.

Foster, William, Fred Gruen, and Neil Swan. 1994. 'Economic Effects on the Host Community' in H. Adelman, A. Borowski, M. Burstein, and L. Foster, eds, *Immigration and Refugee Policy: Australia and Canada Compared*. Vol. 2. Toronto: University of Toronto Press, pp. 445–71.

Frideres, James S. 1993. *Native Peoples in Canada: Contemporary Conflicts*. Scarborough, ON: Prentice-Hall.

George, M.V., M.J. Norris, F. Nault, S. Loh, and S.Y. Dai. 1994. *Population Projections for Canada, Provinces and Territories 1993–2016*. Catalogue 91-520. Ottawa: Minister of Industry, Science and Technology.

George, M.V., Shirley Loh, Ravi B.P. Verma, and Y. Edward Shin. 2001. *Population Projections for Canada, Provinces and Territories 2000–2026*. Catalogue 91-520. Ottawa: Ministry of Industry.

Globe and Mail, The. 2001a. '69 Per Cent Don't Trust Screening of New Canadians', 26 Dec., p. A8.

——. 2001b. 'Japan Reluctant to Accept Much-Needed Immigrants', 28 Aug., p. A12.

——. 2000a. 'Poll Shows Opposition to Minorities Rising', 11 Mar., p. A8.

———. 2000b. 'The Boat People's Big Gamble', 22 July, p. A7.

———. 1999. 'Migrants Not Owed Free Ride, Poll Says: Sympathy for Newcomers Lowest in B.C.; Public Split on Need for Refugee Hearings', 31 Aug., p. 1.

———. 1998a. 'Stop Spending on Immigrants', 3 Jan., p. D6.

———. 1998b. 'The Language of Immigration', 5 Mar., p. A22.

———. 1997a. 'Corporate Cash Registers Ring in Chinese New Year', 7 Feb., pp. A1, A6.

———. 1997b. 'Ottawa Offers Immigration Deal', 27 Feb., pp. A1, A3.

———. 1997c. 'B.C. to Abolish Welfare Rule', 6 Mar., pp. A1, A4.

———. 1996a. 'Toronto Firm Takes to Heart Cultural Lessons', 30 Aug., p. B6.

———. 1996b. 'Immigration Levels Reflect Backlash', 30 Oct., pp. A1, A6.

———. 1995a. 'Chasing After the Ethnic Consumer', 18 Sept., p. A6.

———. 1995b. 'Banks Woo Asian Clients', 21 Nov., p. C1.

———. 1995c. 'White Flight, Chinese Distress', 30 Sept., pp. D1, D2.

———. 1994a. 'Streets a Fear of Losing the Old Canada', 11 Mar., p. A2.

———. 1994b. 'Canadians Should Shake Off Their Insecurity RACISM/As Reports Tell of a Diminishing West, East Asia Is Booming. That's One Reason Canada Is Intolerant of Visible Minorities', 28 Mar., p. A13.

———. 1994c. 'How Many Immigrants Should Canada Admit?', 4 Feb., p. A23.

———. 1994d. 'Canadian Values', 22 Mar., p. A26.

———. 1993. 'Canadians Want Mosaic to Melt, Survey Finds', 14 Dec., pp. A1, A2.

———. 1992. 'Poll Showed Hostility to Immigrants', 14 Sept., p. A4.

Goldlust, John, and A.H. Richmond. 1974. 'A Multivariate Model of Immigrant Adaptation', *International Migration Review* 8(2): 193–225.

Grant, Mary L. 1999. 'Evidence of New Immigrant Assimilation in Canada', *Canadian Journal of Economics* 32(4): 930–55.

Green, Alan G. 1995. 'A Comparison of Canadians and US Immigration Policy in the Twentieth Century' in D.J. DeVoretz, ed., *Diminishing Returns: The Economics of Canada's Recent Immigration Policy*. Toronto and Vancouver: C.D. Howe Institute and Laurier Institute, pp. 31–64.

Green, Alan G., and David A. Green. 1999. 'The Economic Goals of Canada's Immigration Policy: Past and Present', *Canadian Public Policy* 25(4): 425–51.

———. 1995. 'Canadian Immigration Policy: The Effectiveness of the Point System and Other Instruments', *Canadian Journal of Economics* 28(4b): 1006–41.

Halli, S.S., S.Y. Dai, M.V. George, and R.B.P. Verma. 1996. 'Visible Minority Fertility in Canada, 1981–1986', *Genus* 52(1–2): 181–9.

Harrison, Paul. 1992. *The Third Revolution: Population, Environment and a Sustainable World*. London: Penguin.

Harrison, Trevor. 1996. 'Class, Citizenship, and Global Migration: The Case of the Canadian Business Immigration Program, 1978–1992', *Canadian Public Policy* 22(1): 7–23.

Hawkins, Freda. 1988. *Canada and Immigration: Public Policy and Public Concern*, 2nd edn. Montreal: McGill-Queen's University Press.

Health and Welfare Canada. 1989. *Charting Canada's Future: A Report of the Demographic Review*. Ottawa: Minister of Supply and Services Canada.

Henry, Frances. 1989. *Who Gets the Work in 1989?* Ottawa: Economic Council of Canada.

———. 1973. *Forgotten Canadians: The Blacks of Nova Scotia*. Don Mills, ON: Longman.

Henry, Frances, and Effie Ginzberg. 1985. *Who Gets the Work? A Test of Racial Discrimination in Employment*. Toronto: The Urban Alliance on Race Relations and the Social Planning Council of Metropolitan Toronto.

Henry, Frances, Carol Tator, Winston Mattis, and Tim Rees. 2000. *The Colour of Democracy: Racism in Canadian Society*. Toronto: Harcourt.

Hiebert, Daniel. 2000. 'Immigration and the Changing Canadian City', *The Canadian Geographer* 44(1): 25–43.

——. 1999. 'Immigration and the Changing Social Geography of Greater Vancouver', *BC Studies* 121(spring): 35–82.

Holdren, John P. 1991. 'Population and the Energy Problem', *Population and Environment* 12(3): 231–55.

Horan, Patrick M. 1978. 'Is Status Attainment Research Atheoretical?', *American Sociological Review* 43(4): 534–41.

Howard-Hassmann, Rhoda E. 1999. '"Canadian" as an Ethnic Category: Implications for Multiculturalism and National Unity', *Canadian Public Policy* 25(4): 3–17.

Huang, Evelyn, and Lawrence Jeffery. 1992. *Chinese Canadians Voices from a Community*. Vancouver: Douglas & McIntyre.

Human Resources Development Canada. 2001. 'Earnings and Employment Patterns', *Applied Research* 7(1): 8–9.

Immigrant Investor Program Advisory Panel. 1995. *Refocusing the Immigrant Investor Program*. Ottawa: Minister of Supply and Services Canada.

Immigration Legislative Review. 1997. *Not Just Numbers: A Canadian Framework for Future Immigration*. Ottawa: Minister of Public Works and Government Services Canada.

Isajiw, Wsevolod W. 1990. 'Ethnic Identity Retention' in R. Breton et al., eds, *Ethnic Identity and Inequality*. Toronto: University of Toronto Press, pp. 34–91.

Isbister, John. 1996. *The Immigration Debate: Remarking America*. Hartford, CT: Kumarian Press.

Jasso, Guillermina, and Mark R. Rosenzweig. 1995. 'Do Immigrants Screened for Skills Do Better Than Family Reunification Immigrants?', *International Migration Review* 29(1): 85–111.

Jenson, Jane. 2000. 'Social Cohesion: The Concept and Its Limits', *Plan Canada* 40(2): 8–10.

Johnson, Victoria, and Robert Nurick. 1995. 'Behind the Headlines: The Ethics of the Population and Environment Debate', *International Affairs* 71(3): 547–65.

Johnston, Hugh J.M. 1989. *The Voyage of the Komagata Maru: The Sikh Challenge to Canada's Colour Bar*. Vancouver: University of British Columbia Press.

Kalbach, Warren E., and Madeline A. Richard. 1990. 'Ethno-Religious Identity and Acculturation' in Shiva S. Halli, Frank Trovato, and Leo Driedger, eds, *Ethnic Demography: Canadian Immigration, Racial and Cultural Variations*. Ottawa: Carleton University Press, pp. 179–98.

Kalin, Rudolf, and John W. Berry. 1996. 'Interethnic Attitudes in Canada: Ethnocentrism, Consensual Hierarchy and Reciprocity', *Canadian Journal of Behavioural Science* 28(4): 253–61.

Kallen, Evelyn. 1982. 'Multiculturalism: Ideology, Policy and Reality', *Journal of Canadian Studies* 17(1): 51–63.

Kazemipur, Abdolmohammad, and Shiva S. Halli. 2001. 'The Changing Colour of Poverty in Canada', *Canadian Review of Sociology and Anthropology* 38(2): 217–38.

——. 2000a. 'Neighbourhood Poverty in Canadian Cities', *Canadian Journal of Sociology* 25(3): 369–81.

——. 2000b. 'The Invisible Barrier: Neighbourhood Poverty and Integration of Immigrants in Canada', *Journal of International Migration and Integration* 1(1): 85–100.

——. 1997. 'Plight of Immigrants: The Spatial Concentration of Poverty in Canada', *Canadian Journal of Regional Science* 20(1, 2): 11–28.

Kelly, Ninette, and Michael Trebilcock. 1998. *The Making of the Mosaic: A History of Canadian Immigration Policy*. Toronto: University of Toronto Press.

Kobayashi, Audrey, and Linda Peake. 1997. *Urban Studies Research on Immigrants and Immigration in Canadian Cities*, report prepared for Strategic Policy, Planning and Research and Metropolis Project. Ottawa: Citizenship and Immigration Canada.

Langlois, Claude, and Craig Dougherty. 1997. 'The Longitudinal Immigrant Database (IMDB): An Introduction', paper presented at the CERF-CIC Conference on Immigration, Employment and the Economy, 17–18 Oct., 1997, Richmond, BC.

Ley, David. 1999. 'Myths and Meanings of Immigration and the Metropolis', *The Canadian Geographer* 43(1): 2–19.

Ley, David, and Heather Smith. 1997. 'Immigration and Poverty in Canadian Cities, 1971–1991', *Canadian Journal of Regional Science* 20(1, 2): 29–48.

Liberal, The. 1995. 'Ethnic Concentrations Causing Conflict', 25 June, p. 3.

Li, Peter S. 2001a. 'The Market Worth of Immigrants' Educational Credentials', *Canadian Public Policy* 27(1): 1–16.

———. 2001b. 'The Racial Subtext in Canada's Immigration Discourse', *Journal of International Migration and Integration* 2(1): 77–97.

———. 2001c. 'The Economics of Minority Language Identity', *Canadian Ethnic Studies* 33(3): 1–21.

———. 2000. 'Earning Disparities between Immigrants and Native-Born Canadians', *Canadian Review of Sociology and Anthropology* 37(3): 289–311.

———. 1999. 'The Multiculturalism Debate' in Peter S. Li, ed., *Race and Ethnic Relations in Canada*, 2nd edn. Toronto: Oxford University Press, pp. 147–76.

———. 1998. *The Chinese in Canada*, 2nd edn. Toronto: Oxford University Press.

———. 1997. 'Asian Capital and Canadian Business: The Recruitment and Control of Investment Capital and Business Immigrants to Canada' in Wsevolod W. Isajiw, ed., *Multiculturalism in North America and Europe*. Toronto: Canadian Scholars' Press, pp. 363–79.

———. 1996. *Literature Review on Immigration: Sociological Perspective*, report submitted to Citizenship and Immigration Canada for distribution to the Centres of Excellence on Immigration.

———. 1994a. 'Unneighbourly Houses or Unwelcome Chinese: The Social Construction of Race in the Battle Over "Monster Homes" in Vancouver, Canada', *International Journal of Comparative Race and Ethnic Studies* 1(1): 47–66.

———. 1994b. 'A World Apart: The Multicultural World of Visible Minorities and the Art World of Canada', *Canadian Review of Sociology and Anthropology* 31(4): 365–91.

———. 1993. 'Chinese Investment and Business in Canada: Ethnic Entrepreneurship Reconsidered', *Pacific Affairs* 66(2): 219–43.

———. 1992. 'The Economics of Brain Drain: Recruitment of Skilled Labour to Canada, 1954–86' in Vic Satzewich, ed., *Deconstructing a Nation: Immigration, Multiculturalism & Racism in '90s Canada*. Halifax: Fernwood, pp. 145–62.

Li, Peter S., and B. Singh Bolaria. 1979. 'Canadian Immigration Policy and Assimilation Theories' in John A. Fry, ed., *Economy, Class and Social Reality*. Toronto: Butterworths, pp. 411–22.

Li, Peter S., and Yahong Li. 1999. 'The Consumer Market of the Enclave Economy: A Study of Advertisements in a Chinese Daily Newspaper in Toronto', *Canadian Ethnic Studies* 31(2): 43–60.

Lockwood, Matthew. 1995. 'Development Policy and the African Demographic Transition: Issues and Questions', *Journal of International Development* 7(1): 1–23.

McDade, Kathryn. 1988. *Barriers to Recognition of the Credentials of Immigrants in Canada*. Ottawa: Institute for Research on Public Policy.

McDonald, James T., and Christopher Worswick. 1998. 'The Earnings of Immigrant Men in Canada: Job Tenure, Cohort, and Macroeconomic Conditions', *Industrial and Labor Relations Review* 51(3): 465–82.

———. 1997. 'Unemployment Incidence of Immigrant Men in Canada', *Canadian Public Policy* 23(4): 343–73.

Manpower and Immigration Canada. 1974a. *Immigration Policy Perspectives*. Ottawa: Information Canada.

———. 1974b. *The Immigration Program*. Ottawa: Information Canada.

———. 1974c. *Immigration and Population Statistics*. Ottawa: Information Canada.

———. 1974d. *Three Years in Canada: First Report of the Longitudinal Survey on the Economic and Social Adaptation of Immigrants*. Ottawa: Minister of Supply and Services Canada.

———. 1970. *Immigration and Population Statistics*. Ottawa: Information Canada.

Marger, Martin N., and Constance A. Hoffman. 1992. 'Ethnic Enterprise in Ontario: Immigrant Participation in the Small Business Sector', *International Migration Review* 26(3): 968–81.

Marr, Bill, and Pierre Siklos. 1999. 'Immigrant Class and the Use of Unemployment Insurance by Recent Immigrants in Canada: Evidence from a New Database, 1980–1995', *International Migration Review* 33(3): 561–93.

Marr, W.L., and M.B. Percy. 1985. 'Immigration Policy and Canadian Economic Growth' in John Whalley, ed., *Domestic Policies and the International Economic Environment, Studies of the Royal Commission on the Economic Union and Development Prospects for Canada*. Vol. 12. Toronto: University of Toronto Press, pp. 57–109.

Mata, Fernando, and Don McRae. 2000. 'Charitable Giving among the Foreign-Born in Canada', *Journal of International Migration and Integration* 1(2): 205–32.

Mercer, John. 1995. 'Canadian Cities and Their Immigrants: New Realities', *Annals of the American Academy of Political and Social Science* 538(Mar.): 169–84.

Miedema, Baukje, and Nancy Nason-Clark. 1989. 'Second Class Status: An Analysis of the Lived Experiences of Immigrant Women in Fredericton', *Canadian Ethnic Studies* 21(2): 63–73.

Miles, Robert. 1987. *Capitalism and Unfree Labour: Anomaly or Necessity?* London: Tavistock Publications.

———. 1982. *Racism and Migrant Labour*. London: Routledge & Kegan Paul.

Moogk, Peter N. 1994. 'Reluctant Exiles: Emigrants from France in Canada before 1760' in Gerald Tulchinsky, ed., *Immigration in Canada: Historical Perspectives*. Toronto: Copp Clark Longman, pp. 8–47.

National Post. 1999. 'Minister Condemns Smuggling of Humans', 3 Sept., p. A10.

Naylor, R.T. 1987. *Canada in the European Age, 1453–1919*. Vancouver: New Star Books.

———. 1975. *The History of Canadian Business, 1867–1914*. Toronto: James Lorimer and Company.

Nevitte, Neil. 1996. *The Decline of Deference*. Peterborough, ON: Broadview Press.

Nodwell, Evelyn, and Neil Guppy. 1992. 'The Effects of Publicly Displayed Ethnicity on Interpersonal Discrimination: Indo-Canadians in Vancouver', *Canadian Review of Sociology and Anthropology* 29(1): 87–99.

Norton, Thomas T., Stephen Dovers, H.A. Nix, and David H. Elias. 1993. *An Overview of Research on the Links Between Population and Environment*. Boulder, CO: Westview Press.

O'Brien, K.G., J.G. Reitz, and O.M. Kuplowska. 1976. *Non-Official Languages: A Study in Canadian Multiculturalism*. Ottawa: Minister of Supply and Services Canada.

Ornstein, Michael D., and R.D. Sharma. 1981. 'Adjustment and the Economic Experience of Immigrants in Canada: 1976 Longitudinal Survey of Immigrants', paper prepared for Employment and Immigration Canada.

Owen, Carolyn A., Howard C. Eisner, and Thomas R. McFaul. 1981. 'A Half-Century of Social Distance Research: National Replication of the Bogardus Studies', *Sociology and Social Research* 66(Oct.): 80–99.

Pal, Leslie A. 1993. *Interests of State: The Politics of Language, Multiculturalism, and Feminism in Canada*. Montreal and Kingston: McGill-Queen's University Press.

Palmer, Howard. 1997. *Canadians' Attitudes Towards Immigration: November and December 1996, and February 1997 Surveys*, report prepared for Program Support, Strategic Policy,

Planning and Research Branch, Citizenship and Immigration Canada.

Panitch, Leo, ed. 1977. *The Canadian State: Political Economy and Political Power*. Toronto: University of Toronto Press.

Parai, L. 1965. *Immigration and Emigration of Professional and Skilled Manpower During the Post-war Period*. Ottawa: Economic Council of Canada.

Patterson II, E. Palmer. 1972. *The Canadian Indian: A History Since 1500*. Don Mills, ON: Collier-Macmillan.

Pendakur, Krishna, and Ravi Pendakur. Forthcoming. 'Speak and Ye Shall Receive: Language Knowledge as Human Capital', *International Migration Review*.

———. 2000. 'Ethnicity and Earnings' in Ravi Pendakur, *Immigrants and the Labour Force: Policy, Regulation, and Impact*. Montreal and Kingston: McGill-Queens University Press, pp. 159–91.

———. 1998. 'The Colour of Money: Earnings Differentials among Ethnic Groups in Canada', *Canadian Journal of Economics* 31(3): 519–48.

Pendakur, Ravi, and Fernando Mata. 1998. 'Patterns of Ethnic Identification and the "Canadian" Response', *Canadian Ethnic Studies* 30(2): 125–37.

Pentland, H. Clare. 1981. *Labour and Capital in Canada, 1650–1860*. Toronto: James Lorimer.

Pereira, Pedro Telhado, and Lara Patricio Tavares. 2000. 'Is Schooling of Migrants' Children More Like That of Their Parents, Their Cousins, or Their Neighbours?', *Journal of International Migration and Integration* 1(4): 443–59.

Peterson, William. 1958. 'A General Typology of Migration', *American Sociological Review* 23(3): 256–66.

Pitman, Walter. 1977. *Now Is Not Too Late*, report submitted to the Council of Metropolitan Toronto by Task Force on Human Relations.

Porter, John. 1965. *The Vertical Mosaic*. Toronto: University of Toronto Press.

Portes, Alejandro. 1998. 'Social Capital: Its Origins and Applications in Modern Sociology', *Annual Review of Sociology* 24: 1–24.

Portes, Alejandro, and Leif Jensen. 1989. 'The Enclave and the Entrants: Patterns of Ethnic Enterprise in Miami Before and After Mariel', *American Sociological Review* 54 (Dec.): 929–49.

Potrebenko, Helen. 1977. *No Streets of Gold: A Social History of Ukrainians in Alberta*. Vancouver: New Star Books.

Price, John. 1979. *Indians of Canada: Cultural Dynamics*. Scarborough, ON: Prentice-Hall.

Privy Council. 1999. 1999-525, 25 March, *Canada Gazette*, Part II, vol. 133, no. 8, pp. 1029–34.

———. 1993. 1993-1626, 4 Aug., *Canada Gazette*, Part II, vol. 127, no. 17, pp. 3410–84.

———. 1990. 1990-2317, 25 Oct., *Canada Gazette*, Part II, vol. 124, no. 23, pp. 4888–93.

———. 1989. 1989-2440, 7 Dec., *Canada Gazette*, Part II, vol. 123, no. 26, pp. 4939–44.

———. 1985. 1985-3246, 31 Oct., *Canada Gazette*, Part II, vol. 119, no. 23, pp. 4582–6.

———. 1978. 1978-486, 23 Feb., *Canada Gazette*, Part II, vol. 112, no. 5, pp. 757–88.

———. 1967. 1967-1616, 16 Aug., *Canada Gazette*, Part II, vol. 101, no. 17, pp. 1350–62.

———. 1962. 1962-86, 18 Jan., *Canada Gazette*, Part II, vol. 96, no. 3, pp. 126–44.

———. 1956. 1956-785, 24 May, *Canada Gazette*, Part II, vol. 90, no. 11, pp. 545–8.

Public Policy Forum. 1994. *Developing a Ten-Year Strategic Framework For Canadian Citizenship and Immigration Policy and Programs: Finding the Right Consultative Process*.

Rajagopal, Indhu. 1990. 'The Glass Ceiling in the Vertical Mosaic: Indian Immigrants to Canada', *Canadian Ethnic Studies* 22(1): 96–105.

Rao, Someshwar, and Constantine Kapsalis. 1982. 'Labour Shortages and Immigration Policy', *Canadian Public Policy* 8(3): 374–78.

Ray, Brian K., and Eric Moore. 1991. 'Access to Homeownership among Immigrant Groups in Canada', *Canadian Review of Sociology and Anthropology* 28(1): 1–29.

Reitz, Jeffery G. 2001. 'Immigrant Skill Utilization in the Canadian Labour Market: Implications of Human Capital Research', *Journal of International Migration and Integration* 2(3): 347–78.

———. 1998. *Warmth of the Welcome: The Social Causes of Economic Success for Immigrants in Different Nations and Cities*. Boulder, CO: Westview Press.

———. 1980. *The Survival of Ethnic Groups*. Toronto: McGraw-Hill Ryerson.

Reitz, Jeffery G., and Raymond Breton. 1994. *The Illusion of Difference: Realities of Ethnicity in Canada and the United States*. Toronto: C.D. Howe Institute.

Revised Statutes of Canada. 1952. *An Act respecting immigration*, c. 325.

———. 1985. *An Act respecting immigration to Canada*, c. I–2.

Richard, Madeline A. 1991a. *Ethnic Groups and Marital Choices*. Vancouver: University of British Columbia Press.

———. 1991b. 'Factors in the Marital Assimilation of Ethno-Religious Populations in Canada, 1871 and 1971', *Canadian Review of Sociology and Anthropology* 28(1): 99–111.

Richmond, Anthony H. 1988. *Immigration and Ethnic Conflict*. New York: St. Martin's Press.

———. 1984. 'Immigration and Unemployment in Canada and Australia', *International Journal of Comparative Sociology* 25(3–4): 243–55.

———. 1974. *Aspects of Absorption and Adaptation of Immigrants*. Ottawa: Minister of Supply and Services Canada.

Richmond, Anthony H., and Warren E. Kalbach. 1980. *Factors in the Adjustment of Immigrants and Their Descendants*. Catalogue 99-761E. Ottawa: Minister of Supply and Services Canada.

Roberts, Lance W., and Rodney A. Clifton. 1982. 'Exploring the Ideology of Canadian Multiculturalism', *Canadian Public Policy* 89(1): 88–94.

Roy, Arun S. 1997. 'Job Displacement Effects of Canadian Immigrants by Country of Origin and Occupation', *International Migration Review* 31(1): 150–61.

Roy, Patricia E. 1989. *A White Man's Province: British Columbia Politicians and Chinese and Japanese Immigrants, 1858–1914*. Vancouver: University of British Columbia Press.

Samuel, T.J., and B. Woloski. 1985. 'The Labour Market Experiences of Canadian Immigrants', *International Migration* 23(2): 225–50.

Samuel, T.J., and T. Conyers. 1987. 'The Employment Effects of Immigration: A Balance Sheet Approach', *International Migration* 25(3): 283–90.

Sanders, Jimy M., and V. Nee. 1987. 'Limits of Ethnic Solidarity in the Enclave Economy', *American Sociological Review* 52(Dec.): 745–73.

Sassen, Saskia. 2001. *The Global City: New York, London, Tokyo*, 2nd edn. Princeton, NJ: Princeton University Press.

Satzewich, Vic. 1991. *Racism and the Incorporation of Foreign Labour: Farm Labour Migration to Canada Since 1945*. London: Routledge.

Satzewich, Victor, and Peter S. Li. 1987. 'Immigrant Labour in Canada: The Cost and Benefit of Ethnic Origin in the Job Market', *Canadian Journal of Sociology* 12(3): 229–41.

Scassa, Teresa. 1994. 'Language Standards, Ethnicity and Discrimination', *Canadian Ethnic Studies* 26(3): 105–20.

Seward, Shirley B. 1987. *The Relationship Between Immigration Policy and the Canadian Economy*. Ottawa: Institute for Research on Public Policy.

Sewell, William H., Archibald O. Haller, and George W. Ohlendorf. 1970. 'The Educational and Early Occupational Status Attainment Process: Replication and Revision', *American Sociological Review* 35(6): 1014–27.

Sewell, William H., and Robert M. Hauser. 1975. *Education, Occupation, and Earnings: Achievement in the Early Career*. New York: Academic Press.

———. 1972. 'Causes and Consequences of Higher Education: Models of the Status Attainment

Process', *American Journal of Agricultural Economics* 54(5): 851–61.

Shamsuddin, Abdul F.M. 1998. 'The Double-Negative Effect on the Earnings of Foreign-Born Females in Canada', *Applied Economics* 30(9): 1187–1201.

Simon, Julian. 1981. *The Ultimate Resource*. Oxford: Martin Robertson.

Smith, James P., and Barry Edmonston, eds. 1997. *The New Americans: Economic, Demographic, and Fiscal Effects of Immigration*. Washington, DC: National Academy Press.

Stanbury, W.T., and John D. Todd. 1990. *The Housing Crisis: The Effects of Local Government Regulation*. Vancouver: Laurier Institute.

Star Phoenix, The. 2001. 'Canada Too Lax on Immigration, but Border Security OK, Poll Finds', 5 Nov., p. A12.

———. 1992. 'Investors in ICC Get Day in Court', 30 Dec., p. A4.

———. 1992. 'Investors Want to Be Heard at Hearing in ICC Control', 21 Dec., p. A9.

———. 1992. 'Immigrants Say Investments Misused', 17 Dec., p. D1.

Statistics Canada. 2001. *Imports and Exports of Goods on a Balance-of-Payments Basis*. < www.statcan.ca > Canadian Statistics, International Trade.

———. 1999. *The Daily*. 16 Nov.

———. 1998a. Table 93F0025XDB96001 (n01_1303.ivt): *Total Population by Aboriginal Identity (7) and Registered Indian Status (3), Showing Indian Band/First Nation Membership (3) for Canada, Provinces, Territories, and Census Metropolitan Areas*. 1996 Census of Canada.

———. 1998b. *The Daily*. 17 Feb.

———. 1997. Table 93F0023XDB96001 (n01_0411.ivt): *Total Population by Immigrant Status (4A), for Canada, Provinces and Territories, 1911–1996 Censuses*. 1996 Census of Canada.

———. 1996. *Public Use Microdata File On Individuals: Documentation for 1996 Census*.

———. 1993. *Ethnic Origin: The Nation*. 1991 Census of Canada, Catalogue 93–315. Ottawa: Minster of Industry, Science and Technology.

———. 1990. *Public Use Microdata File On Individuals: Documentation and User's Guide*.

———. 1984. *Population: Ethnic Origin*. 1981 Census of Canada, Catalogue 92–911, Vol. 1. Ottawa: Minister of Supply and Services Canada.

———. 1983. *Historical Statistics of Canada,* 2nd edn. Ottawa: Minister of Supply and Services Canada.

———. 1974. *Population: Ethnic Groups*. Catalogue 92-723, Vol. 1, Part 3, Bulletin 1.3. Ottawa: Minister of Industry, Trade and Commerce.

Statutes of Canada. 2001. *An Act respecting immigration to Canada and the granting of refugee protection to persons who are displaced, persecuted or in danger*, c. 27.

———. 1995. *An Act to amend the Auditor General Act*, c. 43.

———. 1992. *An Act to amend the Immigration Act and other Acts in consequence thereof*, c. 49.

———. 1986 *Employment Equity Act*, c. 31.

———. 1982. *Canada Act*, c. 11.

———. 1976–7. *An Act respecting immigration to Canada*, c. 52.

Sydney Morning Herald, The. 2002. 'The Great "Children Overboard" Lie', 14 Feb., p. 1.

Suryadinata, Leo. 1997. *Chinese and Nation-Building in Southeast Asia*. Singapore: Singapore Society of Asian Studies.

Sweetman, Arthur. 2001. 'Immigrants and Employment Insurance' in Saul Schwarts and Abdurrahman Aydemir, eds, *Essays on the Repeat Use of Unemployment Insurance*. Ottawa: The Social Research and Demonstration Corporation, pp. 123–54.

Teixeira, Carlos. 1998. 'Cultural Resources and Ethnic Entrepreneurship: A Case Study of the Portuguese Real Estate Industry in Toronto', *Canadian Geographer* 42(3): 267–81.

Thomas, Derrick. 1990. *Immigrant Integration and the Canadian Identity*. Ottawa: Employment and Immigration.

Thompson, John Herd, and Morton Weinfeld. 1995. 'Entry and Exit: Canadian Immigration Policy in Context', *Annals of the American Academy of Political and Social Science* 538(Mar.): 185–98.

Timlin, Marble T. 1960. 'Canada's Immigration Policy, 1896–1910', *Canadian Journal of Economics and Political Sciences* 26(4): 517–32.

Toronto Star, The. 1997. 'Well-Off Chinese Are Big Spenders', 10 Jan., A1, p. A24.

———. 1996a. 'Courting New Fund Customers', 15 Sept., p. C4.

———. 1996b. 'Edging into the Mainstream', 10 Nov., p. B10.

———. 1996c. 'Immigration Levels Concern About 60%', 19 Aug., p. A1.

———. 1995a. 'Mayors Condemn Comments on Chinese', 16 Sept., p. A4.

———. 1995b. 'Bell Stands Her Ground', 22 Aug., p. A6.

———. 1995c. 'Markham Declares Truce with Chinese', 27 Sept., p. A6.

———. 1988. 'The New, Upscale Chinatown Prospering in Scarborough', 21 Nov., p. A6.

———. 1984. 'Chinese Centre Parking "Chaos" Draws Ire of 500', 29 May, p. A7.

Trovato, Frank, and Carl F. Grindstaff. 1986. 'Economic Status: A Census Analysis of Immigrant Women at Age Thirty in Canada', *Canadian Review of Sociology and Anthropology* 23(4): 569–87.

Tulchinsky, Gerald. 1994. *Immigration in Canada: Historical Perspectives.* Toronto: Copp Clark Longman.

United Nations Conference on Trade and Development. 1996. *World Investment Report: Investment, Trade and International Policy Arrangements.* New York and Geneva: United Nations Publication.

United Nations Development Programme. 1999. *Human Development Report 1999.* New York: Oxford University Press.

Vancouver Sun, The. 2000. 'Survey Finds Less Tolerance for Immigrants', 11 Mar., p. A11.

———. 1997. 'Ottawa Poised to Balance B.C.'s Immigration Cost Inequity', 28 Feb., p. A3.

———. 1995. 'Average Chinese-Canadian Consumer Well-Heeled', 13 Sept., pp. C1, C3.

———. 1989. 'Hong Kong Connection: How Asian Money Fuels Housing Market', 18 Feb., p. A8.

Wang, Shuguang, and Lucia Lo. 2000. 'Economic Impacts of Immigrants in the Toronto CMA: A Tax-Benefit Analysis', *Journal of International Migration and Integration* 1(3): 273–303.

Ward, W. Peter. 1978. *White Canada Forever: Popular Attitudes and Public Policy Toward Orientals in British Columbia.* Montreal: McGill-Queen's University Press.

Wellman, David T. 1977. *Portraits of White Racism.* Cambridge, UK: Cambridge University Press.

Western Living, The. 1988. 'Big Houses', Nov., pp. 31–41.

Whitaker, Reg. 1977. 'Images of the State in Canada' in Leo Panitch, ed., *The Canadian State: Political Economy and Political Power.* Toronto: University of Toronto Press, pp. 28–68.

Wilson, Kenneth L., and Alejandro Portes. 1980. 'Immigrant Enclaves: An Analysis of the Labour Market Experiences of Cubans in Miami', *American Journal of Sociology* 86(2): 295–319.

Wilson, Kenneth L., and W. Allen Martin. 1982. 'Ethnic Enclaves: A Comparison of the Cuban and Black Economies in Miami', *American Journal of Sociology* 88(1): 135–60.

Wong, Lloyd L. 1997. 'Globalization and Transnational Migration', *International Sociology* 12(3): 329–51.

———. 1995. 'Chinese Capitalist Migration to Canada: A Sociological Interpretation and Its Effect on Canada', *Asian and Pacific Migration Journal* 4(4): 465–92.

———. 1993. 'Immigration as Capital Accumulation: The Impact of Business Immigration to Canada', *International Migration* 31(1): 171–90.

Wong, Lloyd L., and Michele Ng. 1998. 'Chinese Immigrant Entrepreneurs in Vancouver: A

Case Study of Ethnic Business Development', *Canadian Ethnic Studies* 30(1): 64–85.

World Bank, The. 2000. *World Development Report 1999/2000: Entering the 21st Century*. New York: Oxford University Press.

———. 1999. *World Development Report 1998/1999: Knowledge for Development*. New York: Oxford University Press.

World Committee on Environment and Development. 1987. *Our Common Future*. New York: Oxford University Press.

World Trade Organization. 2001. *Annual Report 2001*. Geneva: WTO Publications.

Wotherspoon, Terry, and Vic Satzewich. 2000. *First Nations: Race, Class, and Gender Relations*. Regina, SK: Plains Research Centre.

Wright, Erik Olin. 1979. *Class Structure and Income Determination*. New York: Academic Press.

Zhou, Min. 1992. *Chinatown: The Socioeconomic Potential of an Urban Enclave*. Philadelphia: Temple University Press.

Zhou, Min, and Carl L. Bankston III. 1996. 'Social Capital and the Adaptation of the Second Generation: The Case of Vietnamese Youth in New Orleans' in Alejandro Portes, ed., *The Second Generation*. New York: Russell Sage Foundation, pp. 197–220.

Zhou, Min, and John R. Logan. 1989. 'Returns of Human Capital in Ethnic Enclaves: New York City's Chinatown.' *American Sociological Review* 54(Oct.): 809–20.

Author Index

Subject Index